CONTEMPORARY AMERICAN THEATRE

Contemporary American Theatre

Edited by
Bruce King

St. Martin's Press   New York

First published in the United States of America in 1991

Printed in Hong Kong

ISBN   0-312-06141-2

Library of Congress Cataloging-in-Publication Data

Contemporary American theatre / edited by Bruce King.
   p.   cm.
Includes index.
ISBN   0-312-06141-2
1. Theater—United States—History—20th century.
2. American Drama—20th century—History and criticism.
I. King, Bruce Alvin.
PN2266.5.C66   1991
792'.0973'09045—dc20   90–26675
                                                         CIP

To Nicole's Friends

Contents

List of Plates

Notes on the Contributors

Bruce King is co-editor of the Modern Dramatists series and editor of the English Dramatists. He has written *Coriolanus, Dryden's Major Plays, Marvell's Allegorical Poetry, The Macmillan History of Seventeenth-Century Literature, New English Literatures* and *Modern Indian Poetry in English*.

Barbara Kachur is Director of Theatre in the Department of Communication, University of Missouri – St Louis.

Dennis Carroll is Professor of Drama, University of Hawaii, author of *Mamet* in the Modern Dramatists series and *Australian Contemporary Drama, 1905–1982*.

David Savran teaches in the English Department, Brown University, and is author of *The Wooster Group: 1975–1985, Breaking the Rules* and *In Their Own Words*, a book of interviews with contemporary American dramatists.

Holly Hill teaches in the Drama Department, John Jay College, City University of New York. She is editor of *Playing Joan*, interviews with actresses. She reviews New York theatre for *The Times* of London.

Alexis Greene teaches at New York University and is a theatre critic.

S E Gontarski is Professor of English at Florida State University, Tallahassee, and author and editor of several books on Samuel Beckett including *The Intent of Undoing, Endgame: Samuel Beckett's Production Notebook, Shaping the Mess: the Composition of Samuel*

Beckett's Happy Days and *Krapp's First Tapes: Beckett's Manuscript Revisions of Krapp's Last Tape*. He is also a theatre director.

Glenn Loney   is Professor in the Department of Theatre, Brooklyn College and the Graduate School of the City University of New York and author and editor of many books including *Twentieth-Century Theatre, Musical Theatre in America, California Gold-Rush Plays* and *Peter Brook's Royal Shakespeare Company Production of A Midsummer-Night's Dream*.

Lenora Champagne   is a well-known perfomance artist, writer and director. She edited *Out From Under: Women on Sex and Death and other Things*, a collection of writing by solo women performers. She teaches at the State University of New York – Purchase.

Mel Gordon   is Head of the Theatre Programme, University of California – Berkeley, and author/editor of *Expressionistic Texts, Dada Performance, Grand Guignol: Theatre of Fear and Terror, Lazzi: Comic Routines of the Commedia dell' Arte* and *The Stanislavsky Technique: Russia*.

Theodore Shank   is Professor in the Theatre Department, University of California – San Diego, La Jolla, and author of *American Alternative Theatre* in the Modern Dramatists series. He is a well-known theatre and opera director and contributing editor to *New Theatre Quarterly*.

Alisa Solomon   is drama critic for *The Village Voice* and various theatre journals. She teaches in the English Department, Baruch College, City University of New York.

Don Shewey   was editor of *Seven Days* and author/editor of *Out front: contemporary gay and lesbian plays, Sam Shepard, Caught in the act* and other books.

Gerald Rabkin   is Professor of Theatre at Rutgers University, theatre critic and author of *Drama and Commitment: Politics in the American Theatre of the Thirties*.

Jim Carmody   is Professor in the Department of Theatre, University of California – San Diego.

Introduction

BRUCE KING

Although students of contemporary American theatre are well served by Ruby Cohn's *New American Dramatists: 1960–1980*, Helene Keyssar's *Feminist Theatre* and Theodore Shank's classic *American Alternative Theatre*, I and others feel it is already time for another examination of the directions drama and alternative forms of theatre have been taking in recent years. There is enough justification for a book in the increasing importance of Richard Nelson, Emily Mann, Christopher Durang, August Wilson, Stephen Sondheim, David Henry Hwang, Laurie Anderson, Wendy Wasserstein, Tina Howe, the directing of Peter Sellars, the success of women playwrights on Broadway, new forms of feminist theatre and discussions of post-modernism, post-structuralism and multiculturalism, along with the emergence of the new performance artists, site-specific works, dance drama and the new vaudeville. This collection of essays looks at American theatre after the cultural revolution of the 1960s, after the achievements of Sam Shepard, early Robert Wilson and early Mamet. What are the significant developments in American drama since the late 1970s and throughout the 1980s?

Cultural forms, conventions and performers change rapidly in relation to the desire for novelty, the need for the modern artist to top predecessors and in relation to the influences or forces of cultural production. This is especially true of the theatre. The need for an audience and the economics of performance which make theatre inherently more conservative than music or painting also make theatre continually change; innovations in acting, form, themes, conventions, scenery, playing spaces and performers are reflections of their time. Being highly public the theatre is sensitive and immediately responsive to changes in the general mood. What could be a more direct response to the McCarthy anticommunist witch hunt than Arthur Miller's *The Crucible* (1953) or Miller's

1

adaptation of Ibsen's *An Enemy of the People* (1950)? What could be more late 1960s than The Living Theatre and its *Paradise Now* (1968)?

The place of theory and deconstructionism during the 1970s and 1980s can be seen in the projects of the Wooster Group and the problem of how to move beyond the resulting fragmentation is seen in the directing of Peter Sellars. The on and off flirtation of the avant-garde with rock music, its mass audience and popular culture is shown by the various stages of Laurie Anderson's development as a performance artist. If the post-1960s intense concern with the private subjective individual self is expressed in many performance art pieces, especially in the confessional monologues and expressionistic psychodramas, the consciousness and concern of mainstream American culture for the problems of African Americans and of women is shown by the success on Broadway of such dramatists as Tina Howe, Wendy Wasserstein and August Wilson. The continuing exploration of ways to move theatre beyond literary drama can be seen in the plays of Adele Shank, Laura Farabough and Laura Harrington. Their plays also show that new, original drama is alive and well outside New York, especially in California.

There are still good critics who feel that when all is said and done worthwhile theatre remains that which is written down and published as plays. If so, the major dramatists at present include David Mamet, Tina Howe, Christopher Durang and Richard Nelson; but that is a limited view of theatre and culture. It would be like saying that the only really significant jazz can be found on recordings. There has always been a tension in theatre between the text, the aspiration for the permanence of classical art, and the performance, that which exists in the present and is a product of actors, directors, stage designers, comedians, dancers and other performers. Some of the best art of our time rejects the permanent and universal for the improvisational, temporal and immediately relevant. This in itself is a reflection of changing sensibilities and ideological positions, whether in challenging the status of elite art and the culture with which it is associated or in various commitments ranging from politics to the desire to live fully in the present. But then most modern art pretends to be an anti-art, pretends to the revolutionary, to the democratic; that is the style of the age and still the best way to obtain notice.

The cultural revolution of the 1960s brought radical changes to the American theatre, changes that coincided with the broadening of the role of avant-garde art which lost much of its elitism and rejection of mainstream culture. Indeed mass culture became one of its sources of inspiration. The counter culture for a time broke through barriers between high, middle and low forms of art and entertainment creating a new sensibility, new tastes and an openness to the unconventional. Such tastes were carried between New York and San Francisco by *Evergreen Review*, rock music, protest movements, the expansion of the universities, various new endowments to support the arts and by a new, university educated, upper middle class in the once more growing cities of middle America and the Sun Belt. The results can be seen in the network of serious little theatres throughout the country performing plays formerly only possible in the Village (before the Village was supplanted by SoHo, the lower East Side and other venues). Another change is the loss of prestige of the older, middle brow, Broadway theatre which is increasingly being bled into anaemia through its bloated production costs and its failure to incorporate the new theatre of the counter-culture.

Among significant influences on recent theatre are the collapse of distinctions between high and popular art, the influence of television in popularising many forms of innovative entertainment, the increasing importance of university drama departments in providing a home for the avant-garde, the interest in contemporary opera, the breakdown of established theatre and literary genres, the change in sensibility from elite modernist high culture to the catch-all post-modernism of today, the feminist movement and the increasing significance of multiculturalism in our society.

That the theatre has changed is obvious. Somehow roles have reversed and it is off Broadway and the avant-garde that creates much of the new musical theatre while Broadway imports musical comedies from England! The most successful recent American musical, *A Chorus Line*, began below 14th Street in an art theatre. The one widely acclaimed Broadway composer, Stephen Sondheim, is considered somewhat of an elite taste for writing lyrics to fit character and dramatic situations. Unlike the compositions used in earlier musicals, his do not have the 'hook lines' and obvious forms of popular songs, are not repeated or used as a reprise. Increasingly Sondheim's songs are performed in concert halls or his plays revived by light opera groups.

Those curious and seemingly unproductive counter-cultural happenings of the 1960s have developed into performance art, a serious theatre form, discussed by Leonora Champagne, which is extremely popular and seemingly on the verge of establishing itself as a genre with its own sub-genres, including confessional monologues. Among the better-known performers Karen Finley, Spalding Gray, Meredith Monk and Laurie Anderson are radically different and each deserves an essay about their work. As Mel Gordon shows, Laurie Anderson has at times been situated between various kinds of performance art and other arts. She is a multimedia performance artist who especially makes use of voice, dance and progressive rock; but she might also be seen in the context of those who have attempted some fusion between jazz improvisation, theatre and dance. Leonora Champagne is herself a well-known performance artist and I find interesting her notes on the difference in critical reaction to solo performance art by men and women. But then this is perhaps to be expected when the feminist movement and critical theory have made all art seem ideological and a reflection of gender roles. Theatre by women has itself increased to the point where there are now recognised subdivisions, including feminist performance art, feminist theatre groups and acceptance of possible conflicts in aims between, say, the women playwrights on Broadway, discussed by Barbara Kachur, and the more ideologically directed feminist theatre, discussed by Alisa Solomon. Other major changes in cultural taste and form include the rise of dance drama, discussed by Theodore Shank, and the extension of serious cultural recognition to such popular arts as the new vaudeville.

August Wilson, as Holly Hill says, illustrates the new strength of black serious drama as it finds a place within the mainstream of American culture. *Ma Rainey's Black Bottom* combines treatment of the situation of blacks within America with celebration of black culture and history. It represents a way of bringing together elements of protest drama with the black musical, and recognition that the history of jazz and blues might provide the basis of serious plays and has as much right on stage as, say, the use of an impressionist painter or an eighteenth-century composer as subject matter.

David Hwang's international success with *M Butterfly* might be attributed to a combination of excellent stagecraft and theatrical-ity with an increasing interest in and acceptance of minorities, multiculturalism and homosexuality. The ways in which many of the strands of the 1960s are now assimilated into a new general liberal cultural consensus can be seen by comparing Hwang's play, and its success, with the shock that used to accompany productions of the plays of Genet. Hwang's play has many similar themes and concerns as Genet's but in the intervening years they have moved from the fringes to be generally acknowledged. It is not necessary to make inflated claims for *M Butterfly* to see it at the intersection of many present concerns including the tensions between the First and Third World, the anxieties produced by the increasing contact between East and West, the importance of the new immigrant communities and their cultures, and our sense that cultural values are relative and individuality may be a social creation, a form of theatre. It also makes use of our present feeling that all texts are intertextual and forms of parody. Such feelings are not new to the theatre where acting itself calls into question the nature of self and the supposed imitation of reality. What is new is the bringing of all this together in an international hit.

Cultural change is often a product of improved communications. Many of the new developments can be explained by the importance of television in bringing the tastes of New York to the former cultural provinces. The need to find interesting entertainments has led to national exposure of the new vaudeville, and particularly of The Flying Karamazov Brothers. The latest discovery in New York may within a year be know in the cities of mid-America through the stamp of approval of a national television show. Urban mid-America has proved receptive to new forms of theatre, especially comedy, in ways that would have been thought unlikely a few generations ago. If the centre of theatre culture in America remains New York, especially below 14th Street, the tastes of the avant-garde have a way of being communicated to others rapidly through television and such means as *The New Yorker*, *The Village Voice*, the Public Broadcasting System, National Public Radio and university drama departments. While it is still necessary to visit New York to see the Wooster Group, and it may be necessary to visit London to see productions of the plays of Richard Nelson, the works of Tina Howe, Marsha Norman, Christopher Durang, August Wilson, Wallace Shawn and others are acted often in the larger cities and university campuses, although often to small audiences in art theatres.

This is a different situation than in the 1940s and 1950s when serious theatre usually meant Broadway and the unconventional was limited to a small avant-garde. When I was in school near Philadelphia there was little in the way of innovative local drama – indeed, even art house cinema was likely to be another phrase for sexy – but there were plays trying out before opening on Broadway and they included works by T S Eliot, Christopher Fry, Jean-Paul Sartre, Jean Cocteau and Jean Giraudoux. Not only have the theatre economics discussed by Glenn Loney in Chapter 8 impaired the vitality of the musical but a new division within American society means that the shared values that enabled both musical comedies and serious elite drama to appear on Broadway has now long fragmented. If Broadway has lost the stamp of approval to below 14th Street, the provinces are more open to innovation, as can be seen by the Houston premieres of John Adams's opera *Nixon in China* and Philip Glass's *The Making of the Representative for Planet 8*. It may still be necessary to go to New York or Europe to make a reputation; but in the long run culture follows money and there is a wealthy class in many larger American cities willing to purchase the prestige of name art and originality as well as a section of the middle class interested in the arts and willing to accept modern drama in its more experimental forms.

While it is common to say that after the radical experimentation of the 1960s there was a return to realism, the realism of recent decades, as Dennis Carroll and David Savran show, is different from the realism of the past. Narrative, plot and consistency of theme have returned, but there are often amazing gaps or leaps in characterisation, action and setting. For those used to an earlier realism the realism of the present must seem rather odd. Formal experimentation, along with the influence of television and cinema, has led to a looser, more arbitrary, self-conscious, self-referential realism.

Television, in creating an audience with a short attention span, has undoubtedly contributed to the episodic, sketchy plots of recent plays, the jumps in time, the way everything seems foregrounded, the telling through images rather than narrative. Sam Shepard seemed to understand that a contemporary audience is likely to wander off without violence, noise, shock and other means of getting attention. Is it my imagination or do the plays I see with kitchen sinks look more like the image of a room on television that the kitchen sinks in naturalistic drama in the past? There is a foregrounding, up front, a brightness of colour, as if the conventions of realism have changed.

Another influence is the general cultural awareness of the questions raised by structuralism, post-structuralism and Marxist theories about the nature of art forms, an awareness foregrounded in the productions of the Wooster Group. Their plays seem to ask what is theatre, what is an image, what happens if we act this in the dark or under glaring lights, how much distance and alienation can an audience take, what is the relation of this play to other plays and the usual critical assumptions about American classics? Suppose we begin with a structural analysis and critique of some classic, where will it take us? Suppose we add some element of chance, what is the effect of juxtaposing video images? What other cultural products in our society can be examined by incorporation into the play? Born out of the analytical mood of the 1970s, the Wooster Group tends rather more towards the fragmentary, juxtapositional and spatial than the narrative.

Still another influence on contemporary American theatre is the return to psychology, especially as see in the way European expressionism has become the basis for dance theatre. Even within the Wooster Group there is its opposite, Spalding Gray's auto-biographical monologues, which along with Laurie Anderson's recordings and film are perhaps the best known examples of kinds of performance art. The continuing importance of Elizabeth LeCompte to the Wooster Group, of Lee Breuer to Mabou Mines and Richard Foreman to the Ontological/Hysterical Theatre should put an end to the once common claim that whereas the European avant-garde is a director's theatre the American is communal, the product of a group rather than an individual.

There is perhaps no clear break between the formalism and minimalism of the 1970s and the new autobiographical and psychological arts of the 1980s. The dance theatre depends on formal repetition and symbolic structures for its overall organisation, while the seeds of the new expressionism were already present within the minimalist analytical art of the 1970s. The communalistic theatre groups that have continued to be influential and evolve have done so because some strong individual saw that the group expressed his or her own preoccupations. Even the supposedly new hedonism and 'me-ism' of the 1980s can be seen in the 1960s demand for instant satisfaction and 'Paradise Now'.

One characteristic of post-modernism is that the avant-garde has become popular, more an up-to-date fashion in taste, like this year's hemline and colours, than part of a radical rejection of bourgeois culture. Experimentation and anti-realism have lost much of their content. Eighty years of familiarity with modernism, including over thirty years of American universities teaching modernism as the continuation of the greattt tradition of western culture, means that its shock effects are now well known and likely to be part of the repertoire of rock and roll groups. *1000 Airplanes*, a collaboration between David Hwang, Philip Glass and scenic designer Jerome Sirlin, received a full page spread in *Time*. When I read about William Irwin's mime in *The New Yorker*, and when such avant-garde venues as La Mama, The Performing Garage and P.S. 122 are listed under *The New Yorker's* 'Goings on about Town' (which now includes sections called 'Edge of Night Life' and 'In Another Category'), I realise that this year's latest off off Broadway excitements will next year be part of the Brooklyn Academy of Music's New Wave and will probably be playing within a few years in a crowded high school auditorium in Indianapolis the week after the Bolshoi ballet and a week before Les Ballets Trockadero de Monte Carlo.

David Savran asks whether in such a situation the radical criticism of American society in the plays of Emily Mann, David Mamet and Richard Nelson is not co-opted and made part of the entertainment of those liberals with a guilty conscience over the evils of capitalism. This is an old problem which has exercised the Left in the past and which has no more solution now than it had when George Orwell questioned how it is possible to write communist novels in a capitalist society. In questioning possible contradictions in the work of some of our more radical writers Savran's concern is representative of many Marxist and feminist theorists at present who, in my view, have somehow talked themselves into a position not much better than those who objected during the 1930s that progressive novelists had failed to portray happy victorious peasants and workers. The recognition that art may be situated, often by the critic, ideologically quickly degenerates into a demand for propaganda and the privileging of politics, usually of a simplistic kind, over the rest of life – personal, sexual, moral, religious, aesthetic – with little space for dialogue, conflict, nuance or reality. Theatre, like other arts, thrives on complexity, ambiguity, the ironies of history, the actualities of lives. When Mamet shows the way such opposites as ideals and corruption or dreams and evil are mixed in the American character we recognise a criticism of capitalism and patriarchy which would only be weakened by offering some glimpse of an alternative.

In *Principia Scriptoriae* and *Some Americans Abroad* Nelson is concerned with those, whether academics or politicians, who, due to their own interests or agenda, deny the reality of contemporary art and the actual experience of the individual as politically relevant. If Nelson's plays, whether comic or serious in tone, imply that all is political, the language of politicising and moralising is questioned. Both Left and Right are subjected to demystification by someone on the Left. The dramatist, the artist, belongs to a class which is exploited by Left and Right. For those who ask where they can find a first rate American dramatist with a sophisticated awareness of politics, an American Brecht or Dario Fo, they might have a look at Nelson's plays. They seem to me to be the most interesting new American textual drama since Shepard and Mamet. Although written in the contemporary realistic manner with a thin, episodic narrative, they are rich in American speech, complexity, irony, moral probing and depth while having recognisable situations. I am always amazed at how Nelson and Mamet both find the poetic within the ungainliness, ugly contours and shoddiness of American speech. Their jerky idiomatic realism is perhaps the nearest equivalent we have to poetic drama. I am always impressed by the way Mamet criticises and satirises while avoiding an easy mocking dismissal of the American Dream. He sees its possibilities, energy and attractions along with the costs, vulgarity, violence, inherent imperialism and self-deception.

As I think of significant dramatists, directors and performers not included here or only discussed briefly, I realise it is already time for still another book about contemporary American theatre. At present there is a vitality resulting from the intersection of traditions, the counter-culture of the 1960s, theory, other cultures and recent technology and forms of communication. Where is the chapter on video and theatre with an analysis of the ways the use of video screens on stage provide juxtapositions, demystification, extra playing space and distance? Emily Mann and the Wooster Group have made good use of video. But then I wish I could have found some way to get in the amusing, poetic surrealist plays of Kenneth Koch, or the extravagant caricature transvestite theatre of Charles Ludlam.

It is perhaps time to ask whether the West Indian dramatist Derek Walcott should now be considered part of American drama, especially after his use of American Indian culture in *Ghost Dance*, in view of his prolonged residence in Boston and the fact that his plays are so often performed in the United States? He is a major dramatist and his poems are included in anthologies of black American literature. Or are we to be like the French who still refuse to consider Samuel Beckett part of French literature? There is need for awareness of the broad spectrum of the new multiculturalism in America and its effects on drama. David Henry Hwang and the dramatist and performance artist Ping Chong are basically crossover dramatists successful with a white theatre public. They are in a similar position to August Wilson. But just as there is a black theatre seldom attended by white audiences so there is an impressive new ethnic theatre in America, especially in Spanish.

Drama history is based on major changes, the new directions culture takes or those who can gain attention. Much is left out, especially in histories of American culture that give emphasis to innovation and which like to think that in a democracy each individual is a self-invention and the American artist a discoverer of more new worlds. Will there be a place for A R Gurney's studies in the conflicts and pieties of waspdom? They are witty, well made in the contemporary episodic mode, and have the same anger at the inhibiting effects of family life and other orthodoxies as the more radical dramatists of our time. Do not WM-ASPs have a right to join the revolution? His work shares with the plays of John Guare and Mamet a concern for the denial of dreams. Whether expressionist or in what might be termed the expressionist naturalistic mode of Lanford Wilson, so much of American drama contrasts dreams with a reality of dreary small towns, shabby hotels, loveless isolated lives, self-deceptions, violence. In the attention and prestige given the avant-garde we now tend to neglect, as worn out, one of the major traditions of American theatre, a tradition that Sam Shepard revitalised by making it mythic and giving it an energy it too often lacks.

I will conclude by mentioning Martin Sherman, best known for *Bent*. Although born and educated in the United States, he lives and works in London where his plays premiere before transferring to the United States. He is representative of an increasing number of contemporary American theatre artists who have found recognition abroad. Despite the broadened base of serious theatre in America and its undeniable vitality it is a shamefully small, minority art in comparison to the situation of contemporary drama in Europe. It is still true that most Americans are ignorant of American artists and often only learn about them from London or Paris.

PART I
Textual Drama

1

Women Playwrights on Broadway: Henley, Howe, Norman and Wasserstein

BARBARA KACHUR

Although American women have been writing plays since Mercy Otis Warren penned *The Adulateur* in 1772, it was not until the early decades of the twentieth century, roughly coterminous with the first women's movement, that a significant number of exceptional dramatists (such as Susan Glaspell, Rachel Crothers, and Sophie Treadwell) would emerge, write the first feminist plays, and vie for their share of both space and acclaim in the theatre arena.[1] This initial emergence of a feminist force in the theatre, a force made strong by the comparative plethora of women writers and bolstered by a relatively receptive political climate, proved so unique that it prompted commentary and coverage in daily newspapers and weekly magazines[2] – not unlike Gussow's recent *New York Times* articles on the newest surge of women dramatists in the 1970s and 1980s – and remains the seminal point of American feminist drama. As theatre history informs us, however, despite the auspicious beginnings of *fin de siècle* feminist political solidarity and artist accomplishment, not the least of which was Zona Gale's 1921 Pulitzer for *Miss Lulu Bett*,[3] the strong, articulate and united voice of American women dramatists did not endure and increase, but rather modulated, eventually attenuated, and regrettably, for approximately the next forty-odd years that is, found resonance only when such isolated and individual playwrights like Lillian Hellman, Mary Chase and Lorraine Hansberry occasionally broke the silence.

The status of women playwrights (as well as women theatre artists in general) began to change markedly when in the late 1960s a second women's movement, this one more energised and forceful, refocused attention on women's sociopolitical status, reopened artistic avenues for women, and redefined both the nature and artistic expression of women's experiences. Although initially forced to produce their plays in off off Broadway and fringe theatres during the 1960s and much of the 1970s, women dramatists eventually made their way back to Broadway – gaining considerable recognition first with Ntozake Shange's *For Colored Girls* (1976) and building unprecedented momentum with writers such as Beth Henley (whose 1981 Pulitzer for *Crimes of the Heart* made her the first woman to win that coveted award in twenty-three years), Marsha Norman (who followed two years later with a Pulitzer for '*night Mother*), Tina Howe, Cindy Lou Johnson, Susan Nanus, Wendy Wasserstein (the most recent recipient of the Pulitzer, in 1989, for *The Heidi Chronicles*) and many others.

The success of these contemporary writers on Broadway, not unlike their early twentieth-century predecessors, has not come without heavy costs and serious recriminations, however. Although these women have collectively enjoyed commercial success and renown on Broadway for a comparatively brief time (just over a decade), the attacks against their plays on critical and theoretical grounds already threaten to minimise their accomplishments and marginalise their texts. In this, history is repeated. Indeed, as far back as 1909, the critic Walter Eaton cavilled that Crothers's play, *A Man's World*, missed 'the masculinity of structure' (Barlow, 1981, p. xxix), while public and critical disapprobation forced Gale to alter the ending of *Miss Lulu Bett* so that the titular heroine, rather than reject her suitor and search for autonomy as is in the original, opts to marry and live in sentimental wedded bliss (Alder, 1987, pp. 4–6). Decades later, critics would pejoratively refer to Henley's 'homespun' humour and 'gossamer women' in *Crimes* (Barnes, 1981, p. 137; Betsko and Koenig, p. 219), while Wendy Wasserstein would fail to get *Uncommon Women and Others* moved to Broadway because, unlike Gale, she refused to change the ending to depict one of her heroines, Holly, marrying a rich and willing suitor (Betsko and Koenig, p. 426). Clearly women's fight for recognition and acceptance in the male-dominated theatre continues, but the battleground has now been extended into the academy; not only do women struggle against the gender bias of self-empowered critics and producers who can reject their creativity and invalidate their artistic expression, they are also under attack by some feminist scholars for capitulating to the commercial theatre which, by its very financial motives, panders to mainstream ideology and reinforces the status quo.

Because these critical postures dominate much that has been written of late about contemporary women dramatists and significantly influence the manner in which their plays are typically interpreted, it is necessary to outline them briefly in order to place these dramas in the historical–critical context that forms the starting point for almost any discussion on current women writers in the commercial theatre. Broadly speaking, these critical perspectives centre on questions about universality and dramaturgical paradigms. One the one hand, critics (mostly male) often summarily dismiss women playwrights for a lack of universal vision: specifically, for writing about the mundane, quotidian aspects of women's lives which neither address nor elucidate those weighty metaphysical and transhistorical issues ostensibly at the root of male-authored texts, thereby making their plays accessible only to a coterie audience of women and feminists and not to the ubiquitous 'generic' spectator.[4] Henley perhaps best responded to this indictment when, in commenting on the negative reactions to *The Miss Firecracker Contest* as a 'petty play about a beauty context', said that reviewers 'wouldn't look for any of the deeper meaning or the spiritual levels in the play. Whereas if a man wrote a play about a baseball game, critics might be more inclined to find deep meanings about the Lost American Dream' (Betsko and Koenig, p. 219). At the same time, some feminist scholars object to the plays by women writers in the commercial theatre because that forum precludes deployment of the more preferred subversive modes and themes found in contemporary experimental drama and performance art by women. Objection is also raised on more theoretical grounds because their plays not only rely on the traditional realistic dramaturgy which reinscribes women's position as object, a fetishised image, but also, and more nefariously, locates her within the very domestic locale that has negatively defined and insidiously confined women without offering a means of either re-visioning them within that context or a way to escape it. Henley's dramas have been used as a case in point in their failure 'to advance positive images of women [because of] her consistent and unimaginative dependence on the forms and modes of the dominant male tradition of American drama.'[5]

These critical attacks – the first levelled against women playwrights since the turn of the century and the latter a new development within the nascent discipline of feminist performance theory – will continue until the much needed definition of a feminist poetics is articulated. In the meantime, however, these perspectives have, either deliberately or unwittingly, reinscribed the fallacious assumption that women's plays are identical thematically and dramaturgically, and that women playwrights are a segregated group (either separated by the author's sex, as the male reviewers would have it, or according to their commercial forum, as some feminist theorists have divided them) that share more commonalities than they are separate voices, each resonating her own unique artistry – and surely such misconceptions are not eradicated but rather mediated by those few newspaper articles, both past and present, in which reviewers lump all women playwrights together and imply a similarity in their vision and dramaturgy.

Because much has been written to jeopardise the general acceptance of these dramatists as diverse artists, it is crucial that their works begin to be analysed not just as a collective voice promulgating a specific feminist agenda or mediating traditional perceptual modalities, but rather also as individual writers responding to different artistic, thematic and dramaturgical impulses so that their specific and sundry contributions – unlike the unheralded differences between Glaspell's slice-of-life drama *Trifles* and Treadwell's expressionistic tragedy *The Machinal* – receive the same celebration and recognition for diversity that has long been reserved for such male counterparts as Durang, Rabe, Shepard and Gurney. This chapter hopes to afford a starting point for such inquiries by charting the dramaturgical and thematic variety afforded by four of the most prominent writers on Broadway: Beth Henley, Tina Howe, Marsha Norman and Wendy Wasserstein. Space restrictions limit a definitive discussion, but the attempt is made to highlight some of their more noteworthy playwriting characteristics; it is interesting that what partially emerges out of this brief inquiry is, at turns, evidence of the very universal themes and non-realistic dramaturgical strategies which have often been eclipsed by other, more reductive discussions.

BETH HENLEY

By the time Beth Henley's first full-length play, *Crimes of the Heart*, had won the Pulitzer and The Drama Critics Circle Award even before it had its Broadway debut, she had also completed writing and arranging rehearsals for *The Miss Firecracker Contest* and *The Wake of Jamey Foster*.[6] These three dramas, composed around the same time and to date Henley's most well known, display such similarities in technique, theme and characterisation that critics have readily identified the quintessential Henley play. Most noticeable is the southern ambience which has sparked comparisons with Flannery O'Connor and Tennessee Williams: the characters' colourful and poetic dialect, compelling and graphic narratives and storytelling, eccentric behaviour, strong family bonds – all depicted within the frame of Gothic humour, an admixture of bizarre tragic situations and grotesquerie with a comic and absurd guise. Her plays are intricately plotted – Rich (1980), for example, said *Crimes* had 'enough plot for about three Faulkner novels' – and seldom does she allow a single protagonist to dominate, but rather brings on a host of characters, each afforded individual nuances, rich complexities and her moment at centre stage.

Although Henley's positioning of women within domestic, family environments has, as noted earlier, garnered considerable criticism and debate and surely affords volumes about mother–daughter relationships, female sibling rivalry, patriarchal conditioning and domestic confinement, Henley uses female characters less to paint a domestic portrait of women than to embody her larger ontological concerns about spiritual bankruptcy and the individual's isolation: 'I want to look at the world. . . . What is amazing to me is the existential madness that we – everyone – are born into' (Betsko and Koenig, p. 221). Her female protagonists are victims of broken dreams and unfulfilled lives, but they concomitantly symbolise the human's indomitable will to survive by striving to find meaning and happiness in a world that can guarantee little else but pain, disappointment and death. Indeed, perhaps no contemporary playwright so underscores the relationship between death and comedy, between the rejuvenating, recuperative value of comedy against the darkness of life and its closure through death than Henley, and it is her ability to make us laugh in the face of existential madness that makes her plays brilliantly unique.

Henley depicts this existential condition by mingling comedy with death, bringing death on stage (either referentially or directly) as a centrepiece, and depicting it in such ludicrous terms (such as the aunt who dies after undergoing a gland transplant from a monkey which results in her growing ape hair all over her body) that she not only forces us to laugh despite ourselves (not unlike the Magrath sisters who fall into a paroxysm of laughter over their grandfather's dying coma) but also undercuts the seriousness with which her characters (and by extension us) take life's disappointments as the end of the world. Her existential vision precludes resolutions and closure; rather, her plays conclude on a caesura in which characters grab at whatever amount of happiness exists to assuage their despair, knowing full well that tomorrow may bring pain and anguish, and perhaps the real closure that is death.

Crimes of the Heart (1980), set in the small town of Hazlewood, Mississippi, concerns the three Magrath sisters' reunion, instigated by Babe's (the youngest at twenty-four) recent shooting assault on her husband. All three women are victims of irrational crimes of the heart, feelings of isolation and despair initiated some sixteen years before when their mother, who had been abandoned by her husband, hanged herself (with her pet cat). Of the three children, Meg (now twenty-seven) was the one to find her mother's body, and since that time she has been unable to feel love and has deliberately anaesthetised herself against emotions (forcing herself, after her mother's death, to look at pictures of crippled children and animals to condition her stamina against future pain). Thirty-year-old Lenny was left to take care of their grandfather who has manipulated her into subservience by fostering her belief that she is an old maid and worthless because of a deformed ovary. Babe sought solace in a loveless marriage to a lawyer who physically abused her, and it is Babe who, throughout the play, repeatedly talks about their mother's death, questions why her mother would hang the cat also, and is herself driven to attempt suicide. By the end of Act Three, the sisters experience emotional changes: Meg, after an evening with her old boyfriend, realises that she can feel passion without fear; Lenny rejects the notion of her worthlessness, contacts her ex-boyfriend and rekindles their romance; and Babe is spared a jail sentence but more importantly understands why her mother killed the pet: 'she needed him with her 'cause she felt so all alone' (p. 69). The play ends with a moment of celebration as all three voraciously dig into a huge birthday cake for Lenny, and the curtain falls on a picture of them locked in a transitory moment of familial bonding and love: 'The sisters freeze for a moment laughing and catching the cake; the lights change and frame them in a magic, golden, sparkling glimmer'(p. 72).

Explaining *Crimes*'s theme, Henley said it was 'about overcoming ghosts of the past and letting go of what other people have said you are, what they have told you to be' (Betsko and Koenig, p. 218), a theme she also attributes to her next play, *The Miss Firecracker Contest* (1981, 1984). Set in Brookhaven, Mississippi, the play concerns Carnelle Scott, a twenty-four-year-old waif raised by her recently deceased aunt and two cousins, who tries to combat her feelings of rejection and isolation by entering a beauty contest, a victory she believes, said Henley, 'would make her feel like she is somebody' (Betsko and Koenig, p. 220). The family is united when Carnelle's cousins, Delmount and Elain, return home: Elain (a previous contest winner) to deliver a speech at the pageant and to find refuge from her wealthy, overly attentive husband, and Delmount to escape from his state job of retrieving dead dogs from the highway and to claim the house his mother bequeathed him.

At the end, Elain returns to her husband, Delmount intends to attend college and study philosophy so he will 'be able to let everyone know why we're living' (p. 102), and Carnelle, after losing the contest (coming in last), accepts herself as she is, looks into her dressing-room mirror at her hair (dyed crimson red for the contest) and says proudly: 'It used to be brown. I had brown hair. Brown' (p. 110). Although still not sure exactly what happiness life has to offer – ' I just don't know what you can, well, reasonably hope for in life' (p. 106) – Carnelle joins Delmount to watch the evening fireworks, celebrating her independence from the expectations and definitions of her by others and caught in the moment of festive rejoicing.

While *Crimes* and *Miss Firecracker* met with critical success, enjoyed long runs, and received film adaptations, Henley's next play, *The Wake of Jamey Foster* (1982), ran for only two weeks.[7] This comedy is set in Canton, Mississippi at Marshael Foster's home where friends and relatives gather to pay respects to Marshael's alcoholic ex-husband, Jamey, whose body (tackily clad in an orange and yellow plaid jacket) is on display in an open coffin in the front parlour. Around this gaudy and gruesome centrepiece the bizarre

Foster clan display their sibling rivalry, petty resentments, personal secrets (even accidentally dropping food on Jamey's corpse), and revealed behind all the animosity is a group of insecure, unhappy people, Marshael in particular, who, looking back over her failed marriage to Jamey, tries desperately to grapple with the rejection she felt when he left her for another woman and to understand how one's hopes and dreams can diminish into indifference and emotional death. In the final scene, as the coffin is removed and all leave for the funeral, Marshael refuses to attend, symbolically breaking her emotional ties with the past and finally, after days of insomnia, finding momentary peace as she lies down and is sung to sleep by her friend, Brocker, as the sun comes up on Easter morning.

After the ill-fated *Jamey Foster*, Henley wrote two plays, both unsuccessful. *The Debutante Ball* (unpublished) is axiomatically about a young debutante's coming-out party held for her by her wealthy southern family; staged in California (1987), it never made it to New York. *The Lucky Spot*, initially staged in Williamstown (1986) and then at the Manhattan Theatre Club (spring 1987) where it ran for less than one month, is a Depression-era western set in Pigeon, Louisiana. It concerns Cassidy, a fifteen-year-old child whom Reed (the forty-year-old proprietor of the Lucky Spot Dance Hall) won in a poker game and impregnated. Although the play aims at themes about salvation through faith and rebirth through love (symbolised by Cassidy being pregnant on Christmas eve), it digresses into a TV western (complete with obligatory bar-room brawls) and, even worse, centres around the rivalry between Cassidy and Sue Jack for Reed's affections. The rampant chauvinism and exploitation of women (men come to the Lucky Spot and pay to dance with the women) are not made palatable despite Henley's deliberate antedating.

'Her authentic voice has gone astray', concluded Rich (1987) about Henley's last play, an accurate assessment of the play-wright's shift away from centring women not only as protagonists, but also as signifiers of more than the general female: as victims symbolising the universal human condition of alienation, suffer-ing and pain, and yet as survivors whose tenacity and resilience affords them a strength and dignity (unlike Williams's Blanche) seldom attributed to women in modern American drama. Perhaps after the failure of her last two plays, Henley will return to her authentic voice which raised women above the domestic landscape and positioned them within the larger picture of life's tragicomic terrain.

TINA HOWE

Tina Howe began her career as a playwright in the early 1970s with two absurdist comedies about women in domestic roles,[8] but these social satires proved so radically feminist that Howe had difficulty getting her works staged, was dropped by her agent, and decided that her survival in the theatre meant reassessing and reshaping her strategy. What evolved out of her regrouping was a surrealistic style that capitulated neither her feminist voice nor her absurdist view of life. Typically, her comedies juxtapose the familiar with the outrageous thus force a revisioning of the real, palpable world, and they concomitantly foreground universal questions about life and death, humankind's quest for immortality through creation (of other life or art works), and our need for such creations as a means of explicating the purpose and importance of existence itself. All of which make her plays among the most dramaturgically and thematically complex in contemporary literature. The metatheatrical (the artist within the artwork) questions reality and fiction, the permanence of art, the ephemerality and closure of life. The theatrical performance ironically reconstructs all of these. Her plays elevate the metaphysical and metatheatrical to new meaning by continually valorising and centring woman as the primary 'creator–artist'.

Museum (1978), Howe's first play after changing her style, takes place at a museum gallery's exhibition of modern art where some forty characters, representing a cross-section of art consumers, meander through.[9] The centre-piece of the exhibit and the play, however, is the sole woman's exhibit, a series of animal-bone sculptures made by Agnes Vaag, and it is around this artwork that Howe orchestrates her most potent messages about an artist's self-abandonment and anguish in descending into her creative forces, the phenomenological search for universal truths and sublime visions ostensibly captured and articulated by artists' works, women's need to unlock the sublimity of another woman's artworks, and the mystical, spiritual power of female artist–creators. Tink Solheim, a friend of Agnes, begins a 'grisly aria', as Howe described it ('Antic Vision', 1985, p. 12), detailing her search with

Agnes for found objects and accidentally coming upon her as she was licking and nibbling on the bones of a skeleton, a graphic monologue that unnerves and repulses the crowd. Momentarily, Tink begins manically to search the sculptures for the special surprise that Agnes told her was hidden in each, and when she finds the switch and 'releases the miracle buried' inside, the lights dim, floodlight pours down on the statue, and Bach's organ music swells from the pedestal (p. 64). The viewers are enthralled, spiritually awakened, and stand motionless for several minutes as they take in its unique beauty and mystery. From this climax the gallery-goers are led into an orgiastic revelry in which they tear apart and steal an exhibit in their 'desire', explained Howe, 'to possess what's beautiful and immortal' (Betsko, p. 230), a coda instigated by the epiphany from Agnes's miracle.

Although in her next play, *The Art of Dining* (1979), Howe places her heroine, Ellen, in the typical female role of cook, the nineteenth-century townhouse-cum-restaurant setting subverts a realistic, domestic view: 'a surreal nostalgia suffuses the room. Things are on the verge of lifting off the ground or disappearing entirely. Nothing is quite what it seems' (p. 7). In this surreal environment customers (not unlike the art consumers in *Museum*) feast voraciously in orgiastic ecstasy on the famous culinary creations of master-chef Ellen.[10] Howe uses food partly to symbolise contemporary spiritual starvation, and again she valorises women as the source of nurturing, nourishment and salvation. Two characters embody the woman–artist: Ellen, the gourmet chef who elatedly and lovingly whips up the exotic cuisine, and Elizabeth Barrow Colt, a young anorexic writer with a neurotic fear of food. At the conclusion, these two women meet physically and spiritually, and they not only help each other toward self-expression but also lead the entire crowd into a ritualistic moment of community. As Ellen ignites and serves complimentary crêpes to the guests, Elizabeth narrates the universal, communal significance of Ellen's festive gift: 'long, long ago when men ate by a fire . . . and shared in the feast' (p. 96). Elizabeth then joins the others and 'for the first time all evening, she eats' (p. 96). Everyone gathers closer around the flame, 'Ellen's face glowing with a fierce radiance' (p. 97). As all the characters come together to share in one common, spiritualised humanity, 'purified of their collective civilization and private grief' (p. 97), the playwright engenders in her audience a correlative communal experience that is the essence of live theatre.

In her next and finest play, *Painting Churches* (1983), Howe brings together all the thematic and metatheatrical strands from the earlier plays; here, as she acknowledges, her 'feminist and aesthetic voices were fused at last' ('Antic Vision', p. 14). The play concerns Mags, an impressionist painter who returns to her Boston home to paint a portrait of her elderly parents, Fanny and Gardner Church (hence the title). While the play probes issues about a child's quest for parental approval (through Mags's need for Fanny and Gardner to like her painting of them), the need to find self-expression separate from parents' ideologies (evident by Mags's aria about finding her own painter's materials and impressionist vision), the degradation of growing old and facing death (symbolised by Fanny who takes care of her senile husband), beneath these surface themes Howe underscores the artist's to need combat time's flux and death's inevitability by capturing life so that it can be re-experienced, relished and shared, a means for the artist to gain immortality and give immortality to others.

Howe orchestrates this metatheatrically: a painting with a play. Mags paints the picture of her parents, which will be forever locked in time, while audiences observe her through a playscript similarly immutable. Howe's opening stage directions indicate that 'it's several years ago' (p. 9), which is to say it is history, already fact and artifact. At the conclusion, Howe merges the painting with the play: after Fanny and Gardner see the painting (which the audience does not), it recalls for them a Renoir with a couple dancing and then they begin to dance, picking up speed as far-away strains of Chopin are heard, as 'the lights become dappled . . . and the curtain falls' (p. 83). On stage, Fanny and Gardner have become transformed into their painting. Mags, 'moved to tears', has captured her parents forever, the child has given the parents immortal life, and the pain that Mags has felt years ago in realising that, while swimming with her father, time was passing and 'you were slipping from my grasp' (p. 78) is now avenged. As the dappled lights fade and Fanny and Gardner seem almost to disappear before Mags's eyes, we realise that this last fading moment of them, this transformed life-painting by Mags, is as much now a memory to Mags (since this happened 'several years ago') as it is now for us (as the play concludes) – the real life of these characters has faded into a memory, yet, like the painting, remains immortal in Howe's script.

After *Painting Churches*, Howe's writing changed markedly. Gone is the antic humour, the surreal note, the metatheatricality, and the centring of women's creative, artistic expression. In *Coastal Disturbances* (1986), Howe attempted to write an 'extremely female play about falling in love from a woman's point of view' which could also 'celebrate the tenderness of men' (Bennetts, 1986, p. 18), but what emerges is a cliché story about a puerile young woman, Holly, who settles for her manipulative and shallow ex-lover rather than the compassionate and tender beach life-guard. Similarly, Howe's latest effort, *Approaching Zanzibar* (1989), which depicts the Blossom family travelling cross-country to visit Olivia, a dying aunt, is a slice-of-life comedy, relatively straightforward with occasional bits of symbolism. Although both plays broach issues about women as creator–artists through the myriad references to childbearing as well as through the photography of Holly and Olivia (a site-specific artist), neither exhibits the thematic resonance or the dramaturgical intricacy of the earlier plays.

When Howe adjusted her dramaturgical style and composed *Museum*, she elatedly realised 'I found my niche at last. I would write about women as *artists*, eschew the slippery ground of courtship and domesticity and move up to a loftier plane' ('Antic Vision', p. 12). For some unexplained reason, Howe has recently fallen from that loftier plane and positioned women marginally within the very domestic, courtship canvas she sought to avoid. Except for a few poignant moments that intimate women's potential salvation through each other (as in *Zanzibar's* conclusion where the young girl rejuvenates Olivia from a dying stupor), Howe's latest plays indicate, regrettably, that she has only moved full circle.

MARSHA NORMAN

Marsha Norman began her career at Actors' Theatre, Louisville, where she enjoyed her first success with *Getting Out* in 1977, and since then she has written six plays, most notably *'night Mother*, which earned her the Pulitzer in 1983 and a movie adaptation in 1986. Norman's plays to date, unlike those by Henley, Howe or Wasserstein, are not only serious in tone, but also reveal both an eclecticism in style and diversity in theme. Dramaturgically, her plays range from an experimental technique of the split protagonist in *Getting Out* to a strict observance of naturalism and neoclassical unities in *'night Mother*, a style used not merely as a device to heighten the drama's poignancy by underlining the realness of the characters' lives but also, and more consistent with her concern about probing into the effects of psychological and emotional traumas, to accentuate that, as in reality, behind the seemingly content exterior and activities of others (from the mundane tasks of doing laundry, making cocoa or sharing gossip) there often resides a troubled soul and spirit. Thematically, Norman's plays can run the gamut, from embracing issues about female autonomy and identity to underscoring the existential *malaise* of modern society. Norman achieves this range – with the exception of her most recent drama, *Traveler in the Dark* (1984) – by positioning women as protagonists, allowing them at turns to signify the negative socialisation of women, their victimisation within the patriarchal society, and the lack of bonding in mother–daughter relationships, as well as to represent the more global verities of familial emptiness, human isolation and spiritual bankruptcy within the contemporary landscape.

Getting Out, Norman's most overtly feminist play, dramatises the first day of Arlene Holsclaw's release after an eight-year prison term for killing a cab driver during a robbery. The play's title is deliberately ambiguous and ironic: ambiguous because while it denotes Arlene's physical release from prison it also signifies her attempt to liberate herself from the psychological, physical and emotional degradation she has endured at the hands of her sexually abusive father, negligent and battered mother, manipulative pimp and sexist prison guards; ironic because although Arlene gains physical and psychological freedom, as a woman she remains incarcerated (symbolised by the bars on her apartment window) in the larger prison of a patriarchal society which defines the limited potential and parameters of women's sexual, economic and personal freedom.

To dramatise Arlene's journey to self-esteem and autonomy Norman used a split-protagonist device: Arlene, in her late twenties, is shown in the present, and as she reacts to her new life outside prison – combatting an attempted rape by the prison guard who brought her home, defending her search for a new identity and self-fulfilment against her mother's degrading recriminations, and fending off her ex-pimp who attempts to seduce her back to prostitution – she experiences flashbacks which detail parallel

dehumanising incidents which had earlier molded her into a rebellious and volatile teenager, Arlie. The juxtaposition of past and
present incidents, acted out by two separate characters, does more
than make concrete the depth of the emotional and psychological
victimisation which Arlene must confront and exorcise: it also
underscores the reality that Arlene (a symbolic prisoner) battles
subjugation all her life and that as a woman her definition and
role in society has been and will continue to be predetermined.
While Arlene completes her exorcism, at the play's conclusion she
faces a life of abject poverty because, as an ex-convict (in terms of
being a prisoner of patriarchal victimisation), the world affords
her little opportunity to break out of its insidious confinement.

Between *Getting Out* and *'night Mother*, Norman wrote four
plays, but only one, *Third and Oak: The Laundromat* (1979), dealt
exclusively with women, curiously the only successful one of
the group.[11] *The Laundromat* takes place in a lonely laundromat
in a small southern town where a young girl, Deedee, and a
middle-aged woman, Alberta, meet at 3:00 am (a clock on the
wall indicates the time and runs throughout the play). Each is
isolated by her own private grief – Deedee by the knowledge that
her husband is not at work but is cheating on her, and Alberta with
the pain from the recent death of her husband. Only after each is
able to admit and share her private grief are they able to help one
another toward growth: accepting life alone. While this positive
self-realisation portends female autonomy, the emotional texture
of the play is paramount: from their breaking down the barriers,
exposing and facing the truth, they form a quasi-mother–daughter relationship (coincidentally, their last names are the same,
Johnson) which neither had previously enjoyed. Although each
will go their separate way, they form a rare, momentary human
bond which Norman will resurrect and develop in *'night Mother*.

In *'night Mother*, Norman's most studied and successful drama,
the playwright merges the issues of psychological devastation,
familial bonding and human isolation to create a powerful existential tragedy. Despite the realistic, domestic interior, Norman, as
her set description indicates, aims at ubiquity: the 'nowhere that is
everywhere' (p. 7).[12] Moments into the play, the thirty-eight-year-
old Jessie announces to her mother Thelma that she will commit
suicide that evening, and what takes place during the following
ninety minutes (tracked by the clock on stage) is the relentless,
inexorable move toward that fate, despite Thelma's strategic

attempts to prevent it. Because the issues of human despair and suicide spring from the quotidian details within this domestic women's arena and not from the abstract terrain of Beckett's tramps, critics ineluctably and misguidedly look for some socio-psychological pathology to explain Jessie's decision.[13] Admittedly, the script affords tempting explanations – Jessie is epileptic and has self-imposed her confinement in her mother's home, she is divorced, has a criminal son, never had a loving relationship with her parents, and they, in turn, never loved each other – but while these facts emerge and form the fabric of dialogue between Jessie and Thelma, Norman deftly and carefully avoids ascribing any particular reason because it is none of these, yet it is all of these and still it is even more. Indeed, *'night Mother* is not a disquisition on the socialisation of women but an exploration into existential despair, and how Jessie got there is as irrelevant as how Vladimir and Estragon arrived on their barren road. What is important, however, are Jessie's feelings of isolation and despair, and in this palpable despair she becomes a microcosm of the universal human condition: 'I read the paper. I don't like how things are. And they're not any better out there than they are in here'(p. 23).

Jessie's sense of helplessness and alienation came to her in one lucid moment when the epilepsy dissipated and the medicine brought clarity, and she now demands control of her life, and, as Norman said, 'she will have the courage to take that control' (Gussow, 1983). Before she goes, however, she needs to relieve her mother of any sense of guilt or responsibility which survivors of suicide suffer: 'I only told you so I could explain it, so you wouldn't blame yourself. . . . There wasn't anything you could say to change my mind. . . . I just wanted you to know' (p. 48). What Jessie is also hoping for – and what eventually transpires – is their first evening of a mother–daughter relationship which neither has ever enjoyed. Norman insists 'They have never been so close as they are on this evening. It is calling the question that produces the closeness' (Betsko, p. 328). While their reasons for disclosure vary (Jessie to explain her feelings, and Thelma to find some words to dissuade her daughter), a bond forms from their honest questions to each other, questions which would have otherwise never been asked and knowledge of each other that otherwise would have never been shared.

All of Thelma's delaying tactics are worthless, of course, and even her suggestions for change – crocheting, rearranging the furniture, getting a dog – are meaningless external things (not unlike Vladimir and Estragon's endless games and chatter) which cannot assuage Jessie's deep, internal despair. Norman views Jessie's death, within the play's context, as a positive act: 'Jessie is able to get what she feels she needs. That is not a despairing act. It may look despairing from the outside, but it has cost her everything she has. If Jessie says it's worth it, then it is' (Betsko, p. 339).

In the year following *'night Mother*, Norman wrote her latest play, *Traveler in the Dark* (1984), which details the crisis of faith suffered by Sam, a forty-year-old surgeon: he lacks belief in the religion of his father (a revivalist preacher) and has lost faith in his medical abilities. Having learned that his office-nurse and childhood sweetheart is dying of cancer, which he failed to diagnose in time, Sam gathers his wife and son and retreats to his father's home where he agonises over his mid-life, existential crisis. Although Norman is exploring her usual terrain of love, compassion and self-knowledge as the core of life's meaning, *Traveler* lacks the unsentimentality, subtlety and depth of her earlier, more successful plays. Norman revised the play, which ran for three months at the Taper Forum (1985) to tepid reviews. It has never surfaced again, nor has another new play by Norman.

Traveler in the Dark portends Norman's move away from female protagonists. Although she had earlier written plays that did not foreground women, these have not been critically or commercially successful. Norman's existential vision, her strengths in creating emotionally honest, spiritually impoverished and psychologically devastated characters has occurred only when she uses the materials she knows best: women. The ability in her women characters to represent not the stereotypical domestic female, but rather the universal human condition, is a potent contribution to the canon of women's plays which testify that women can signify more than 'the Other'. The absence of such plays after *'night Mother* leaves a substantial void in this canon.

WENDY WASSERSTEIN

Although Wendy Wasserstein writes wildly comedic plays, behind the witty repartee, one-liners and puns, she dramatises serious issues and conflicts which contemporary women face despite their ostensible social, economic, political and sexual emancipation.

Wasserstein is preoccupied with foregrounding feminist issues, in particular with exploring the positive and negative effects that the feminist movement has had on women. This preoccupation with bringing to the stage the anxiety, despair and confusion women face in their search for self in a contemporary world that continually changes the rules, expectations and definitions of them has resulted in three major plays – *Uncommon Women and Others, Isn't It Romantic,* and *The Heidi Chronicles* – that form a quasi-trilogy (though not intentionally written as such) tracing the myriad changes that women have had to assimilate and reconcile themselves with during the last twenty years.

Wasserstein's first comedy, *Uncommon Women and Others* (1977), is a picaresque memory play recounting the adventures of five college seniors at Mt Holyoke College. The play opens and closes in a restaurant where the women reunite six years after graduation, but it is the fifteen flashback episodes in between, which take place in the dormitory living room, that reveal their conflicts as they prepare to graduate and confront their futures. Each of the five major characters' attitudes and choices *vis-à-vis* the new options and independence open to women represent the spectrum and concomitantly form the fabric of Wasserstein's theme. At one end is Kate, the Phi Beta Kappa headed for law school and a successful corporate lawyer six years later, at the other is Samantha, anxious to dedicate herself to her fiancé and happily married and pregnant at the reunion, and in between the two extremes are those with whom the playwright is most interested: Holly, who longs for a mate yet refuses to live through another, prefers sharing the spotlight within a community of women over the shadow of man, and winds up avoiding any choices by staying in graduate school and accruing three masters degrees; Muffet, a student of feminist history and literature who admits repeatedly that she does not know what to do with her life upon graduation, and ends up an insurance seminar hostess, regrettably single but proud that she can support herself financially; and Rita, an outspoken radical feminist in college who eventually marries but insists that she will someday write a novel and find her full, creative potential. In her cross-section of women, Wasserstein dramatises, as she explained, that 'the Women's Movement has had answers for the Kates of the world . . . or the Samanthas. . . . But for the creative people, a movement can't provide answers. There isn't a specific space for them to move into' (Betsko and Koenig, p. 424). While the career woman and the traditional housewife have found their comfortable niche, for others, the struggle and confusion over the need for emotional happiness and personal autonomy is not so easily reconciled in a contemporary society that has redefined the rules so that these two goals are mutually exclusive, a theme that also dominates Wasserstein's next comedy.

In *Isn't It Romantic* (1981, revised 1983), Wasserstein resurrects Holly, renames her Janie Blumberg, and gives her an old college friend, Harriet Cornwall, as a temperamental and ideological foil. Janie, a twenty-eight-year-old free-lance writer, easily manipulated, an innately 'nice, sweet' Jewish girl whose parents nudge her to marry, she wants 'very badly to be someone else without going through the effort of actually changing [herself] into someone else' (p. 19). Harriet, also twenty-eight and an aggressive business-woman like her mother, wants to have it all: 'married or living with a man, have a good relationship and children that you share equal responsibility for, and a career, and still read novels, play the piano, have women friends and swim twice a week' (p. 45). When Harriet, who has enjoined Janie with her feminist rhetoric not to marry out of loneliness, announces her engagement to a man she has known for only two weeks, Janie feels betrayed and launches into a tirade denouncing Harriet's hypocrisy and capitulation to the newest social dictum: 'Then you almost turn thirty and *Time Magazine* announces "Guess what girls, it's time to have it all"' (p. 54). Despite her earlier complacency and bewilderment over her life's choices, Janie ultimately, unlike her idol Harriet, learns to change her life, to respond to her own inner voice, and to take a stand: she turns down a comfortable marriage to her nice but unsuitable fiancé because she refuses 'to turn someone into the answer for me' (p. 54), and concludes the play with finally unpacking and moving into her apartment – she has found the courage to live by her feminist convictions, to construct her own identity, and to face the world alone if necessary, regardless of what others may say about her choices.

While *Romantic* picks up where *Uncommon Women* left off, in it Wasserstein also takes issue with the newest wrinkle in the feminist polemic: the myth of the superwoman. Wasserstein avers angrily that 'the notion of "having it all" is ridiculous . . . No man has had the pressure during the past ten years of having a different article come out every two weeks dictating how he should live his life' (Betsko and Koenig, p. 422). After the 'either–or' choices promulgated during the *Uncommon Women* era came society's new way of mythologising women: to demand that if they seek successful careers they have to be able to maintain home and family as well – gruelling demands never placed on men. As someone who has experiences the continually shifting definitions of 'woman' that have surfaced over the last two decades, Wasserstein is intrigued by the course of the women's movement, and, after *Romantic*, she expressed interest in writing a play about its history and depicting 'someone who went through it and how it affected them personally' (Betsko and Koenig, p. 432). That play would be *The Heidi Chronicles*, which premiered at Playwright's Horizon (1988), moved to Broadway's Plymouth Theatre, and won Wasserstein the Pulitzer Prize for drama, the Tony Award for play-writing, the Outer Critics Circle, the Susan Smith Blackburn Prize and numerous other awards.

Called '*The Big Chill* of feminism' by Brustein, *The Heidi Chronicles* takes a retrospective, rueful and nostalgic look at the past twenty years of the women's movement by chronicling thirteen episodes from the life of Heidi Holland. After a brief initial episode in 1989 showing Heidi, an art historian, lecturing to her college class about forgotten women Renaissance artists, the action regresses to 1965 and traces Heidi's trek from the pre-feminist era in 1965 when she was sixteen, through the political activism of the late 1960s, the women's consciousness-raising groups in the early 1970s, the peaceful feminists' protests on college campuses during the mid-1970s, the superwoman era of the early 1980s, and yuppiedom of the mid-1980s. Throughout these myriad sociopolitical changes during her last twenty years, Heidi clings tenaciously to her generation's feminist ideals and values, and now, in the late 1980s, as she hears other women, her contemporaries as well as the younger post-feminist generation, trivialise the sacrifices and imply a vacuity in her generation's fight for the ideals of individuality, peace and sisterhood, Heidi feels like an alienated anachronism. She articulates her disillusionment and isolation when, at a 1986 alumnae luncheon, she delivers an extemporaneous, impassioned speech entitled 'Women, Where Are We Going', which describes women in her aerobics class: on one ideological side, the elderly grey-haired lady who extols the virtues of women writers, and at the other two 'hot shot' young women who are more into designer clothes than discussions about women's literary contributions. Heidi's remorse over the post-feminist fissure between the generations of women is conveyed poignantly in her speech's summation: 'It's just that I feel stranded. And I thought the whole point was that we wouldn't feel stranded. I thought the point was we were all in this together' (pp. 94–5).

Wasserstein concludes *The Heidi Chronicles* with her heroine remaining a 'true believer' (p. 116) to the most basic of feminist ideas: the right to choose. But Heidi's choice at the play's conclusion to adopt a daughter has sparked cavilling by feminists who regard it either as a cop-out or, ironically, the wrong choice. Likewise, *Uncommon Women* has been faulted for not offering 'alternatives to or a substantial critique' of the limited opportunities open to women (Keyssar, 1984, p. 154). Wasserstein would agree, but she might respond, as she implied in a recent lecture,[14] that she cannot posit solutions, for to do so would not only be to make the very dogmatic prescriptions and proscriptions she views as the source of women's current confusion and divisiveness, but also, and more pointedly, would be to belie her convictions, those born out of the feminist movement, that every woman must make her own choices irrespective of the current rhetoric or rules of others, and furthermore must be embraced by other women for her courage to choose even if her decisions are not theirs personally. Curiously, to demand a doctrinaire Wasserstein is to confirm tacitly her themes about women's lack of and continued search for a solid solution to their life's choices, and, more telling, to deny her characters the right to choose is to confirm the very breakdown in feminist solidarity which has engendered contemporary feelings of isolation, alienation and separation among women. Wasserstein cannot dictate, she can only explore the terrain, and can only do so from where society forces her to sit.

Within the last decade, some 200 years after Mercy Otis Warren put pen to paper and composed her propagandist pamphlets and plays, American women dramatists, spurred by the same political, social and economic unrest that precipitated the first feminist movement, have propelled themselves into every possible theatre arena – from fringe theatres, to regional stages, academic theatres, performance art and to Broadway – with a force and vigour that Glaspell and her contemporaries could never have envisioned. Bolstered by the new academic discipline of women's studies, these writers are garnering personal support and critical attention from a coalition of scholars that their predecessors in the early twentieth century could not have imagined and, could they have had the benefit of such, would not have suffered obscurity for over fifty years.

If history has taught us anything, however, it is that women playwrights can come to a virtual halt and be excluded from the commercial theatre – which, for better or worse, is the one arena that promotes women playwrights and their voice to national and international prominence – with perhaps little more than passing comment in one brief article by reviewers like Gussow or Kerr. Indeed, had Glaspell been told that within a few decades her voice and that of her compeers would diminish and fall to near silence, she would have pointed to the strong feminist coalition as well as to the accomplishments by her and other (like Zona Gale's Pulitzer), and certainly would have agreed with Howe's comment in a recent interview for *The New York Times* (7 May 1989) that 'we are just emerging as forces to contend with in the theatre.' If history does have an inscrutable way of repeating itself, then the recent signs by Henley, Howe and Norman of moving away from centring women as strong, potent characters intimates perhaps an early sign of attenuation not unlike that experienced fifty years ago.

Henley, Howe, Norman and Wasserstein represent the pioneers of this second generation of women playwrights, and although they suffer criticism for their ostensible lack of universality or their dearth of experimentation in developing new dramaturgical paradigms, their works not only prove otherwise, but also exhibit an impressive degree of thematic and structural diversity which has, like that of the first group of pioneer dramatists, gone relatively unnoticed or are obscured in theatrical reviews or scholarly disquisitions that intentionally or inadvertently deflect attention away from the very types of crucial discussions that celebrate the play-writing contributions of their male counterparts. While working toward a feminist poetics, scholars concomitantly need to isolate these women as individual dramatists, underscore their uniqueness of voice and dramatic expression, and celebrate the play-writing diversity that has been both the impressive trademark and legacy of women dramatists throughout American history.

NOTES

1. For excellent historical surveys of American women theatre artists, see Helen Kritch Chinoy and Linda Walsh Jenkins, *Women in American Theatre* (New York: Theatre Communications Group,

1987), and Judith Olauson, *The American Woman Playwright* (New York: Whitston, 1981).

2. See, for example, Virginia Frame, 'Women Who Have Written Successful Plays', *Theatre Magazine*, vol. 6 (October 1906), nos. ix–x, pp. 264–7, and Lucy France Pierce, 'Women Who Write Plays', *The World Today*, vol. 15 (June 1908), pp. 725–31.

3. After Gale and before the arrival of the new wave of feminist writers, only four women were awarded the Pulitzer Prize: 1931, Susan Glaspell, *Alison's House*; 1935, Zoe Atkins, *The Old Maid*; 1945, Mary Chase, *Harvey*; 1958, Kitti Frings, *Look Homeward, Angel*.

4. For an excellent discussion about the canonisation of women's plays see Jill Dolan, *Feminist Spectator as Critic* (Ann Arbor: UMI Research Press, 1988), and 'Bending Gender to Fit the Canon: The Politics of Production', in Linda Hart, *Making a Spectacle* (Ann Arbor: University of Michigan Press, 1989).

5. Jonnie Guerra, 'Beth Henley: Female Quest and the Family-Play Tradition', in Hart, pp. 118–19. Not all feminist scholars agree; for this discussion, see, for example, Dolan, Forte, Keyssar, Morrow, Spencer and both Laughlin and Harbin in Barranger, *Southern Quarterly*, 1987.

6. *Crimes* had its initial staging in Actors' Theatre of Louisville in 1979; then, after some difficulty, it was staged at the Manhattan Theatre Club in December 1980, and finally at Broadway's Golden Theatre on 4 November 1981. During this time, Henley had made arrangements for *Miss Firecracker* and *Jamey Foster* to begin rehearsals at Buffalo's Studio Theatre and Connecticut's Hartford Stage, respectively. Henley's first play was a one-act entitled *Am I Blue*, written in 1972 and presented by the Circle Repertory Company in 1982.

7. From 14–23 October 1982 at the Eugene O'Neill Theatre.

8. *The Nest* (1970), which opened at the Mercury Theatre and closed after one performance, examined the ritual of courtship and the savagery between women as they battle for husbands; there is no extant published copy. *Birth and After Birth* (1973), an absurdist look at women's roles as mother, wife and child-bearer, has never been produced; it is anthologised in Honor Moore, *The New Women's Theatre* (New York: Random House, 1977).

9. Howe believed that reviewers saw a play as an indictment against modern art, its consumers and its critics (Simon, 1986, for example), and, feeling uncomfortable about being satirised, they reacted negatively to the detriment of the play's run (Betsko and Koenig, p. 229). *Museum*, which opened at the Los Angeles Actors' Theatre in April 1976, had a brief New York run at the Public.

10. For a discussion of female hunger and self-expression, see Nancy Backes, 'Body Art: Hunger and Satiation in the Plays of Tina Howe', in Hart.

11. *Third and Oak: Pool Hall*, a one-act companion piece to *Laundromat*, involves two men, one the proprietor of the pool hall and the other

the son of his closest friend. *Circus Valentine* (1979), a roman-ticised portrait of a travelling circus and written during Norman's residency at Actors' Theatre, was poorly received in New York, and *The Holdup* (1983), a western comedy based on her grandfather's tales, had only a workshop production at San Francisco's American Conservatory Theatre (Gussow, 1981, 1983; Stout, 1983).

12.   The regional and social specificity of *Getting Out* and *Laundromat* (southern lower class) engendered reductive interpretations of these plays; Norman admitted retrospectively that if she were writing *Getting Out* today it would have a less specific locale. Norman consciously corrected this problem in *'night Mother* (Betsko and Koenig, p. 337).

13.   For example, Gilman glibly summed that 'epileptics, neglected children and abandoned wives have a hard time in "coping"', and Rich (1983) attributes Jessie's despair to all her personal problems, in addition to the fact that she is 'a fat, lumpy, anonymous-looking woman'. Even Dolan, who has written extensively on this play and its existential resonance, laments its 'unwillingness to discuss Jessie's dilemma in terms of a wider social context' (Dolan, 'Bending Gender', p. 336).

14.   The Women's Club of Washington University, St Louis, Missouri, 13 November 1989.

BIBLIOGRAPHY

Adler, T. P. (1987) *Mirror on the Stage: The Pulitzer Plays as an Approach to American Drama* (West Lafayette, Indiana: Purdue University Press).

Barlow, J. E. (1981) *Plays by American Women: The Early Years* (New York: Avon).

Barnes, C. (1981) '*Crime* is a Prize Hit that's all Heart', *New York Critics' Review*, pp. 42, 137

Barranger, M. S. (1987) 'Southern Women Playwrights', *Southern Quarterly* (special issue), spring, vol. 25, no. 3.

Bennetts, L. (1986) 'Theatre: Tina Howe Writes a Love Story Set on a Beach', *New York Times*, 16 Nov.

Betsko, K. and Koenig, R. (eds) (1987) *Interviews with Contemporary Women Playwrights* (New York: Beech Tree Books).

Brown, J. (1979) *Feminist Drama* (Metuchen, N.J.: Scarecrow).

Brustein, R. (1989) 'Women in Extremes', *The New Republic*, 17 April, pp. 32–4.

Carlson, S. L. (1984) 'Comic Textures and Female Communities, 1937–1977: Clare Booth and Wendy Wasserstein', *Modern Drama*, Dec., vol. 28, no. 4, pp. 564–73.

Chinoy, H. K. and Jenkins, L. W. (1987) *Women in American Theatre* (New York: Theatre Communications Group).

Cohen, E. (1988) 'Uncommon Woman: An Interview with Wendy Wasserstein', *Women's Studies*, vol. 15, nos 1–3, pp. 257–70.

Dolan, J. (1988) *Feminist Spectator as Critic* (Ann Arbor: UMI Research Press).

Forte, J. (1989) 'Realism, Narrative, and the Feminist Playwright: A Problem of Perception', *Modern Drama*, March, vol. 32, no. 1, pp. 115–27.

Gilman, R. (1983) 'Theatre', *Nation*, 7 May, p. 586.

Gussow, M. (1981) 'Theatre: Women Playwrights Show New Strength', *New York Times*, 15 Feb., pp. 4, 24.

———. (1981),'Theatre: Beth Henley's *Crimes of the Heart*', *New York Times* 5 Nov., pp. 21ff.

———. (1983) 'Women Playwrights: New Voices in the Theatre', *New York Times*, 1 May, pp. 22ff.

Hart, L. (1989) *Making a Spectacle* (Ann Arbor: University of Michigan Press).

Henley, B. (1982) *Am I Blue* (New York: Dramatists Play Service).

———. (1982) *Crimes of the Heart* (New York: Dramatists Play Service).

———. (1983) *The Wake of Jamey Foster* (New York: Dramatists Play Service).

———. (1985) *The Miss Firecracker Contest* (New York: Fireside Theatre Edition).

———. (1987) *The Lucky Spot* (New York: Dramatists Play Service).

Howe, T. (1979) *The Art of Dining* (New York: Samuel French).

———. (1979) *Museum* (New York: Samuel French).

———. (1984) *Painting Churches* (New York: Samuel French).

———. (1985) 'Antic Vision', *American Theatre*, Sep., pp. 12, 14.

———. (1987) *Coastal Disturbances* (New York: Samuel French).

———. (1989) *Approaching Zanzibar* (New York: Samuel French).

Keyssar, H. (1984) *Feminist Theatre* (London: Macmillan).

Laughlin, K. L. (1986) 'Criminality, Desire and Community: A Feminist Approach to Beth Henley's *Crimes of the Heart*', *Women and Performance*, vol. 3, pp. 35–51.

Morrow, L. (1988) 'Orality and Identity in *'night Mother* and *Crimes of the Heart*', *Studies in American Drama*, vol. 3, pp. 23–39.

Norman, M. (1979) *Getting Out* (New York: Dramatists Play Service).

———. (1980) *Third and Oak: The Laundromat* (New York: Dramatists Play Service).

———. (1983) *'night Mother* (New York: Dramatists Play Service).

———. (1985) *Third and Oak: The Pool Hall* (New York: Dramatists Play Service).

———. (1987) *The Holdup* (New York: Dramatists Play Service).

Rich, F. (1980) 'Stage: *Crimes of [the] Heart*, Comedy About 3 Sisters', *New York Times*, 22 Dec., p. 16.

———. (1983) 'Theatre: Suicide Talk in *'night Mother*', *New York Times*, 1 April, p. 3.

———. (1987) 'Stage: *Lucky Spot* by Beth Henley ', *New York Times*, 29 April, p. 22.

Simon, J. (1986) 'The Powers That Will Be', *New York*, 22–9 Dec., pp. 96–7.

———. (1987) 'Lucky Spot', *New York*, 11 May, pp. 83, 84.

Spencer, J. S. (1987) 'Norman's *'night Mother*: Psycho-drama of Female Identity', *Modern Drama*, Sep., vol. 30, no. 3, pp. 364–75.

Stout, K. (1983) 'Marsha Norman: Writing for the "Least of Our Brethren"', *Saturday Review*, Sep./Oct., pp. 29ff.

Wasserstein, W. (1978) *Uncommon Women and Others* (New York: Dramatists Play Service).

——. (1985) *Isn't It Romantic* (New York: Dramatists Play Service).

——. (1988) *The Heidi Chronicles* (New York: Fireside Theatre Edition).

'Women in Theatre', (1985) *The Theatre Annual* (special issue), vol. 40.

'Women Playwrights: Themes and Variations', (1989) *New York Times*, 7 May, pp. 1, 42.

2
Not-Quite Mainstream Male Playwrights: Guare, Durang and Rabe

DENNIS CARROLL

Guare, Durang and Rabe: what do they have in common except that they are all male, with Roman Catholic backgrounds and with careers that germinated in the rich, explosive period of the late 1960s and early 1970s? For one thing, they do not fit into the mainstream of steady financial success or critical acceptance. The content of their plays and their restlessly exploratory techniques for dramatising it are too maverick for that, even if they have had major 'successes'. Similarities are revealed by their use of scenography, language, social ritual and structure. But it is in the area of thematic exploration that their kinship is revealed most clearly.

Though all three have apparently conformed to the international trend towards a greater realism in the last fifteen years, this has made possible for them a more subtle dramaturgy, a more complex articulation of their concerns. In their use of scenography, they still foreground their major metaphors, but less obviously. Dialogue is more important as style-marker or distancing screen than as a traditional tool to suggest subtext or reveal character; indeed, their characters often use it as defensive or offensive weaponry to conceal themselves. Long 'arias' impose their own tonal and structural idiosyncrasies on the plays. 'Social rituals', earlier used to satirise social conformity, are later insidious palliatives consciously chosen by characters to deflect genuine contact with another. Often the structure of the more recent plays appears to be more 'well-made' than that of the more obviously episodic earlier ones, but this is deceptive.

All three continue to be absorbed by three major themes. The most intimate and personal concerns the dilemma of the family member – most often the son – who feels unloved and unwanted, and who seeks both an identity and a personal fulfilment that transcends the role that the family has delimited him to play. On a broader, sociopolitical level, the playwrights explore the nuclear or extended family as an institution in tense dialectic with the more impersonal forces of the surrounding society, and the threat of the family's breakdown or destruction. The third theme spirals out beyond the sociopolitical arena altogether. All these playwrights were raised as Roman Catholics, and in different degrees all have come to question or reject their faith. Along with lapsed faith is the consequent terrified protest at the meaningless and random patterning of life, and an urge to find some transcendent substitute for received religion.

JOHN GUARE

John Guare's career has been more pock-marked by scattershot critical commentary than that of most major American playwrights. Of influential reviewers, only *Newsweek's* Jack Kroll has been consistently perceptive in illuminating Guare's developing techniques and objectives as a playwright. Guare's major endeavour as a playwright to date is still incomplete – the planned tetralogy known as the 'Lydie Breeze' plays. The two plays of the tetralogy so far released in published form are *Lydie Breeze* and *Gardenia*, both first performed in 1982.

A bizarre tonality, very disconcerting to some, is at the core of Guare's distinctiveness as a playwright. He himself described his best-known play *The House of the Blue Leaves* (1971) as the child of a marriage between Strindberg and Feydeau – and the style and technique was suggested by him seeing *The Dance of Death* and *A Flea in Her Ear* on two successive evenings at Britain's National Theatre (*Los Angeles Times*, 1972, p. 26). Ross Wetzsteon has described Guare's style as being coloured by 'outbursts of macabre violence in the midst of bizarre comedy' (1982, p. 36). The label 'black comedy', fashionable in the 1960s, hardly applies to Guare's strategies, because in his hands the violence and the comedy do not blend into an easily digestible mixture for audiences. There are disconcertingly sudden shifts from farce to violence and back. In *The House of the Blue Leaves*, for example, the Queens apartment of the hero is suddenly invaded by a paramedic with a strait-jacket, who chases the mentally distraught Bananas, wife of the hero; at the same time the AWOL son of the family, trying to assassinate the visiting Pope with a home-made bomb, is pursued Feydeau-like fashion about the room by military police. The son gives the bomb, in gift-wrapping, to a visiting Hollywood starlet, who goes off with some visiting nuns to see the Pope. There is a tremendous offstage explosion, and in the following scene we learn that the nuns and starlet have been killed. Most other maniacal farcical Guare plays are given sudden about-faces in tone, and in appropriate audience response, by similar 'bombs' of brutal and unexpected violence.

Guare's early scenic strategies show signs of the wildly experimental off off Broadway scene of the late 1960s, in which the emphasis was on ingenious and telling presentational props and scenic units, rather than on a fully developed and expensive 'set'. In the early plays, Guare often uses costumes and props to develop funny visual business, to cue 'transformations', to underline satirical social rituals, or even excursions beyond the proscenium for 'audience participation'. In the later plays, the scenography becomes more restricted in its active uses and at the same time more precise and startling, though always justified by the sometimes unusual circumstances of the action. Sometimes the arresting images are subchronic, as in *Lydie Breeze*, where the stage represents an austere double-storey house on Nantucket threatened by a vast expanse of sea and sand-dunes in turn punctuated by the ruins of an upturned, ruptured boat. Sometimes they are diachronic, as in the successive, and wildly contrasting, scenic images in *Bosums and Neglect* (1979): a hospital room and a chic Manhattan apartment stuffed with books and art objects – or, even more extreme, the open beach and the closed prison of the two acts of *Gardenia*. Perhaps nowhere is Guare's visual imagination more surreally in evidence than in the setting for *Marco Polo Sings a Solo* (1976), which combines on stage bizarrely incongruous images on an iceberg off the coast of Norway in 1999: Grieg's grand piano, a baby carriage, heat-lamps, and work-room furniture.

Guare's highly individual way with dialogue underlines his characters' difficulties in living an authentic life under the weight of literary models and a cultural consciousness. More so than with most modern American playwrights, Guare's dialogue is witty, literate – and full of references to other plays, other writings. Guare assumes that his audience is educated, smart and highly sophisticated theatrically. Thus they may share the characters' problems of finding authenticity of behaviour and feeling through the smokescreen of role-models their own literary and cultural awareness provides. For example, *Rich and Famous* (1974) deals with The World's Oldest Playwright's difficulties with playmaking and with transcending artistic influences and 'show biz' pressures. *Marco Polo Sings A Solo* piles up references to nineteenth- and twentieth-century literary and theatrical works as a way to indicate the weight of cultural heritage, good and bad, by 1999. The lovers of *Bosums and Neglect* struggle to reach each other through walls of books and publications, and the role-models provided by their knowledge of literature, before giving way to violence as a way of primal communication – triggered, significantly, when he knifes up her books. In *Gardenia* and *Lydie Breeze*, the key dramatic importance of numerous letters, writings and manuscripts foregrounds the difficulty of creating original literary art against the weight of a heritage by which it will be measured.

The Guare dialogue is also characterised by arias – long uninterrupted set speeches which characterise the work of some other important contemporary American playwrights, and which pull their plays away from parameters of literal naturalism. Faced with the challenges of surmounting prescribed behaviour, Guare's characters go on the defensive into monologue, which is sometimes soliloquy, other times addressed to the theatre audience as confidant. This device suggests in Guare the strength, even pigheadedness, of the characters' dreams, but alsso their basic insularity, their unfitness for communicating their dreams and ideals to other characters. Sometimes the dream is a confidence, a cherished ideal, as in *Muzeeka* (1967), for instance, where the hero tells the audience of his plan to infect people with the dancing spirit of the Etruscans through muzak. Sometimes the aria is aggressive, a piece of weaponry, as in *Cop-out* (1968), where the cop rattles off a litany of conformity and solidarity with the force, even priding himself on his vasectomy which he underwent because of his brother officers' example. For Guare the playwright, as distinct from his characters, however, the arias have another function. As Wetzsteon has put it, Guare's 'fantasies kept spilling over the edges of his scripts' (1982, p. 35), and this has been especially possible through the arias, for it is through them that the density of narrative and poetic exposition that is a major characteristic of Guare's signature style is chiefly driven home.

Guare's extensive use of music and song is a stylistic characteristic not shared by Durang and Rabe. It can provide an entertaining parody of other forms of musical theatre; a Brechtian distancing of key themes; or an underlining of period style.

Parodic social rituals, and the conformity and constriction they connote, loom large in the early Guare plays. In *Home Fires* (1969), the satirical action centres around two funerals in 1918 after the First World War, and much of the comedy accrues from the way that they are disrupted. In *Cop-out,* Marilyn Monroe sleeps with a succession of US presidents; in *Muzeeka,* a prostitute invades the audience area and gives out her calling card, and an assignation is disrupted with stagehands assisting and hampering the action by adding and removing scenery. *The House of the Blue Leaves* is framed with the hero's salving social ritual of playing his awful songs to the audience in a piano bar.

Guare's structural conventions, especially in the early plays, have seemed chaotic to many critics. There has been the predictable charge of the plays being 'episodic', and further charges of a lack of expositional and narrative coherence. The most successful play with audiences and critics so far, *The House of the Blue Leaves* is possibly the easiest to follow at the level of narrative and in terms of linear development. Some of the later plays appear to be more structurally conventional, but in fact they are marked by various gaps and disjunctions even though they appear more 'unified'. In the 'Lydie Breeze' plays, gestures towards a more conventional form are partly strategies to foreground the devices of nineteenth-century drama. (This foregrounding appears in other ways too: in the Ibsenesque technique of past-as-nemesis, for instance, and in the motif of transmitted venereal disease so important in the climactic events of *Lydie Breeze.*) If in Ibsen and Chekhov major events happen offstage or in the past, in Guare this is emphasised to the point where it becomes mannerist and, in the opinion of some critics, undramatic. The act of murder, central to both the 'Lydie Breeze' plays, and the later suicide of Lydie, are not shown on stage, but constantly refracted through discussion and reminiscence. But this dramatic obliqueness underlines Guare's insistence that the 'present', whether it be that of a group of individuals, a family or a nation, is chiefly characterised by a refracted consciousness of a 'past' defined and fixed by events of a higher profile than the present is usually able to match or counter.

In other Guare plays, there are similar gaps, undramatised offstage events, and surprising narrative developments which are unconventional and often exhilarating and which embody in diverse ways his stated intention of bringing to the stage the density and excitement of multi-stranded novelistic narrative (Harrop, 1987a, p. 155). One of the most structurally interesting plays is *Landscape of the Body* (1977), which uses flashback, a dead narrator, and a careful progression of short scenes that are presented independently of her – all to the net effect of revealing multi-stranded narrative information that the characters themselves never learn. This reinforces a distancing irony in what otherwise could have been merely an affecting but simple-minded play.

Guare is very much concerned with the two family-centred themes of the individual's place in the family, and the way that larger societal fores impinge on it. The figure of the son who must compulsively prove himself recurs in several Guare plays from the time of the early *Home Fires*. Perhaps it is in *Bosums and Neglect* that the figure is most movingly evoked – the hero's failure to deeply connect with the mother he loves is equated with his earlier failure to connect with other women in his life.

It is the way the son feels that he must prove himself as a successful member of the family and be accepted by the parent that allows Guare to intimate the power of larger social pressures on the family and its individual members. The son's desire to be 'rich and famous', to gain an identity and be accepted by the parents, is a side-effect of the cult of 'celebrity', which is dehumanising because it creates two races apart: those who fashion themselves into media cut-out figures, and their audiences who mindlessly accept them as gods and heroes. In *The House of the Blue Leaves* and *Rich and Famous* especially, Guare investigates the dehumanising qualities of 'celebrity' on both human products and consumers. The hero of *Rich and Famous* still wants those attributes, even though he aware of their drawbacks – to be accepted by his parents, to limn his self-worth, to overcome limitations in realising himself. In *Marco Polo Sings A Solo*, Guare presents the other side of the coin: that personal growth is only possible when one can control the unlimited possibilities for self-fulfilment that being rich and famous can create. In the 'Lydie Breeze' plays, Guare also investigates the extended family commune, an ideal strong in the 1960s. The germinal situation of the tetralogy is the decision of the nurse Lydie Breeze, and three of her ex-Civil War soldier patients, to found a commune on Nantucket dedicated to the education of former slaves. Lydie marries one of the men, Hickman, to facilitate the practicalities of its establishment, but, partly through this action, rivalries are engendered that ultimately split it apart. As in the 1860s, so in the 1960s, Guare implies.

Enveloping the social and familial themes in Guare is yet another: the yearning for some kind of transcendence. Guare seems to feel that the Roman Catholic religion is no answer, though this conclusion seems more wry than angry. In *The House of the Blue Leaves*, the Pope is just another superstar elevated to celebrity status by media exposure; the little nun, sole survivor of the bomb explosion, is delighted at the end over her decision not to go back to the convent. But if not religion, then what? In Guare, terror at the disorder and randomness of life seems more independent of religious causes than it does in Durang. Guare recognises this terror, however, and the later plays increasingly investigate salves for it.

Nantucket symbolises for Guare a place of healing and regeneration. *Lydie Breeze* and *Gardenia* are largely set there, and these are the two of Guare's plays so far in which he examines the solace of a Whitmanesque transcendentalism. The chronology of the plays is significant: *Lydie Breeze*, premiered before *Gardenia* but with an action that chronologically follows it, is suffused with a mystic affirmation; it shows the protagonist Hickman having outfaced the ghosts of his past and reconciled with his young daughter, with her 'on the beach at night alone'. *Gardenia* makes clear the terrible price of this 'transcendence', however. The major theme of the play is the acceptance of limitations – Hickman, in prison for the murder of his friend and rival Dan, lambasts false idealism and the kind of 'transcendentalism' willed and performed rather than lived and experienced. Yet he is forced to compromise by destroying his revised manuscript, a document that authenticates his pain and could give shape and meaning to his odyssey of crime and redemption. He does this both to win his freedom from prison, and to stare his 'petty furies in the face and name them and lose them' (*Gardenia*, 1982, p. 59). This act of compromise, paradoxically both courageous and cowardly, also has a selfishness that brings about Lydie's suicide. Only at that price does Hickman win his physical and spiritual freedom, and Guare suggests that it is a price too dear to pay. In any case, *Gardenia* is the necessary measure through which the apparently positive and mystical ending of *Lydie Breeze* must be qualified.

CHRISTOPHER DURANG

Jerry Zaks, a director who admires both Durang and Guare, has commented that they both have the ability to 'get the audience laughing, laughing, laughing and then shock them. It's not a manipulation. It's the greatest sleight of hand, because it's grounded in reality' (*New York Times*, 1986, p. 16). The tone of Durang's best work can be compared to Guare's, but it is more high-key, more obviously satirical, and somehow more unified in tone in that the shifts from comedy to the disequilibrium of violence are not usually so drastic or unexpected. Perhaps, though, the best of Durang's plays are those in which these shifts are the most disconcerting.

Striking metaphor and visual virtuosity are not as important in Durang's work as they are in Guare's Many of the early plays utilize a bare or amorphously set stage that can serve for several different locations, and even the later plays depend on somewhat neutral scenographic solutions for the shifting locations Durang requires. Loren Sherman devised a series of sliding plum-coloured panels for *The Marriage of Bette and Boo* (1985) to convey an almost cinematic flow from one location to the next, as Durang's afternotes to the published version make clear (p. 97). Similarly, for the first off Broadway production of *Beyond Therapy* (1981), the several locations of the action were ironically played out in the same slickly amorphous Manhattan-chic space that did duty for all of them (Gussow, 1981, p. C11). The only play in which more elaborate stage settings are important is *A History of the American Film* (1976), where the subject matter of the play is scenically embodied in a double-duty theatre balcony and stalls with roll-away seats; the stalls area can thus represent both a movie-watching audience and what they are seeing. If the setting is often extremely simple, however, the costumes in

Durang play an unusually important part in defining the moral or spiritual state of the characters. Examples are afforded by the costumes of the students who come to Sister Mary dressed in the 'improvised garb' of the holy family for their pageant play in *Sister Mary Ignatius Explains It All For You* (1979); the elegant red and black formal wear of the Emissaries from God in *The Nature and Purpose of the Universe* (1975); and the increasingly deracinated wedding garb that the title characters wear all the way through *The Marriage of Bette and Boo*.

When one turns to Durang's dialogue it is obvious that there is not the same literary allusiveness as in Guare, though it is there in a more moderate form. Certain plays, such as the short *The Actor's Nightmare* (1981), make much use of the audience's presumed familiarity with the great works of dramatic literature, old and new, while *A History of the American Film* depends for much of its satirical thrust on the audience's cinematic literacy.

One convention does stand out: a pseudo-objective narrative device as used by authorial surrogates or commentators, notably the Emissaries of God in *The Nature and Purpose of the Universe* and Matt the son in *The Marriage of Bette and Boo*. The former play, Durang's first, is a fable of a deracinated Roman Catholic family told as Gothic horror comic. The central figure is Eleanor, a wife and mother abused and terrorised by husband and sons and betrayed by a 'redeemer' figure in the form of a Fuller brush salesman, and forced to flee to Iceland when her husband supports a radical nun in a *putsch* to assassinate the Pope. The elegantly clad Emissaries, who are both narrators and puppet-masters, narrate the fable in the style of a children's bedtime story. Their moral authority as fable-makers is not confronted until the savage cruelty of the ending, when Eleanor is denied even the consolation of death to put her out of her misery. With Matt in *The Marriage of Bette and Boo*, this dramatic movement is reversed. At the beginning, his comments on the marriage of his parents and his mother's series of miscarriages express his own emotional deadness, his distance – both moral and empathetic – from the formative years. Eventually we begin to empathise with him as narrator and character, however, when this attitude is recognised by him, confronted, and perhaps finally abandoned.

The arias of Durang's characters have a similar function to Guare's, but are a little less independent of their immediate context in the play. They often convey the self-absorption or paranoia of the characters. For example, Bette's long 'interior monologue' following her marriage present the interior landscape of her limited mind and imagination; her 'phone call aria' to a friend in Florida she has not seen for many years has a similar if more 'realistic' function, and indicates the developing emptiness that she feels both in her marriage and in her relationships with her relatives. The technique is at its most emphatic, however, in *Sister Mary Ignatius Explains It All For You*. The title character, in her theatre–'classroom', first lectures the theatre audience, cast by implication as her current pupils; and the only interruption to her lectures is afforded by her favourite pupil, a boy who provides monosyllabic answers, usually correct, to her questions on well-drilled material. But then the classroom is invaded by some ex-students who feel betrayed by both her and her religion; and her determination to dominate and control, symbolised in the arias, is formally challenged by the climactic answering aria of Diane, who exposes the shortcomings of Sister Mary's teachings in her own desperate confession of loss of faith. The 'lighter' plays – *Beyond Therapy* and *A History of the American Film*, for example – which Durang told David Savran he expected to be his 'hits' (Savran, 1988, p. 25), contain nothing comparable in terms of length and intensity.

Ritualised action – both religious and social, reported and acted out – is a stronger stylistic hallmark in Durang than in Guare. Often considerable dramatic play is made with the subversion or breakdown of social rituals or ceremonies. *Titanic* (1974) begins aboard a ship with a formal dinner which is undermined by the hilarious revelation of marital infidelity on both sides, and the play continues in a pattern of breakdown of social proprieties. The early scenes of *The Nature and Purpose of the Universe* take their shape from the way that Eleanor's housewifely rituals are viciously subverted by the casual violence perpetrated on her by her menfolk. *Beyond Therapy* begins with a 'blind date' at a restaurant engineered by 'personals' and ends, at another restaurant, with a very forced dinner party that is initiated by gunfire, while much of the rest of the comedy in this play arises from aborted social rituals, including the ritual of psychiatric analysis. The entire action of *A History of the American Film* is ritualised through the conventions of genre, which gradually break down and become more and more scrambled. *The Marriage of Bette and Boo* begins with a wedding, replete with a disrupted family portrait setting (incomplete) and Schubert cello music (unplayed). The wedding ceremony itself is presented in a surreal and montaged form. The play has many scenes in which social rituals collapse or turn awry – Christmas dinners, Thanksgivings, anniversaries, and of course the anxious family gatherings at hospitals at Bette's imminent childbirths, which turn out to be still-births – accented by the savage device of a doctor throwing a doll to the floor. The play takes its closure from the final such ritual: a hospital sick-visit which becomes a death-watch and a requiem.

Durang's handling of structure is more conventional, and adroit, than he is sometimes given credit for. Savran has stated that each play is a 'more or less tightly coordinated series of sketches whose impact finally is the result more of accumulation than linear development' (1988, p. 19). In *A History of the American Film*, this 'accumulation' is negative in the sense that, as the parameters of genre expectation break down, the structure becomes an image of a progression towards moral and narrative chaos. But *The Marriage of Bette and Boo* can be given almost a conventional structural cohesion by a design similar to that of the original production, which makes the changes of locale nominal and facilitates a cinematic smoothness; and *Sister Mary Ignatius Explains It All For You* is, in fact, an extended one-act play that preserves the unities.

Even more severely than Rabe and Guare, Durang lambasts the nuclear family for failure to deliver on promises of intimacy and individual fulfilment. He is particularly concerned with the failure of communication between parents and children. The key situation of the absurdist *Baby With the Bathwater* (1983) is that a couple is so out of touch with their child that they rear him as her for fifteen years. The more representational *The Marriage of Bette and Boo* movingly reveals Matt's guilt at not being able to communicate with either parent, in the two scenes which are out of chronology with the rest of the action. And he cannot bring himself to even visit for long the mother he feels close to. One of the achievements of the play is that, paradoxically, Durang suggests a genuine love which seems to persist in the Bette–Boo relationship in spite of the biological blood-battle which keeps aborting their children, and in spite of Boo's alcoholism. The play's final scene is an ironically brief vision of concord between the parents – but only after their divorce and just before Bette's death.

Other Durang plays present families or ur-families as horror-systems which promise love, order and stability and deliver chaos, cruelty and betrayal. In _The Nature and Purpose of the Universe_, the standard apple-pie vision of the American family is ridiculed, the widely held attitude condoning the American housewife as _mater dolorosa_ savagely questioned. Eleanor becomes the victim of repeated violence by her husband and three sons (a dope pusher, a homosexual and a eunuch) and a horny school coach. Similar horrors beset the racist family in _The Vietnamization of New Jersey_ (1977), but there is still more confusion when it is revealed that the Asian wife is, in fact, an American imposter. The families of _A History of the American Film_ are parodies of cutesy stereotypical families from various film genres. In _Titanic_, an upper class Edwardian family is split apart by an hilarious farrago of past and present adultery and homo- and heterosexual seduction, including the antics of a _femme fatale_ who keeps a hamster up her vagina. In _Beyond Therapy_, the bisexual hero wants marriage and children with a woman, but also a handy male lover in a flat above a two-car garage – even if, at the end, he has apparently settled for a woman only. The play suggests that the family might be more viable as an institution if it engendered fewer promises of personal fulfilment; that its stability and permanence would be more certain if its promises to deliver such qualities were less extreme.

On the broader scale, Durang is concerned with larger institutional systems which impinge on both the family and its individual members and impose similar constrictions and compensatory promises on an even grander scale. On all levels, the individual seems to be constricted by systems that not only establish order but spuriously claim that there can be meaning, pattern and purpose in all human activity. These systems include institutionalised medical and therapeutic palliatives, such as psychiatry and counselling (_Beyond Therapy_); the comforts of narrative genres and their myths (_A History of the American Film_); of culturally induced ethnic stereotyping (_The Vietnamization of New Jersey_); the territorial imperatives of wealth and class (_Titanic_); and the cultural weight of past art and literature (_The Actor's Nightmare_). Such institutionalised targets are important in Durang, and the one that takes precedence over all of them is Roman Catholicism.

Durang's disappointment at the unrealised promises of order, meaning and purpose held out by his religion is at the heart of his three most powerful plays. Seemingly most offensive to him is the idea propagated by the Church that there is purpose in suffering, and that suffering is a cross inflicted on an individual for a reason. At the denouement of *The Nature and Purpose of the Universe*, in a savage commentary on the Abraham and Isaac story, Eleanor begs to be killed rather than live on in suffering. In *Sister Mary Ignatius Explains It All For You*, Diane in her climactic aria relates the traumatic experiences that made her realise that the Church's promises of meaning and order in life were utterly spurious. She tells how her mother died of cancer and the same day she was raped by an intruder in her home and 'Somehow the utter randomness of things . . . *this randomness seemed intolerable*. I found I grew to hate you, Sister, for making me once expect everything to be ordered and to make sense' (p. 147). Diane's protest at the imposition of inimical order-systems leads to her death at the hands of Sister Mary, who shoots her. Shortly afterwards, she also shoots another ex-student, a homosexual who has recently gone to confession, and so can enter 'Heaven' in a state of grace. At the end of the play, still wielding the revolver, she has imposed her belief-pattern, and that of her Church, once again. It is significant that several critics called this Durang's 'revenge' play against the Roman Catholic Church. In *The Marriage of Bette and Boo*, Matt reaches similar insights as Diane about the absurd randomness of much of experience – but not as disastrously, and with a possibility for growth. He comes to believe that suffering is not God's punishment for a specific sin meted out to an individual, and that perhaps individuals, for God, do not exist: 'I think He punishes people in general, for no reason' (p. 84). It is in these three plays that Durang's personal anger and heartache boils up out of the depths and gives them an energy and memorability that the other plays simply do not have.

But if disorder and the randomness of life cannot be stared at and accepted, what is the alternative? Images of apocalypse and total breakdown loom over the endings of several Durang plays. In *A History of the American Film*, a 'The End' sign, which comfortably closed down several genre episodes earlier, rises at the final resolution scene with a great deal of uncertainty, shell-shocked and with some of its letters missing. Carried aloft with it is the archetypal Loretta Young character, who needs its rosy reassurances most. Both remain in a state of semi-ascension at the end, with the onlookers uncertain of what will happen. *The Nature and Purpose of the Universe* finishes with the final situation unresolved; *Titanic* ends with an aborted funeral, decomposing bodies, and the drifting liner about to sink; *'dentity Crisis* (1975) with several adulterous and incestuous couples kissing and making cuckoo sounds. Some transcendental alternative to religion is nowhere in sight.

DAVID RABE

David Rabe came to national attention in 1971 as the first American playwright to deal in depth with the Vietnam War – subject-matter that has made it difficult for critics to recognise some more basic, underlying themes of his work as a whole. His early breakthrough with Joseph Papp and the American Place Theatre, who presented *The Basic Training of Pavlo Hummel* (1970) and *Sticks and Bones* (1971), ensured proper attention and production for some more problematic plays to come. Not as prolific as Guare, he was the early recipient of critical respect, even adulation, on the basis of his first two plays. When this later became more equivocal, it did not stop him from taking creative risks, a trait he shares with Guare and Durang.

The tone of Rabe's work is different to that of the other two playwrights considered here. There is not the swing from near-farce to violence. Though sections of Rabe plays – notably the recent *Hurlyburly* (1984) and *Goose and Tomtom* (1986) – can be uproarious, the progression to and away from comedy is usually fairly gradual. Less well-educated working-class characters are more prominent in the plays, and partly for this reason they contain less self-reflexiveness and less literary allusion.

At least in the early plays, the distinctive feature of Rabe's scenography is a thrust stage platforming at the back – a paradigm not unlike that of the Elizabethan public theatre, with the spatial demarcation of specific locales often fluid. This is significant because a recurring theme in Rabe is the way that personal identity and the family solidarity that can nurture it is connected with a kind of territorial integrity. In *The Basic Training of Pavlo Hummel*, *In the Boom Boom Room* (1973; revised 1986) and *The Orphan* (1973), for example, private or familial space is menaced from the background by some sort of 'tower' or raised structure symbolising institutionalised depredation of the 'personal'. In *In the Boom Boom Room* , several men – the father, the brutal lover and the gay neighbour – manage to gain admittance to Chrissy's

apartment without a key; the precise boundaries of the apartment remain uncertain on the large thrust stage. Even in the
later plays, in the kitchen-living-room of *Hurlyburly* or the cadre
room barracks of *Streamers* (1976), there is a feeling that personal
space is violable or non-existent. At the climax of *Goose and Tomtom*, the grubby interior of Goose and Lorraine's apartment, with
its multiple locks and cheap furnishings, is invaded by mysterious, extraterrestrial forces that break down the doors and walls.
Even more than is true with Durang and Guare, scenic metaphors
embody and epitomise the major dramatic movement of the play:
the elevated 'cages' of the go-go dancers in *In the Boom Boom
Room*, the military training tower in *The Basic Training of Pavlo
Hummel*, the jungle-like plants outside the windows of the Hollywood house in *Hurlyburly*, the mysterious immensity of the night
sky, with its distant stars and planets, in *Goose and Tomtom*. Often
there is the juxtaposing of would-be-domestic interiors against a
pattern of animal or natural imagery which bespeaks the power
of all-enveloping animistic or metaphysical forces.

Two kinds of dialogue tend to be juxtaposed in the early Rabe:
the dialogue of individualised expression, a kind of 'poetry', in
which arresting metaphors are placed in startling, near-surreal
juxtaposition; and the cliches of domestic routine and institutionalised ritual. These two modes are central to the action and conflict
of *Sticks and Bones* and they also inform the gradual development
(or reduction!) of Pavlo in *The Basic Training of Pavlo Hummel*.
In the later plays, the two modes increasingly blur together;
language is used more tortuously by the characters and with
more deliberate opacity by the playwright. Various characters try
to express a barely glimpsed identity through it, or use it to guard
themselves against a commitment or communication which may
frighten them. The tortured attempts at self-definition of Chrissy
in *In the Boom Boom Room* or Billy in *Streamers* develop into the
more sophisticated deflections of Eddie and Micky in *Hurlyburly*, in
which the nonsense phrases 'rapeteta' and 'blah-blah-blah' parody
the limitations of casual social discourse but also signal the characters' unwillingness to open themselves up to something deeper;
paradoxically, there are also moments when certain characters,
such as the actor Phil or the go-go dancer Bonnie, are so anxious to
'communicate' or have a 'deep relationship' that their anxiety turns
their language tortuous beyond their listeners' comprehension and
they defeat their own purpose. Only in *The Orphan* – a semaphoric

retelling of the *Oresteia* legend through a post-Vietnam sensibility – does a more rhetorical and literary kind of dialogue predominate, and its leadenness is highlighted by those few sections of the play in which American idiom is used.

Rabe's use of arias is characterised by closer retention of idiom and colloquialism than his colleagues, and most are more realistically justified by context. Their uses are just as complex, however. Some arias are too neatly turned by a character to point out a moral or serve as 'confessional', and so they expose the very insecurity in the character they are meant to conceal. In *Streamers*, for instance, the homophobic Billy tells a long story about a buddy who got hooked by homosexuality after flirting with it for fun, a story which, for Billy's part, seems like a reaction-formation against some of his own more buried tendencies. In *Hurlyburly*, the photo-journalist Darlene, wishing to guard herself against a too unreserved commitment to Eddie, 'confesses' to him in a long aria about a previous simultaneous affair with two men which led to an abortion. Often, the arias more directly and vulnerably indicate a genuine dislocation, self-enclosure or confusion, as well as being an authorial device for underlining major themes and metaphors. At the end of *Streamers*, after Billy and another character have been knifed to death, an alcoholic sergeant with leukemia, who does not know what has happened, tells a long story recounting the way in which a two-car prang on a road proliferated into a multi-car collision of chaotic impact: an image of the theme of once-seeded violence proceeding and growing on its own momentum. Eddie's solo dialogue with Johnny Carson near the end of *Hurlyburly*, Tomtom's feeling of imprisonment inside his ugly body in *Goose and Tomtom*, Ozzie's reminiscences of his decision to settle down in *Sticks and Bones*, are all important illustrations of the same technique.

Ritualised behaviour is very important in Rabe, and more fore-grounded than even in Durang. In *The Basic Training of Pavlo Hummel*, military training is itself a ritual and informs the main title. This ritual ought to be meaningful for the draftees, and does symbolise a rite-of-passage, but in this play it ironically leads to spiritual and physical death. Less formal army-training rituals – push-ups, gymnastics, polishing gear, mopping up quarters – are behavioral modes the characters fall back on in *Streamers* whenever they are pushed too close to risky intimacy or self-disclosure. In *In the Boom Boom Room* the ritual that predominates is, of course, that of go-go dancing. As Janet Hertzbach has remarked, its grinding routines symbolise the women's isolation, victimisation and sexual degradation (1981, p. 181). But they also involve, as does much of Pavlo's training, a physical stamina and skill, seductive in itself as something to master. The cocaine and drink 'rituals' in *Hurlyburly* stunt and maim self-discovery and intimacy rather than facilitate them. The ritual presentationalism of certain moments in *The Orphan*, *Sticks and Bones* and *Goose and Tomtom* suggest the appeasement of metaphysical and animistic forces. In *Sticks and Bones*, empty domestic social rituals are tellingly juxtaposed against exorcistic ritual-like episodes in which the 'ghost' of David's Vietnamese lover is strangled by David's father Ozzie, and a climax in which David is lovingly bled to death by his family, who hold razors, towels and basins to catch his blood.

In Rabe, the structural patterning of the work is often determined by the developing ramifications of how the central metaphors of the plays govern the action and influence the awareness and insights of the major characters. Since the metaphors are often negative in their thematic implications, the plays reach a point of explosion where the central characters fail in their struggle against the forces the metaphor summates; thereafter the play disintegrates into a usually pessimistic but 'open' resolution. In spite of this, many of the later plays appear 'well-made', but all are subverted with various kinds of disjunctions that erode comforting linearity and observance of 'unities'. *Hurlyburly* includes a gap of one year between Acts I and II; *Goose and Tomtom* is invaded with a surreality that increasingly breaks down the realistic parameters of the early action. *The Basic Training of Pavlo Hummel* and *The Orphan* proceed more episodically, with action that is sometimes non-chronological and sometimes simultaneous. Only the action of *Streamers* approaches old-fashioned regularity, and even that is subverted by 'irrelevancies' both of action and speech.

Rabe's major themes are strikingly similar in their fundamentals to those of Durang and Guare. In Rabe, the motif of the family is even more central to his major concerns, especially the way that an artificial or 'extended' family may be turned to as a substitute for a nuclear family that has failed one of its members. But without exception the 'extended' family, too, fails to nurture. The most savage indictment of the 'nuclear' family is in *Sticks and Bones*, where the monstrous family of apple-pie TV archetypes reject their blinded Vietnam-veteran son and engineer his ritual suicide.

On a more representational level, there is Pavlo Hummel, who is illegitimate, lacks love, is overshadowed by a 'successful' older brother, and hopes to find in the army the family he has never really had. Chrissy, in *In the Boom Boom Room*, has had a mother who never really wanted her and a father who perhaps sexually abused her as a child. In Act II of *The Orphan*, the idea of a 'close' family is savagely parodied; and the whole thematic intent of the play, and essential isolation of Orestes, is summated in the play's title. The male characters of *Hurlyburly* are a pathetic 'family' of housemates all shell-shocked by marriages rocked or destroyed by their own instability or the feminism of the 1970s. The urgency of many of these characters to establish a sense of family, and the emotional and territorial security that is supposed to go with it, brings them to ruin. Chrissy precipitately marries a brutal lout who is infantile in his selfishness; Billy dies for compulsively protecting the integrity of his army 'family' space when Richie threatens to desecrate it with a homosexual act; Eddie fails to nurture Phil, his actor friend, within the male room-mate 'family' and cannot prevent him drifting to suicide; Lorraine, Goose and Tomtom, while trying to preserve their family *ménage à trois*, destroy a brother–sister bond through kidnapping and murder and bring upon themselves their 'family's' own destruction.

Once again, organised religion, including Roman Catholicism, is found to be spurious. There is the obvious critique of the representatives of Roman Catholicism in *Sticks and Bones*, in the portrait of the wretchedly ineffectual priest who retreats before David's striking cane; and in *Hurlyburly*, Phil's religion can give him no solace in the face of his disintegrating marriage. In *The Orphan*, Clytemnestra I's contempt for Calchas and the animistic forces to which her daughter is to be sacrificed involves a concomitant belief in the uselessness of all organised religion and a recognition of the immutability of natural forces deaf to man. The Speaker in that play describes the universe as a 'black immensity in which we float like singular particles of dust . . . bits of air . . . molecules in peculiar exile' (p. 26).

Recently, Rabe has seemed more and more to embrace an almost Artaudian sense of catharsis in advocating that man recognise, and tremble at, the dark power of some primordial metaphysical force. This is a different kind of transcendentalism to Guare's, and it is imbued with a strong sense of pessimistic fatality. At the climax of *Hurlyburly*, the suicidally desperate Eddie explodes in rage at the TV screen and gives a harangue about the astronaut who 'went into orbit; he rendezvoused with the moon, and from that vantage what most impressed him was HIS OWN ABILITY TO GET THERE! Hovering in the heavens, what he saw was the MAGNIFICENCE OF MEN AND MACHINES!' (p. 154). In the play's 'Afterword', Rabe underlines a kind of fatalism even more when he suggests that accident and destiny may well be the same: 'Because always under the little we could will and then attain there was some unknown immensity on which we stood and all utterly beyond us' (p. 169). The jewels obsessing the thieves in *Goose and Tomtom* are yoked with astral images of night sky and distant planets and become talismans by which men reach intimations of the beyond. The images of nightmare that run through the play, and the characters' identification with various animals, providing foreshadowing of the strange climax of the play, a satisfying culmination of metaphor if not action-structure. The aggression of Goose and Tomtom, controlled and directed by the queen-bee Lorraine, leads to the murder of a rival criminal, and the crime rebounds on them. The rival's kidnapped sister Lulu is some kind of medium for forces which, in the form of strange men in masks, demolish the walls of the apartment and spirit Lorraine off as propitiation. As Goose and Tomtom attempt to sleep in the ruins of the apartment by the sibylline Lulu, the diamonds are seen glittering on the floor and on the necks of Goose and Tomtom. But the very final image is like a thematic apotheosis, not only of this play but of all Rabe's more recent work: '*In the dark the diamonds glow and the night sky shimmers with stars and specks and bursts of light, the actual presence of far-flung planets recognizable and afire, all visible through the ruins of the walls*' (p. 124).

BIBLIOGRAPHY

Dates given after the play titles in the text are not of writing or publication, but of the first performance of a definitive version.

Aaron, J. (1977) Review of *A History of the American Film*, Mark Taper Forum, Los Angeles, *Educational Theatre Journal*, vol. 29, no. 3, pp. 415–16.
Brustein, R. (1978) 'The Crack in the Chimney: Reflections on Conteporary American Playwriting', *Theatre*, spring, vol. 9, pp. 21–39.
Christiansen, R. (1982) 'A Wickedly Funny Playwright Explains It All For You', *Chicago Tribune*, 20 June, section 6, p. 11.

Cohn, R. (1982) *New American Dramatists 1960–1980* (London: Macmillan) pp. 31–6.

Dasgupta, G. (1981) 'John Guare', in Bonnie Marranca and Gautam Dasgupta, *American Playwrights: A Critical Survey I* (New York: Drama Book Specialists) pp. 41–52.

Dieckman, S. (1981) 'John Guare', in John MacNicholas (ed.) *Dictionary of Literary Biography*, VII: *Twentieth Century American Dramatists* (Detroit: Gale Research Company) pp. 243–7.

Durang, C. (1978) *A History of the American Film* (New York: Avon Books).

——. (1978) *The Vietnamization of New Jersey* (New York: Dramatists Play Service).

——. (1983) *Christopher Durang Explains It All For You: Six Plays* (*The Nature and Purpose of the Universe; 'dentity Crisis; Titanic; The Actor's Nightmare; Sister Mary Ignatius Explains It All For You; Beyond Therapy* (New York: Avon Books).

——. (1984) *Baby With the Bathwater* (New York: Dramatists Play Service).

——. (1985) *The Marriage of Bette and Boo* (New York: Grove Press).

Guare, J. (1970) *Cop-out, Muzeeka, Home Fires: Three Plays* (New York: Grove Press).

——. (1971) *Kissing Sweet* and *A Day For Surprises* (New York: Dramatists Play Service).

——. (1972) *The House of the Blue Leaves* (New York: Viking).

——. (1972) *The Loveliest Afternoon of the Year* and *Something I'll Tell You Tuesday*, in Albert Bland and Bruce Mailman (eds) *The Off Off-Broadway Book: The Plays, People, Theatre* (New York: Bobbs Merrill) pp. 168–79.

——. (1973) *Two Gentlemen of Verona*, written with Mel Shapiro (New York: Holt, Rinehart & Winston).

——. (1977) *Marco Polo Sings A Solo* (New York: Dramatists Play Service).

——. (1977) *Rich and Famous* (New York: Dramatists Play Service).

——. (1978) *Landscape of the Body* (New York: Dramatists Play Service).

——. (1979) *Bosums and Neglect* (New York: Dramatists Play Service).

——. (1982) *Lydie Breeze* (New York: Dramatists Play Service).

——. (1982) *Gardenia* (New York: Dramatists Play Service).

Gussow, M. (1981) 'Stage: *Beyond Therapy* by Durang at the Phoenix', *New York Times*, 6 Jan., p. C11.

Harrop, J. (1987a) '"Ibsen Translated by Lewis Carroll": The Theatre of John Guare', *New Theatre Quarterly*, vol. 3, no. 10, pp. 150–4.

——. (1987b) '"Living In That Dark Room": The Playwright And His Audience' (interview), *New Theatre Quarterly*, vol. 3, no. 10, pp. 155–9.

——. (1987c) 'John Guare', *New Theatre Quarterly*, vol. 3, no. 10, pp.160–77.

Hertzbach, J. S. (1981) 'The Plays of David Rabe: A World of Streamers', in Hedwig Bock and Albert Wertheim (eds) *Essays on Contemporary American Drama* (Munich: Max Hueber) pp. 173–86.

Homan, R. L. (1982) 'American Playwrights in the 1970s: Rabe and Shepard', *Critical Quarterly*, spring, vol. 24, pp. 73–82.

Kerr, W. (1979) *Journey to the Center of the Theatre* (New York: Knopf) pp. 134–7.

———. (1982) 'John Guare – A Distant Way of Doing Things', *New York Times*, 2 May, section 2, p. 5.

Kolin, P. C. (1986) 'Staging *Hurlyburly*: David Rabe's Parable for the 1980s', *The Theatre Annual*, vol. 41, pp. 63–78.

———. (1988) *David Rabe: A Stage History and A Primary and Secondary Bibliography* (New York and London: Garland Publishing, Inc.).

Los Angeles Times (1972), 16 Jan., p. 26.

McGill, D. C. (1982) 'The Warming of Christopher Durang', *New York Times*, 23 May, section 2, p. 4.

Marranca, B. (1977) 'David Rabe's Vietnam Trilogy', *Canadian Theatre Review*, spring, vol. 14, pp. 86–92.

Moe, C. H. (1988) 'Christopher Durang', in D. L. Kirkpatric (ed.) *Contemporary Dramatists*, 4th edn (Chicago and London: St James Press) pp. 130–2.

Moritz, C. (1987) 'Christopher Durang', in C. Moritz (ed.) *Current Biography Yearbook*, vol. 48 (New York: H W Wilson Company), pp. 147–50.

Rabe, D. (1971) *The Basic Training of Pavlo Hummel*, in *Scripts*, vol. 1, no. 1, pp. 56–92.

———. (1972) *Sticks and Bones* (New York: Samuel French).

———. (1975) *In the Boom Boom Room* (New York: Knopf).

———. (1975) *The Orphan* (New York: Samuel French).

———. (1975) *Streamers* (New York: Knopf).

———. (1978) *The Basic Training of Pavlo Hummel* and *Sticks and Bones* (New York: Penguin Books).

———. (1985) *Hurlyburly* (New York: Grove Press).

———. (1986) *In the Boom Boom Room*, (revision to the original two Acts) (New York: Grove Press).

———. (1987) *Goose and Tomtom* (New York: Grove Press).

Richards, D. (1983) 'Durang's Antic Anger', *Washington Post*, 30 Oct., section F, pp. 1, 10–11.

Rose, L. (1984) 'A New American Master', *Atlantic Monthly*, pp. 120–4.

Savran, D. (1988a) 'Christopher Durang', in D. Savran (ed.) *In Their Own Words: Contemporary American Playwrights* (New York: Theatre Communications Group), pp. 18–34.

———. (1988b) 'John Guare', in D. Savran (ed.) *In Their Own Words*, pp. 84–99.

———. (1988c) 'David Rabe', in D. Savran (ed.) *In Their Own Words*, pp. 193–206.

Schmidt, S. (1972) 'Zeroing In (Farce) on Right Now (Craziness)', *Los Angeles Times*, 16 Jan., Calendar, p. 26.

Simard, R. *Postmodern Drama: Contemporary Playrights in American and Britain* (Lanham, MD: University Press of America), pp. 117–30.

Wetzsteon, R. (1982) 'The Coming of Age of John Guare', *New York*, 22 Feb., pp. 35–9.

Winer, L. (1986) 'Playwright John Guare: Nice Guys Can Finish First', *Wall Street Journal*, 15 May, p. 26.

Zaks, J. (1986) *New York Times*, 16 March, p. 16.

3

New Realism:
Mamet, Mann and Nelson

DAVID SAVRAN

> One has heard of double and triple agents who themselves in the end no longer exactly knew for whom they were really working and what they were seeking . . . in this double and triple role playing. . . . There was basically no longer any self that would have been able to 'self'-seekingly obtain advantages from all sides. What is self-interest in someone who no longer knows where his 'self' is?
>
> Peter Sloterdijk, *Critique of Cynical Reason*

After the height of the Cold War and the ordeal of McCarthyism, the modern American experimental theatre was born. Provoked by a presidential assassination, the political crises of the early 1960s (Cuba, Berlin, Vietnam), and the success of European absurdist drama and experimental cinema, it called into question the principles that had dominated American realism: the predominance of linear form and the congruence of character to environment. The experimental theatre challenged the formal and ideological constraints of the well-made play as handed down by Arthur Miller. It suspected that the closure of the fourth wall and the relationship between self-enclosed stage space and consistent and explicable character concealed, or naturalised, the very psychological and social disjunctions that Miller's drama sought to address.

Sam Shepard constructed plays like jazz riffs and Maria Irene Fornes, in *Promenade*, devised a succession of scenes by shuffling cards on which she had written the names of characters and settings. In her transformational plays, Megan Terry sought to assert the multiple and ruptured nature of personality, thereby challenging the dominion of the unified and self-identical subject.

63

In *Box*, Edward Albee probed the disjunction between setting and action, between a perfect cube and the limping speech of an unseen narrator decrying a terrible catastrophe, as if mourning the failure of the well-made play to touch the reality of psychological schism and social atomisation: 'If only they had *told* us!' (Albee, 1969, p. 8).

By the beginning of the 1970s, however, the revolutionary fervour had in large part subsided. The assassinations of Martin Luther King and Robert Kennedy, plus the victory of Richard Nixon in 1968, marked the beginning of a period of political and aesthetic reaction that countermined the revolutionary zeal – as did the protest movement's success in ending the Vietnam War. For those who remained committed to progressive causes during the 1970s and 1980s, the attempt at radical political change was in the main overtaken by a more ideological struggle against the infamous 'culture of narcissism'. According to Christopher Lasch, this culture is marked by a wave of 'competitive individualism, which in its decadence has carried the logic of individualism to the extreme of a war against all, the pursuit of happiness to the dead and of a narcissistic preoccupation with the self' (Lasch, 1978, p. xv). For this acquisitive society, ruled by the demands of style and image and by a fear of moral uncertainties, the drama of the 1960s seemed curiously dated and out of touch – an experimental (that is, aberrant rather than vital) theatre. Self-justifying fictions and escapist entertainments once again ruled the stage. Most of the few surviving dramas of social conscience forswore struggling with the most bristling issues in favour of a move toward what Mac Wellman has called 'the theatre of good intentions', a theatre of clear-cut moral choice that offers 'only the titillation of briefly identifying with the unfortunate one, the injured, the sick, the maimed, the ineluctable victim' (Wellman, 1984, p. 68). As Wellman demonstrates, plays like Pomerance's *The Elephant Man* and Norman's *'night, Mother* finally dismiss the complexities they raise, becoming little more than 'aggregations of explicated motives, . . . wholly knowable and wholly contrived' (Wellman, p. 62). By explaining away social ills they treat their audience like children whose emotions must be coddled and whose guilt assuaged. American realism had been reborn, phoenix-like, from its own ashes.

In opposition to this drama of denial, however, a vital alternative theatre re-emerged. In the work of David Mamet, Emily Mann and Richard Nelson, a radical 'new realism' has carved out its place on the American stage. While retaining bourgeois characters and everyday speech, new realism breaks sharply with many of realism's most salient techniques. Extending and refining the innovations of the 1960s drama (although resisting its tendency toward ideological polarisation), it practices a trenchant critique of social and psychological homilies. A theatre of questions rather than answers, of confrontation rather than reassurance, new realism fragments plot and disrupts the correlation between setting and action to probe the relationship between cultural breakdown and the disenfranchised subject.

Most importantly, however, the 'new realists' question the adequacy of co-called realistic speech by populating their plays with figures unable to express their emotional turmoil or to understand how they are being manipulated, characters robbed of the ability to speak. Rather than dramatise the subject's mastery of language, the new realists demonstrate how the subject is articulated by a discourse over which he or she has little control. Their plays thereby testify to both the hypotrophy and hypertrophy of language, its under- and overdevelopment: the subject either stammers out a broken and wounded speech or talks incessantly. In the former case, characters articulate halting monosyllables and cliches. In the latter, they speak endlessly, trying to fend off the chaos lurking both within and without but in the end falling victim to the very systems they believe they have mastered. Like double or triple agents, spies who have changed sides so many times they no longer know for whom they are working, new realism's dramatis personae lose the ability to discern the difference between fact and projection. Everyone they encounter is suspect, false. Language is just a collection of arbitrary signals. Everything is what it is not.

New realism's relationship to its nineteenth-century predecessor is a complex one, and yet it is key in understanding both the achievements of these new dramatists and their affinity with the 'old' realism of their own time. During the mid-nineteenth century realism emerged as a reaction against philosophic idealism and the conventions of romantic drama and melodrama. For all its variegation – it was as diverse as the many writers associated with it – it remained bound to certain basic tenets which few of the realists questioned. Realism sought above all to be 'true to reality', to extract from life's diverse phenomena 'those that are necessary to create a full, vivid, and organically unified picture' (Becker, 1963, p. 42). As explicated by nineteenth-century writers, realism was rooted in positivism, the reigning philosophy of bourgeois scientists and intellectuals. It appealed incessantly to the methods of the natural sciences for its authority and rejected the subjectivity of Kant – and indeed al such 'metaphysical nonsense' (Becker, p. 48) – in favour of dissection and analysis. Even Flaubert, always uneasy with the label of realist, asserted that 'Great Art is scientific and impersonal' (Becker, p. 95). Accordingly, realism sought to banish that which it believed impeded 'the true depiction of objects'(Becker, p. 80): rhetoric, convention and the concern with the general rather than the individual instance.

For all its appeal to 'true depiction', realism remained as highly conventional a form as those it sought to displace. The vast majority of the realistic playwrights, including Dumas fils, Augier and Ibsen, based their dramas on the well-made play as it had been developed in the 1820s and 1830s by Eugene Scribe. This formula demanded a linear plot (strictly bound to the laws of cause and effect), type characters and the building of the plot to a single crisis, the resolution of which usually pivoted around the release of withheld information.

Although the realists studiously rejected accusations of ideological bias, the major realist work relentlessly probed the relationship between individual and society from a socially critical perspective. More specifically, realism sought to examine the connection between the subjugated individual and the surrounding culture that he or she deemed stifling and oppressive. As naturalism to some extent displaced realism in the 1880s and 1890s, it intensified the investigation. The plays of Strindberg, Zola and Gorky characteristically eliminated the protagonist's recognition (preferring it take place in the mind of the spectator) and placed far greater emphasis on the determination of character by environment. When both realistic and naturalistic plays, therefore, demanded a new scenic convention – the box set – it did so not simply for the sake of authenticity but to examine the site of entrapment. As Raymond Williams explains, 'the dramatic tension, again and again, is between what men feel themselves capable of becoming, and a thwarting, directly present environment. . . . It is even possible to feel that Ibsen had to make rooms on the stage in order to show men trapped in them' (Williams, 1969, p. 335).

Although eschewing political labels – and Ibsen was particularly insistent – the realists during the second half of the nineteenth century launched an incisive, if fitful attack on the mores and social strictures of the bourgeoisie. Throughout a conservative era, one that testified to the failure of the revolutions of 1848, one that prided itself on technological and social progress, the realists wrote against the grain, pointing out the often pernicious effects of mercantile capitalism on the middle and working classes. Ibsen was particularly critical of the mores of his own social class, and in his work he characteristically opposed what Williams calls the 'actively liberating individual' against 'the frustration and stagnation of the available forms of social life' (Williams, p. 106). He accomplished this (and thereby differed markedly from most of the other realists) not by reconstructing the morally polarised dramatis personae of melodrama, but by showing that the protagonist is always already corrupted, both morally and spiritually. In other words, he demonstrated that the individual trapped in a false society is necessarily torn by contradiction as the culture against which he or she rebels. Furthermore, unlike most of his contemporaries, Ibsen seemed fundamentally unsure of the end to which this struggle leads. Inevitably, the climaxes of his dramas, whether Nora's slamming shut the front door or Hedda's final gunshot, remain as difficult and unsettled as the moral issues with which the characters had been wrestling for four acts. Although Ibsen was in the broadest sense a realist, his work – and this remains perhaps its most radical aspect – questioned rather than ratified the unambiguous teleology of the well-made play. While appropriating its form, he more often than not subverted its underlying principles, and in providing an ambiguous ending, refused the very closure that the form characteristically demanded.

Although the new realists are the product of a very different society from Ibsen's (but one still ruled by middle class values and the conflicting demands of competitive capitalism), they have in many ways renovated the very principles that Ibsen used to deconstruct the realism of his day. Like Ibsen before them, they examine the complex relationship between individual and society and the process by which false values are internalised.

Like Ibsen, they have rejected a positivist epistemology, and the use of stereotypical, knowable and morally polarised characters. But the new realists are not simply Ibsen in modern dress. Their act of resuscitation has necessitated a defamiliarisation of those revolutionary techniques employed by Ibsen but incompletely understood by many of his successors.

The new realists, in particular, have had to reject the realism of Arthur Miller, who donned the mantle of Ibsen in 1951 with his adaptation of *An Enemy of the People* and who remains the foremost exponent of the well-made play in America. But for Miller – and this is tellingly reflected in his own plays – Ibsen is less the speculative playwright than the polemicist: 'Ibsen used to present answers. . . . In the *Doll's House* and even in *Hedda Gabler*, we will find – and in Chekhov, too – we will find speeches toward the ends of these plays which suggest, if they don't overly state, what the alternative values are to those which misled the heroes or heroines of the action shown' (Roudane, 1987, p. 36). Miller's refusal to valorise Ibsen's most deeply dialectical gesture does not banish ambiguity from his own work. Instead, his attempt at its suppression merely serves to reinscribe it on a subliminal level, in the gendered breach between liberal polemic and the forces of darkness and mystery, between male 'alternative values' and female manipulation and cruelty. Thus, for example, in *The Crucible*, Miller's indictment of political oppression is compromised by the play's misogynist and oppressive demonstration that tyranny results when a woman is unable to slake her lustful desires. And in *After the Fall* the ubiquity of guilt upon which Quentin insists is belied by the insidiously relentless return of the Mother, the source of betrayal and shame in Miller's post-Edenic confession.

Rather than attempt to squelch contradiction, the new realists have renovated and extended Ibsen's scepticism by calling into question the laws of cause and effect, by disjoining the linear progression of scenes and by fragmenting temporal continuity. These dislocations characteristically require the substitution of what Kenneth Burke refers to as a qualitative progression for a syllogistic one, or a progression defined by an association of ideas or qualities rather than a cause and effect relationship (Burke, 1968, p. 124). Thus, for example, in *Sexual Perversity in Chicago* (1974), David Mamet practices a scenic intercutting closer to the style of the pornographic film that Bernie and Dan watch than that of conventional realism:

Bernie: That break in the action . . . they shifted scenes . . .
          where they changed the camera angle . . . you know
          why they do that? You know why? Because the guy
          came is why, and they shift angles and wait a while
          so it looks like he's fucking for hours.

(Mamet, 1978, p. 56)

By similarly breaking the action and, as it were, changing the
camera angle, Mamet delays climax indefinitely (there is no real
peripeteia in the play, only innumerable adjustments). Constantly
teasing the spectator, he cuts from a scene of Danny and Deborah
in bed talking about genitalia and masturbation to one of Joan
admonishing two toddlers in nursery school for 'playing Doctor'.
The scenes link up not to further the plot (Joan's speech is
irrelevant to the progression of Danny and Deborah's relationship,
which forms the narrative spine of the play) but to point out a
functional similarity between adult and infant sexuality. Their
liaison thereby furthers the play's almost cubistic illumination of
the multifaceted nature, the 'perversity' of erotic relationships in
a fragmented and compartmentalised society.

In the process of disrupting syllogistic form, the new realists have also fractured what Burke elsewhere describes as the
scene–act and the agent–act rations. According to Burke, these
are the relations that guarantee that actions and characters will be
congruent with their setting, realistically reflecting or symbolising
the same characteristics or qualities that the action expresses as
it unfolds (Burke, 1969, pp. 3–5). In *Still Life* (1980) Emily Mann
disrupts the scene–act ratio by placing her three protagonists
behind a long table which sits in front of a projection screen. This
public setting, as well as the intercutting of what amounts to three
monologues delivered by a Vietnam veteran, his wife and his mis-
tress, decontextualises those manifestly private confessions that
a more conventionally realistic playwright might place in three
different domestic settings. Set at odds with their environment
and with each other, the interwoven discourse asks the spectator
to make the psychological and sociological connections that Mann
cunningly omits:

Mark: (To Cheryl) I know I did things to you, Cheryl.
        But you took it.
        I'm sorry.

> How many times can I say I'm sorry to you? (To
> audience) I've, uh, I've hurt my wife.
> Nadine: He is incredibly gentle.
>
> (Mann, 1982, p. 163).

As the action unfolds, however, the setting becomes startlingly apropos as it is gradually revealed to be a courtroom and the spectators the judge and jury who must confront the contradictions directly, without a narrative intermediary or synthesising master perspective.

Richard Nelson, meanwhile, in *The Return of Pinocchio* (1982), shockingly disjoins agent from act, character from his deeds. Appropriating a figure best known from his incarnation in the Disney cartoon as a puppet who becomes a real boy because he learns the value of self-sacrifice, Nelson brings him home to Italy in 1946 in search of his father. What follows is quite unexpected. During his years in Hollywood Pinocchio has been radically transformed by the capitalist Babylon. After his money is stolen by a compatriot, he gladly mops the floor of the cafe where he has just eaten, assuring the proprietress that 'if men stopped paying what they owed the entire free enterprise system would go down the drain. And it wouldn't take much either – it's a beautiful yet fragile organism' (Nelson, 1984, p. 91). Pinocchio uses this rhetoric – unmistakably like that of Ronald Reagan – to conceal his hateful plans. After murdering the man who fleeced him, Pinocchio conceals both the act and its motivation behind a celebration of that 'American spirit' that the Italians lack: 'if you want to do something, you can. It's all up to you. . . . That's what they got to learn. And that's something positive. And that's why the Reds don't have an iceberg's chance in hell against us Americans' (Nelson, p. 100). By so radically disjoining character from act, Nelson ensures that the dramatic tension will be less within the play-world, between protagonists, than in the spectator's mind, between the traditional Italian character and his newly Americanised self.

These three dramaturgical techniques: fragmentation of the action and disruption of the scene–act and agent–act ratios, owe little to the methods of nineteenth-century realism. Instead, they bear a kinship to the techniques of those German playwrights who, like the new realists, subverted the dominant theatrical conventions of their own day: Lenz, Buchner, Grabbe, Brecht, Von Horvath and Kroetz. Each of these playwrights challenged a ruling ideology by fragmenting plotline (and thereby the integrity of both the subject and the social fabric) so that the contradictions by which the working class and the bourgeoisie live, and sometimes prosper, become painfully evident. Most importantly, this critique is accomplished not by providing the subject with the tools for self-realisation but by demonstrating his or her inability to comprehend the process of dispossession. Lenz's tutor, Lauffer, Buchner's Woyzeck and Kroetz's Otto Meier have no real understanding of what is happening to them. They are all parrots whose speech is stripped of authenticity. Dispossessed of language, they are incapable of understanding how they have been exploited or what they might do to alter their condition. 'Their problems', in the words of Kroetz, 'lie so far back and are so advanced that they are no longer able to express them in words' (Kroetz, n.d., p. 8).

Mamet, Mann and Nelson practice a similarly critical dramaturgy aimed at illuminating how the subject of post-industrial capitalism, 'the present-day servant of the system', as described by Peter Sloterdijk, is necessarily radically fragmented:

By day, colonizer, at night, colonized; by occupation, valorizer and administrator, during leisure times, valorized and administered; officially a cynical functionary, privately a sensitive soul; . . . outwardly a follower of the reality principle, inwardly a subject oriented toward pleasure; functionally an agent of capital, intentionally a democrat; . . . objectively a strategist of destruction, subjectively a pacifist; basically someone who triggers catastrophes, in one's own view, innocence personified.
(Sloterdijk, 1937, p. 113)

For this schizoid subject, this double or triple agent, the self is an oxymoron. 'What is self-interest', Sloterdijk asks, 'in someone who no longer knows where his "self" is?' (Sloterdijk, p. 114).

David Mamet dissects this divided self by probing the crisis of contemporary masculinity, torn by the demands of fierce rivalry in the commercial sphere and sensitivity and generosity in the personal one. Time and again his plays demonstrate that all relationships are deeply corrupted by the intuition – derived more from Veblen than Marx – that all personal transactions in capitalist society are ultimately commercial ones: 'It's impossible to have spiritual empathy if you don't have spirit. *That* is what is lacking. . . . How much empathy is there in a society that is founded on the belief and fear that if I go up, you go down?' (Leahy, 1982, p. 3).

Perhaps the most radical aspect of Mamet's dramaturgy, however, remains his mobilisation of a poetry for the theatre based not on eloquence but on the disjunction between language and desire, on the failure of speech to articulate need: 'No one really says what they mean, but they always mean what they mean' (Savran, 1988, p. 137). This technique ensures that intention – or through-line, as Mamet learned from Stanislavsky via Sanford Meisner – will always be expressed subtextually, as ubiquitous and inaccessible as those dynamics of the market-place that corrupt personal relations. In *Sexual Perversity's* final scene, after ogling women on the beach, Bernie's anger suddenly erupts:

> Coming out here on the beach. Lying all over the beach, flaunting their bodies . . . I mean who the fuck do they think they are all of a sudden, coming out here and just flaunting their bodies all over? (*Pause.*) I mean, what are you supposed to think? I come to the beach with a friend to get some sun and watch the action and . . . I mean a fellow comes to the beach to sit out in the fucking sun, am I wrong? . . . I mean we're talking about recreational fucking space, huh? . . . huh? (*Pause.*) What the fuck am I talking about?
>
> (Mamet, p. 68)

Bernie's speech, torn by redundancies, contradictions, ellipses, cliches, false starts and changes in grammatical subject, exposes the basic illegibility of discourse for a character unable to come to grips with his dismemberment. Speaking a language that he has stolen and which simultaneously has been stolen from him, Bernie prattles incoherently. What, finally, is he talking about, what is his babel, if not the stammerings of a culture whose fundamental contradictions are finally as inaccessible to the disenfranchised subject as the Freudian unconscious to the conscious mind?

If the work of David Mamet, in its emphasis on an environmental (that is, economic) determinism, deconstructs the more naturalistic phase of realism, then Emily Mann's work can be seen to deconstruct the domestic realism of Arthur Miller by focusing on the interplay between family structure and sociopathology. Thus

Still Life, for all its attention to the Vietnam War, is fundamentally more concerned with the vicious cycle of domestic violence that produces dysfunctional adults who in turn perpetrate yet more acts of domestic and political brutality (like the Vietnam War). Similarly, *Execution of Justice* (1984) is far less concerned with the facts of the murders of George Moscone and Harvey Milk than with Dan White's family and the production of his attitudes and beliefs. As a result, the central relationship in Mann's plays is always the parent–child one, as she unearths the process by which moral values and patterns of behaviour are passed from adults to their vulnerable and impressionable offspring. In *Still Life*, for example (in a moment that recalls *All My Sons*), the horror of Mark's confession that he killed three Vietnamese children, a mother and a father in cold blood is redoubled by his fear that his own son is 'going to die for what I've done' (Mann, 1982, p. 217). In *Execution of Justice* the Young Woman asks the play's central question after she hears that the jury has acquitted Dan White of first-degree murder: 'What are we teaching our sons?' (Mann, 1986, p. 110).

Both *Still Life* and *Execution of Justice* are documentary dramas insofar as their dialogue is derived from interviews, trial transcripts and reportage. These plays are distinguished from more conventional documentary realism, however, by Mann's fragmentation and recontextualisation of her sources. By structuring the monologues in *Still Life* associatively rather than syllogistically, by juxtaposing different points of view and running the present tense against the past, raw emotional response against intellectual analysis, Mann concretises the always peripheral position of the rationalising subject *vis-à-vis* event. By counterpointing the domestic against the political, she defamiliarises the family structure that Miller honours in *All My Sons* and incites the spectator to examine the family as a well-known yet alien mode of production. Unlike Mamet, she does not exclude moments of self-recognition. Rather, she demonstrates that characters have only partial understanding because they are unable to see the bigger picture – the form as a whole, or a network of relations in which they are always already immersed.

Richard Nelson's work is more variegated in part because his subject matter and technique have changed during his career. As he acknowledges, the first phase of his writing, from 1975 to 1978, is the result of his work as a newspaper reporter and explores the relationship between real events and their reporting. After serving as dramaturg and adaptor of classic plays, he inaugurated what he refers to as his classical period, from 1979 to 1983, in which he appropriated mythological figures (like Pinocchio) to probe the workings of American culture. His most recent work, from 1984 to the present, is concerned more specifically with the relationship between personal trauma and societal breakdown. Testifying painfully to his failure to find either a positive critical response or a wide audience in his native land, these plays focus on characters (usually intellectuals in exile) who are uprooted and displaced, alienated from themselves and incapable of connecting with their environment. In this work he continues his investigation of the process by which action is framed, by shuffling temporal sequence and using suggestive or mysterious scene titles. Reversing Brechtian procedure, he manipulates the titles to create suspense between the spectator's expectations and his or her perceptions of the action, between imposed formal device and lived experience.

In *The Vienna Notes* (1978), perhaps the most complex of the plays written during the first phase of his career, Nelson studies the construction of political discourse by examining the disparity between live action and its almost instantaneous translation into narrative discourse. By presenting both the real events (a murder and attempted kidnapping) and Senator Stubbs's uninterrupted description of them, Nelson shows how reportage subverts event, insofar as the demonic retelling gains a permanence and truth-value absent from the event itself. But Nelson's formal strategy is even more radical than the familiar Derridean deconstruction of the primacy of speech in relation to writing suggests. Somewhat uncharacteristically, for the long central section of the play, he has chosen a realistic domestic interior, a farmhouse outside Vienna (a city between East and West, a city of espionage). Reversing Mann's tactics, he uses the family to defamiliarise political discourse. All the while espousing compassion and family values, the Senator is paralysed by his fanatical need to construct a discursive image for his constituency back home. Indefinitely suspending action with discourse, this unwitting double agent does nothing to help his hostess or to apprehend her husband's murderers, lying in wait just off-stage, announcing their unseen presence with stray gunshots. His ceaseless production of text deconstructs the binary opposition between private and public, as if to answer the popular obsession with the man behind the image, with the quip: there is no self.

Like *The Vienna Notes*, most new realist plays redefine dramatic struggle by pitting a figure who overarticulates against one unable to express his or her trauma. Characteristically these plays omit peripetiea because no fundamental change in this struggle is possible. One of the few plays that breaks this pattern is Mamet's *Edmond* (1982), all of whose characters are radically impaired, a 'proletariat of the speechless', in Kroetz's suggestive phrase (Innes, 1979, p. 223). As if in compensation for this impoverished proletariat, Mamet constructs *Edmond* with a sharply defined linear spine as a negative morality play. In twenty-three short scenes he depicts the gradual disintegration of a modern everyman, struggling for self-gratification in an urban society in which everything can be bought and sold, in which individuals are completely alienated both from each other and from their own needs. In the opening scene a fortune-teller explains to Edmond that there is a complex predetermination of events, by diet, by genes, by stars. She then proceeds to diagnose Edmond's alienation with acuity: 'You are not where you belong. It is perhaps true none of use are, but in your case this is more true than in most. . . . The world seems crumbling around us. You look and you wonder if what you perceive is accurate. And you are unsure what your place is. To what extent you are cause and to what an effect . . .' (Mamet, 1983, p. 16).

This most plot-driven of Mamet's plays then begins to undermine the determinisms of plot and environment by questioning the dynamics of cause and effect. As Edmond, as amalgam of violence and insatiable need, descends into the maelstrom of the New York underworld, he becomes increasingly inflamed, his self-gratification constantly deferred, fleeced by whores and black card-sharks, while his own racist, sexist and homophobic hatred is unleashed. Not until he picks up a waitress in a restaurant is he able to achieve a sexual (rather than spiritual) release, after which he brutally murders her. Set loose in a society that radically dissociates cause and effect, action and responsibility, the spiritually impotent Edmond has at last asserted his will by perpetrating one irrevocable act. Effect suddenly and relentlessly pursues him. But when he is imprisoned, he discovers that nothing has changed. Edmond's attempt at escape

from an intolerable situation (his home) has led him to an even
more oppressive one (his jail cell). The play's master irony lies
in the fact that only in prison, where he is sodomised by his
black cell-mate, does this victim of the law of cause and effect
even begin to address questions of causality and responsibility:
'There is a destiny that shapes our ends. . . . And people say
it's *heredity*, or it's environment . . . but, I think it's something
else' (Mamet, 1983, p. 100). He and his cell-mate then speculate
whether anyone, whether God or some great genius or some
'whacked-out sucker' or new-born infant, 'can see what we are'
(Mamet, 1983, pp. 101–2). They finally recognise that they are,
in the profoundest sense, the playthings of form, where form
signifies both the social totality that eludes their comprehension
and the dramaturgical whole in which they have played the part
of dupes – those who suffer for the sake of the guilty mob.

For all *Edmond*'s linearity and symmetry (framed by scenes of
metaphysical speculation and hinged upon an irrevocable act), it
finally questions the possibility that one can understand destiny
by, in the fortune-teller's words, reading its signs. The play ends
with a startling stage direction: 'Edmond gets up, goes over and
exchanges a goodnight kiss with the prisoner. He then returns
to his bed and lies down' (Mamet, 1983, p. 106). How has
Edmond moved toward this act, both real reconciliation and
its demonic parody? While carefully delineating the results of
Edmond's homicide, Mamet just as studiously omits the steps to
this erotic and spiritual apotheosis. In this sense *Edmond*, like its
title character – and like all new realist plays – is a mystery without
a solution. Edmond is criminal, victim and investigator, the double
or triple agent who no longer remembers for whom he is working.
Like everybody else he meets, he remains utterly alone, incapable
of knowing where his interests lie or of articulating his needs.

Mamet's strategy of fragmenting the hero, strictly limiting
empathy and withholding the solution, finally has the effect
of deconstructing the much-touted disappearance of the author.
His tactic ironically reactivates the authorial voice, now heard
as a distant oracle, speaking a strange, lost tongue, inciting the
spectator to try to translate that long-forgotten language and in
so doing, to postulate the solution that the author artfully omits
– an alternative to psychological and social brutality. Refusing to
provide a traditional sense of closure, Mamet must opt instead for
a formal device, some theatrical equivalent to film's freeze frame

– a sudden and violent suspension of the action. The final stage direction in *Edmond* strikes with the force of such a device. So do Mark's words at the end of *Still Life*, which are emblematic of the ending of all new realist plays: 'It's a still life. I didn't know what I was doing' (Mann, 1982, p. 224). In other words, here is the totality, the spatial and temporal whole, now suddenly and disquietingly revealed. But I, as a character, do not understand my role because I, unlike you sitting in the audience, have been unable to observe the totality. What about the role you play?

Like the nineteenth-century realists before them, Mamet, Mann and Nelson offer a critique of the political reaction following the collapse of social revolutions by militating against the dominant dramatic form of the day. Like double agents, they are infiltrating the commercial theatre to undermine its ideological vocation. And they are not alone. Maria Irene Fornes, Wallace Shawn and Mac Wellman have also written plays that could be called new realist. For these playwrights the contravention of hegemonic forms and values has necessitated a break not just with theatrical realism but with the realism of television and film as well. This break has been accomplished less by rejecting the latter's principles than by subverting its techniques. What is fragmentation of dramatic action if not an exaggeration of cinematic montage? What is the construction of plot by linking short story scenes or monologues if not an analogue to the juxtaposition of sixty-second television news spots? But the new realists employ these techniques to critique the service they offer the mass media (and the interest of Mamet, Mann and Nelson in advertising or journalism is no mere coincidence). Rather than provide a string of disembodied images that decontextualises event – as the Six O'Clock News does every evening – the new realists restore in fragmentary form the historical context that both shapes individual choice and is shaped by it. They have, in effect, renovated the contemporary history play.

Although I believe that the new realists offer a powerful cultural critique, I must also question this critique's efficacy for much of the theatre-going public. David Mamet, in particular, is enjoying increasing popular acclaim as his plays become more linear and less abrasive. Does the popularity of his work mark a radical form's penetration of the commercial market or this form's co-opting by the mainstream? What, in the end, will keep new realism from being devoured by the omnivorous and hegemonic realism that has dominated the American theatre for so many years? Furthermore, what are we to make of the new realist's failure to provide an image of a less radically oppressive society? Why do the utopian figurations in their work retain their bourgeois formulation as personal gratification rather than provide a glimpse of an alternative community? Does this reluctance to articulate what they are *for* signal a failure of nerve? Or does it mark their recognition that cultural criticism can only proceed from within culture? Does it signal the necessary gulf between an onerous present and a radically different future? Does it encode the inaccessibility of the revolutionary moment?

So, finally, one must ask, for whom is the new realist working? What is the real identity of this double agent? Is there nothing to do but wait for history to answer these questions?

BIBLIOGRAPHY

Albee, E. (1969) *Box and Quotations from Chairman Mao-Tse Tung: Two Inter-related Plays* (New York: Dramatists Play Service).

Becker, G. J. (1963) *Documents of Modern Literary Realism* (Princeton: Princeton University Press).

Burke, K. (1968) *Counter-Statement* (Berkeley and Los Angeles: University of California Press).

———. (1969) *A Grammar of Motives* (Berkeley and Los Angeles: University of California Press).

Innes, C. D. (1979) *Modern German Drama: A Study in Form* (Cambridge: Cambridge University Press).

Kroetz, F. X. (n.d.) *Farmyard & Four Other Plays* (New York: Urizen Books).

Lasch, C. (1978) *The Culture of Narcissism: American Life in an Age of Diminishing Expectations* (New York: W. W. Norton).

Leahy, M. (1982) 'The American Dream Gone Bad', *Other Stages*, 4 Nov.

Mamet, D. (1978) *Sexual Perversity in Chicago* and *The Duck Variations* (New York: Grove Press).

———. (1983) *Edmond* (New York: Grove Press).

Mann, E. (1982) *Still Life*, in J. Leverett (ed.) *New Plays, USA, 1* (New York: Theatre Communications Group).

———. (1986) *Execution of Justice*, in J. Leverett and M. E. Osborn (eds) *New Plays, USA, 3* (New York: Theatre Communications Group).

Nelson, R. (1984) *An American Comedy and Other Plays* (New York: Performing Arts Journal Publications).

Roudane, M. C. (ed.) (1987) *Conversations with Arthur Miller* (Jackson and London: University Press of Mississippi).

Savran, D. (1988) *In Their Own Words: Contemporary American Playwrights* (New York: Theatre Communications Group).

Sloterdijk, P. (1987) *Critique of Cynical Reason*, trans. M. Eldred (Minneapolis: University of Minnesota Press).

Wellman, M. C. (1984) 'The Theatre of Good Intentions', *Performing Arts Journal*, vol. 24.

Williams, R. (1969) *Drama From Ibsen to Brecht* (New York: Oxford University Press).

4

Black Theatre into the Mainstream

HOLLY HILL

Like Athena springing from the head of Zeus, playwright August Wilson burst upon the New York theatre scene in the fall of 1984 with his first Broadway drama, *Ma Rainey's Black Bottom*. By the spring of 1988, there had been three Wilson plays on Broadway – *Ma Rainey*, *Fences* (1987) and *Joe Turner's Come and Gone* (1988) – and each had won the New York Drama Critics Prize for Best Play of the Year. *Fences* also took the Pulitzer Prize and the Tony, Drama Desk and Outer Critics Circle Award – the first work ever to win all five Best Play prizes.

Such a record would be remarkable for any dramatist; the fact that Wilson is black makes his success all the more noteworthy. Though Willis Richardson's *Chip Woman's Fortune* had in 1923 become the first one-act play by a black playwright to be presented on Broadway, and two years later came Garland Anderson's full-length *Appearances*, works by and/or about blacks had only trickled into New York mainstream theatre until 1960. That was the year when Lorraine Hansberry's *A Raisin in the Sun* triumphed on Broadway, directed by August Wilson's future mentor, Lloyd Richards.

The 1960s and 1970s saw an upsurge of black dramatists and other theatre artists, of companies dedicated to fostering black artists, and of a new audience – predominantly black but attracting considerable interest from whites. The Black Theatre Movement – which boasted such playwrights as Ray Aranha, James Baldwin, Amiri Baraka/LeRoi Jones, Ed Bullins, Steve Carter, Alice Childress, Gus Edwards, Charles Fuller, Charles Gordone, Adrienne Kennedy, Leslie Lee, Ron Milner, Ntozake Shange, Barbara Ann Teer, Joseph A Walter, Douglas Turner Ward, Richard Wesley, Edgar White and Samm-Art Williams

81

– was one of the most vibrant developments in off Broadway theatre, and is documented by Mance Williams in *Black Theatre in the 1960s and 1970s* (1985).

Broadway was more resistant to black artists and material, but a glance at the nominees for and winners of its highest accolade, the Tony Award, shows the trickle gradually growing. In the 1950s, only Harry Belafonte was a winner; among the nominees were Lena Horne and Juanita Hall (Bloody Mary of *South Pacific*). Though Lorraine Hansberry and Lloyd Richards lost to the author and director of *The Miracle Worker* in 1960, black artists were nominated in six years of the decade, with performance Tonys going to Diahann Carroll, Lillian Hayman and James Earl Jones, and a special Tony being awarded to the Negro Ensemble Company in 1969. *Hallelujah, Baby!* (co-winner as Best Musical 1968) and *The Great White Hope* (Best Play 1969) were about blacks, though created by whites.

In the 1970s, blacks were nominated for Tonys in every year but 1971. Nine performers won, and 1974 and 1975 were special years. In 1974, Joseph A Walker's *The River Niger*, produced by the Negro Ensemble Company, won Best Play, and *Raisin*, based on *A Raisin in the Sun*, was named Best Musical. The next year, John Kani and Winston Ntshona shared the Best Actor Award for Athol Fugard's *Sizwe Banzi is Dead* and *The Island* – the first Tony recognition of black artists from South Africa, and *The Wiz* wone Best Musical as well as Tonys for its black director/costumer, composer and choreographer.

The 1980s contained black Tony nominees every year, and numerous winners. *Fences* garnered Tonys for performers James Earl Jones and Mary Alice, director Lloyd Richards, and playwright August Wilson. *The New York Times* noted in the spring of 1988 (3 March) that 'Broadway has more offerings for black theatre goers than at any other time in memory', and that blacks and whites were crossing over to each others' shows. In that spring, August Wilson's *Fences* and *Joe Turner's Come and Gone*, South African Mbonghemi Ngema's musical *Sarafina!*, and the (white-created) black gospel version of Sophocles's Oedipus story, *The Gospel at Colonus*, played on Broadway at the same time.

Plays and musicals by and/or about blacks appeared regularly on and off Broadway in the 1980s. Broadway featured such revues as *Sophisticated Ladies* (a celebration of Duke Ellington), and *Black and Blue* (a tribute to black blues and jazz song and dance), and the musicals *Dreamgirls* and *The Tap Dance Kid*. Plays on Broadway included Samm-Art Williams's *Home*, Athol Fugard's *A Lesson from Aloes*, *The Blood Knot*, and *Master Harold and The Boys* (which won Best Actor Tony for South African black Zakes Mokae in the same year (1982) that a production of *Othello* starring James Earl Jones won the Tony for Best Revival. One-person shows included *Lena Horne: The Lady and Her Music* and *Whoopi Goldberg*.

Off Broadway had notable successes with shows by and/or about blacks throughout the 1980s. Plays were in constant development in minority-oriented institutional theatres like AMAS, a multi-racial theatre founded in 1960 by black artist Rosetta Le Noire. She had created a musical revue that celebrated Harlem in the 1920s and 1930s. *Bubbling Brown Sugar*, which originated at AMAS in 1976 and moved to success on Broadway. In the 1980–81 season AMAS presented Vy Higgison's gospel musical, *Mama, I Want to Sing*, which moved off Broadway and has been running ever since.

Woodie King Jr's multi-racial New Federal Theatre, founded in 1970, originated Ntozake Shange's *For Colored Girls Who Have Considered Suicide/When the Rainbow Is Enuf* and co-produced it at the New York Shakespeare Festival's Public Theatre in 1976; from there the poem/play about black women moved to Broadway. In 1988, the New Federal's production of Roy Milner's *Checkmates*, a comedy contrasting a marriage of the wartime 'we' generation with a black yuppie 'me' couple, went to Broadway. The Negro Ensemble Company, founded in 1967, is the oldest continuously operating black theatre organisation in New York City history, and the most visible to the mainstream for the productions it has originated and moved to Broadway, and its successes at its original home base on the lower East Side and in the theatre it has occupied near the Broadway district since 1980. There Charles Fuller's *A Soldier's Play*, staged by NEC co-founder and Artistic Director Douglas Turner Ward, enjoyed a long run beginning in late 1981. Fuller's earlier NEC successes included *Zooman and the Sign* (1980), about a father seeking retribution for his murdered daughter, which won an Obie (off Broadway's Tony), and *The Brownsville Raid* (1976), an account of the framing of three companies of black soldiers wrongly accused of shooting up a Texas town in 1906. *A Soldier's Play* is about a black captain's investigation of a black sergeant's murder on a Louisiana army base during the Second World War and is an exploration of hatred within as well as outside the black community in the story. The taut drama won the Pulitzer Prize and the New York Drama Critic's Circle Best Play Award in 1982.

Since the success of Ntozake Shange's *For Colored Girls*, few black women playwrights have been represented in mainstream productions. Vinnette Carroll's musical *Your Arms Too Short to Box with God* ran for 149 performances in 1980–81 and for 69 performances in a 1982–3 Broadway revival, and Micki Grant's musical *It's So Nice to be Civilized* moved from AMAS to Broadway for only eight performances in 1980, but otherwise works by black women were largely relegated to limited runs in institutional theatres. Margaret B Wilkerson collected and edited a volume of these: *9 Plays by Black Women* (1986).

In the spring of 1983, *Poppie Nongena*, a drama with music based upon her book and co-dramatised by South African white Else Joubet, enjoyed an off Broadway run. *Woza Albert!*, by South African black writers Percy Mtwa and Mbongemi Ngema, who co-authored with the white South African director Barney Simon, played off Broadway in the 1983–4 season. Works by black South Africans grew in importance, and the years between 1986 and 1988 offered the most international selection of works by and/or about blacks yet seen in New York.

The Lincoln Center Theater Company presented *Woza Afrika: A Festival of South African Theater* in its off Broadway-size Newhouse Theater in the fall of 1986; the following spring one of the festival's plays, Mbongeni Ngema's *Asinamali!* had a brief run on Broadway. A similar but more successful pattern was repeated in 1987, when Ngema's musical *Sarafina!* (co-composed with Hugh Masakela) about high school students during the Soweto uprising, starring young talents Ngema recruited from South African townships, originated at the Newhouse and moved to Broadway for a long run.

The 1986–8 period also featured the New York premiere of Nobel Laureate Wole Soyinka's *Death and the King's Horseman* at the Vivien Beaumont Theater at Lincoln Center, West Indian playwright Derek Walcott's *Pantomime* off Broadway, and the irreverent new voice of a youthful American black, George C Wolfe, whose satirical revue *The Colored Museum* ran at the New York Shakespeare Festival's Public Theater for 324 performances before going to the Royal Court Theatre and the West End of London. In eleven sketches, that included a spoof of *A Raisin in the Sun*, a fledgling black yuppie struggling with his former radical persona, and a trip aboard a Celebrity Slave Ship where a stewardess demonstrated a 'Fasten Your Shackles' sign, Wolfe examined ideas and feelings about what it means to be black.

Among the 1986–8 offerings by seasoned black American writers were Samm-Art Williams's *Cork*, about black minstrels, Lonne Elder III's *Splendid Mummer*, a one-man play about nineteenth-century black actor Ira Aldridge, Ron Milner's comedy *Check-mates*, and a revival of Philip Hayes Dean's one-man play *Paul Robeson*. *Lady Day at Emerson's Bar and Grill*, white writer Lanie Robertson's one-woman play with music about Billie Holiday, achieved an off Broadway run of 281 performances and went on a national tour.

The pride that black artists felt in their achievements was crys-tallised in the National Black Arts Festival in Atlanta during the summer of 1988. Conceived as a biennial event, entirely run by blacks, and sponsored by corporate and government grants, the 30 July–7 August festival boasted sixty-five events in the performing and fine arts and literature, and received national media coverage.

Theatre works at the festival included *The Apollo*, a revue of classic acts by (actors playing) Jackie 'Moms' Mabley, Nat King Cole, Billie Holiday and others from the Harlem theatre's heyday, directed and choreographed by George Faison (a Tony-winner for *The Wiz*), and a comedy, *Sisters*, produced by an Atlanta regional theatre, Jomandi Productions. *Sisters'* author and co-director Marsha Jackson had to miss her festival opening because she was making her Broadway debut acting in *Checkmates*.

Attracting the greatest festival press coverage was the world premier of the Negro Ensemble Company's production of *Sally*, Charles Fuller's first full-length drama since his Pulitzer Prize winner *A Soldier's Play*. *Sally* is the first in Fuller's projected five-play cycle, *We*, about black Americans in the last half of the nineteenth century.

Sally and the cycle's second play, *Prince*, opened in New York at the Negro Ensemble Company in December of 1988. About recently freed slaves caught up in the Civil War (Sally is a widow with a teenage son who joins the Union army, Prince is an educated former slave who is a sergeant in the army) and learning quickly that even white people from the north will not treat blacks as equals, both plays were judged disappointments – perhaps works still in progress:

One admires the author's intention; he remains one of our more astute historical observers, but in the paired plays he repeatedly reveals the rough edge of his dramaturgy. Each is fragmentary, lacking both structure and development (although they are not lacking in plot). Mr Fuller appears to be taking a long, but not yet a very deep, look at a turning point in our nation's history. "Sally" and "Prince" seem less like finished works of theater than skeletal scenarios.

(Gussow, 1988)

Mainstream New York success is still the pinnacle, at least in prestige, in the imaginations of most theatre artists and audiences. Through the decades of the 1960s and 1970s, however, a national theatre developed in the network of professional regional theatres throughout the US, and with rare exception musicals and plays eventually seen on or off Broadway in the 1980s were developed in workshops and on the main stages of the not-for-profit theatres in and outside New York. Black playwrights have been among the beneficiaries of this process.

An example of such development is George C Wolfe's *The Colored Museum*, which originated at Crossroads Theater Company, a multiracial regional theatre in New Jersey, before gaining success in New York and London. Other productions of the revue then appeared in regional theatres, and *Variety* (1988) noted that *Colored Museum* was the highest-grossing show in history at Los Angeles's prestigious Mark Taper Forum. The 1988 Broadway revival of *Paul Robeson* also originated at Crossroads, then moved from off off Broadway to Broadway and then to a national tour.

August Wilson's appearance on Broadway as a dramatist not of promise but of rich fulfilment was engendered by the regional theatre system, particularly by institutions with programmes for the development of new playwrights. Each of Wilson's plays was first given staged readings at the National Playwrights Conference of the Eugene O'Neill Theater Center in Waterford, Connecticut, followed by full productions at the Yale Repertory Theater, and one or more regional productions before going to Broadway. Through this process Wilson, who had never had a play professionally produced before *Ma Rainey's Black Bottom*, was able to learn – and is still learning with each new work – how to focus his visions for the stage.

Born in Pittsburgh, Pennsylvania, in 1945, Wilson is the son of a white father he barely knew and of a black mother who raised him and five other children in a small cold-water apartment in a black slum. Wilson's mother taught him to read when he was four, and stressed the idea that if he could read, he could do anything. He was, nevertheless, an indifferent student until he was fifteen, when a teacher he liked assigned term papers. Wilson chose Napoleon, who interested him because he was a self-made emperor, and researched and wrote such a good paper that his teacher thought it was plagiarised. Wilson tore up the paper, threw it in the teacher's wastebasket, and dropped out of school.

Not wanting his mother to know he had left school, Wilson spent schooldays reading the classics of world literature, newer work of black writers, and books about the life of blacks in America. He did odd jobs and roamed the streets, where he began to listen to how the people talked and what they said. On the ABC-TV network programme *20/20* (first broadcast 9 December 1988), Wilson told interviewer Bob Brown that he encountered a generation of blacks whose lives and language bridged the gap between slavery and the civil rights movement, and by listening to them he learned how his people had survived – knowledge abundantly used in his plays.

Wilson dates his birth as a poet from 1 April 1965, when $20 he earned by writing a term paper for his sister ('Two Violent Poets – Robert Frost and Carl Sandburg') enabled him to buy his first typewriter. He wrote poetry and short stories, and in the early 1970s some of his poems were published in little-known black magazines. Samuel G Freedman commented that Wilson is 'one part Dylan Thomas and one part Malcolm X, a lyric poet fired in the kiln of black nationalism' (1987).

Wilson became involved in the Black Power Movement in the late 1960s and early 1970s, and was first attracted to theatre as a means of expressing his political beliefs. During the 1960s he co-founded a black activist theatre company which produced his early one-act plays. In 1978 he went to visit a colleague who had become the director of a black theatre in St Paul, Minnesota, and decided to move there. He continued to write plays, and began submitting two one-acts to the O'Neill Playwrights Conference. There his special talents met with and complemented those of director Lloyd Richards, growing into an extraordinary collaboration.

Since his first great success staging *A Raisin in the Sun* in 1960, Richards had become one of the most important figures in American theatre as Artistic Director of the Playwrights Conference and of the Yale Repertory Theater, and Dean of the Yale Drama School. At the O'Neill, and sometimes in subsequent productions at the Yale Rep, Richards has fostered plays by a diverse range of talents, including Lee Blessing, John Guare, Christopher Durang, Wendy Wasserstein, Lanford Wilson, David Henry Hwang, Philip Hayes Dean, Charles Fuller, Arthur Kopit, John Patrick Shanley, Martin Sherman, Wole Soyinka, Derek Walcott and Richard Wesley.

For three years, however, Richards rejected the short plays that Wilson submitted to the O'Neill. Wilson's plays 'had all the earmarks of what ought to be rejected, but my second thought was that all the characters were vital, alive, and I knew them all' (Richards, 1987).

Wilson kept working on the two short plays, ultimately fusing them into *Ma Rainey's Black Bottom*, which was accepted for the O'Neill Playwrights Conference in 1982. All of Wilson's plays spring from specific inspirations with widespread cultural implications; the genesis of *Ma Rainey* was the first blues – a Bessie Smith record – he heard as a youth. He listened to the record twenty-two consecutive times, feeling that someone was speaking directly to him and that he understood instantly and emotionally. He came to see the blues as part of blacks' oral tradition; a way of passing on information that was given an emotional reference by music. The information Wilson received was that there was a nobility and beauty to blacks he hadn't seen.

This nobility and beauty he conveys in his plays in a style and tone that could be likened to a combination of Sophocles and Aristophanes: hauntingly poetic and raucously humorous, inexorable and irrepressible. Though Wilson's settings are realistic, his protagonists are larger-than-life; they are very much themselves and something more. His recurring themes and the stories embodying them (both those dramatised and those told by the characters) raise the black experience in America to epic stature. The dialogue, inspired by Wilson's long-time observation of black speech, is evocative stage poetry in what is said and not said. The pressure of characters struggling with a fate that is both within their own natures and a legacy of being black in America, the threat of being pushed beyond endurance into violence, gives the plays a sense of danger, dramatic tension and high theatricality.

The title *Ma Rainey's Black Bottom*, like all of Wilson's titles and some of his characters' names, is real and metaphoric. It is a song recorded in the play by its female protagonist, who is based upon 'Ma' (Madame) Gertrude Rainey, the Mother of the Blues. The title also suggests white exploitation of blacks, dramatised in the struggle for control between Ma and her white manager and a white recording studio owner. As Ma recognises:

> They don't care nothing about me. All they want is my voice. . . . As soon as they get my voice down on them recording machines, then it's just like if I'd be some whore and they roll over and put their pants on.
>
> (Wilson, 1985, p. 49)

So Ma makes the whites play kiss-her-bottom from the moment she enters, *grande-dame* style with an entourage, until she signs the release papers after the recording session.

Set in 1927, *Ma Rainey's Black Bottom* unfolds on the split-level setting of a Chicago recording studio and an adjacent room for the band. In the four-man band, each player carries a legacy from racism and has developed his own way of coping. The piano player is self-educated and tries to make the others see that awareness of their African heritage, not imitating whites, is the key to their identities and futures. The three others are illiterate but Levee, the fiery young trumpeter, rather than live day-to-day as he sees most blacks doing to get along in the white world, has dreams of fame and fortune as a composer and band leader of jazz. Levee's swing version of the title song wins the studio boss's approval and Ma's contempt: he is the first example of many in Wilson's work of how a black person is thwarted not simply by whites and/or himself but by other blacks.

As the musicians wait to record, they engage in such humorous banter as bets over how to spell 'music' and to say the Lord's Prayer, and a scrap over a train schedule as lively as the Bliss family argument about Paris streets in *Hay Fever*. The characters tell many stories in Wilson's plays; among the provocative solos in *Ma Rainey* are the piano player's recollection of his failed marriage, the trombonist's of a black preacher made to dance all night by a white gang, and Levee's of witnessing, at the age of eight, his mother's rape by a group of white men. The bandsmen's talk flows like the music the rehearse, and the moment when the actors pick up their instruments and actually play a tune (only partly supplemented by recorded music in the Broadway production) is vividly theatrical, as is the recording session when they play and Ma sings.

Wilson's dialogue is earthy, as in a scene where Levee comes on to Ma's sensual young girlfriend:

> Levee: Can I introduce my red rooster to your brown hen?
> Dussie Mae: You get your band, then we'll see if that rooster know how to crow.
>
> (p. 82)

lyrical:

> Ma Rainey: White folks don't understand about the blues. They hear it come out, but they don't know how it got there. They don't understand that's life's way of talking. You don't sing to feel better. You sing cause that's a way of understanding life. . . . The blues help you get out of bed in the morning. You get up knowing you ain't alone. There's something else in the world. Something's been added by that song. This be an empty world without the blues. I take that emptiness and try to fill it up with something.
>
> (p. 82)

and incendiary:

> Levee: God ain't never listened to no nigger's prayers. God take a nigger's prayers and throw them in the garbage. . . . God hate niggers! Hate them with all the the fury in his heart. Jesus don't love you, nigger! Jesus hate your black ass! Come talking that shit to me. Talking about burning in hell! God can kiss my ass!
>
> (p. 98)

While Ma has filled herself up with song, Levee is filled with hatred and desperate hope – a mixture that proves as dangerous as hubris and leads to a tragic ending. Some critics (including this writer) called the conclusion melodramatic, but this judgement is not sustained by a second viewing or a reading of the play: the ending is a logical growth from character and event. Wilson's writing of Levee is so powerful that hope that he will be able to make his own music makes the ending of the play seem as if a phonograph needle has been savagely scratched across a favourite record. The clash between Ma and Levee over their music, the forces that propel each from within and challenge each without, is a battle of giants, and when Levee falls it is from a height he ascended by challenging the gods.

Though Wilson did not set out intending to write a cycle of plays, as *Fences* (set in 1957), *Joe Turner's Come and Gone* (set in 1911) and *The Piano Lesson* (set in 1936) were in various stages of development, he realised that he was creating a play for each decade of the nineteenth century: 'I'm taking each decade and looking at one of the most important questions that blacks confronted in that decade and writing a play about it. Put them all together and you have a history' (DeVries, 1987).

Fences began with the image of a man holding a baby in his arms – it was Wilson's reaction against the stereotype of the irresponsible black man. His protagonist, Troy Maxson, tries to hold closely what is his and to keep out whatever threatens his control – he builds real and psychological fences in the play.

The setting is the porch and dirt yard of an old house off a back alley in an industrial city in 1957. Troy's history unfolds in scenes with his wife, children and brother. The brutalised son of a sharecropper, Troy ran off at fourteen and sowed some wild oats (one resulting in his older son, Lyons) before serving fifteen years in jail for robbery. There he learned to play baseball, and upon release was an outstanding player in the Negro League. Troy blames racism for his not getting into Big League baseball;; his wife tries to remind him that he was nearly forty when he played.

Embittered by lost opportunity (one of Wilson's recurring themes), Troy has scraped together a life as a garbage collector, bought a house with government compensation paid to his brother Gabrial for a First World War head injury, and raised a son with his second wife, Rose. In the play's action, Troy wins one small victory – he challenges the union to become the first black garbage truck driver – while others are mostly pyrrhic. Afraid that sports will once again hold out false hopes, and perhaps envious of an opportunity he did not have, Troy exercises control over his teenage son Cory by refusing to let him accept a football scholarship to college and by turning him out when Cory remains rebellious. The image of the man holding a baby occurs mid-way through the second act, when Troy brings home the baby daughter his girlfriend died having (too conveniently in dramaturgical terms), and asks Rose to bring her up. Rose's reply is 'From right now . . . this child got a mother. But you a womanless man'.

Fences is opulent with humour and pathos, and the sensual texture and rhythm of life that is characteristically Wilson's. Troy and his best friend drink moderately on paydays, and the friend speaks admiringly of the legs and hips of the woman who turns out to be Troy's girlfriend:

> Troy: Legs don't mean nothing. You don't do nothing but push them out of the way. But them hips cushion the ride!
> Bono: Troy, you ain't got no sense.
> Troy: It's the truth! Like you riding on Goodyears!

(p. 5)

There are wrenching scenes between Troy and Rose, and Troy and Cory, who seems to do no right in his father's eyes. Cory asks Troy why he's never liked him, and gets a stinging rebuke (followed by a lecture on responsibility): 'Like you? Who the hell say I got to like you? What law is there say I got to like you? Wanna stand up in my face and ask a damn fool-ass question like that' (p. 37).

Rose tries to explain that Cory wants to emulate Troy, but he answers 'I don't want him to be like me! I want him to move as far away from my life as he can get. You the only decent thing that ever happened to me. I wish him that' (p. 39). His feeling for Rose aside, Troy goes to the other woman, who makes him feel free and fresh, as he tries to explain to Rose in a speech where Wilson uses metaphor to say several things – how the girlfriend makes Troy feel, what that made him do (become the first black driver in his union), and why he wants the expected baby – 'She firmed up my backbone. And I got to thinking that if I tried . . . I just might be able to steal second. Do you understand after eighteen years I wanted to steal second' (p. 70). Troy feels that he is always at bat and usually striking out, his final opponent being death.

Wilson alludes to pagan tradition in the name Troy, and to Christian in Troy's brother Gabriel, the lyrical character in *Fences*. His war-addled brain has led him to fancy himself as the angel Gabriel, spending his time conferring with St Peter and chasing the hounds of Hell. In the play's final moment, Gabriel blows his horn to signal St Peter to open the pearly gates to Troy. No sound comes from the battered instrument, but when Gabriel howls to heaven, his cry is as a trumpet. The symbolic and real actions in *Fences* capture the rage, anguish and yearning of black people in America almost a century after the Civil War.

The grandeur of Wilson's vision is most evident in *Joe Turner's Come and Gone*. The play's setting is a Pittsburgh boarding house in 1911, inspired by black artist Romare Bearden's painting of a boarding house scene that includes an abject man in a coat and hat. Wilson wondered why the man was so abject, and created the character of Herald Loomis – 'Herald, because he's a herald. Loomis, because he's luminous', the playwright told a *New York Post* interviewer (23 March 1988). Loomis is an ominous figure in a black coat and hat, a former church deacon pressed into seven years' labour by Joe Turner, whose villainous history W C Handy made into the blues song that is the play's title.

The boarding house is owned and run by a rigorous northern black named Seth Holly, and his warm-hearted wife. Though an able tinkerer, Seth cannot earn enough to set up his own business; he does jobs for a white peddler whose ancestors were slave-traders. The blacks who take up temporary residence at Seth's are from the south, mostly young people looking for work and attachments but finding exploitation by white bosses who demand kickbacks for jobs, and policemen who arrest them on paydays to take part of their salaries as fines. These characters include an adventurous young man and a sultry woman who stays overnight, just long enough to steal him from the world-weary woman he had newly taken as a room-mate.

Senior by age (sixties) and residence in the house (three years) is Bynum, a conjure man who performs sacrificial rituals offstage and acts as a counsellor and storyteller within the action. Bynum received his vocation – that of binding people who belong together – as a youth in a religious encounter with a 'shiny man' who 'had this light coming out of him. . . . He shining like new money with that light' (p. 9). Bynum has wandered throughout the country performing his rituals and binding people, looking for another shiny man because

> if I ever saw one again before I died then I would know that my song has been accepted and worked its full power in the world and I could lay down and die a happy man. A man who done left his mark on life. On the way people cling to each other out of the truth they find in themselves.
>
> (p. 10)

Bynum's greatest challenge comes with the appearance of Herald Loomis, who has been traveling with his eleven-year-old daughter, searching for the wife from whom Joe Turner forcibly separated him. The white peddler promises to find the wife on his travels, and Seth thinks he knows her whereabouts; the play is not about Herald's search for her but for himself. Joe Turner took part of Herald's soul as well as his body into bondage, and his spirit is still fettered. In Bynum's view, most people are in search of their songs – their identities, a sense of which allows them to connect with other people and the world. He recognises in Herald a man 'who done forgot his song. Forgot how to sing it. A fellow forget that and he forget who he is. Forget how he's supposed to mark down life' (p. 71).

The ending of the first act features a high-spirited Juba – an African song and dance around the Sunday dinner table – interrupted by Herald, who goes into a trance. This is the final goad to Seth, spooked by Herald from the beginning, to ask him to leave at the end of the week. Just when Herald and his daughter are about to move on, the long-sought meeting with the wife occurs – not a sentimental reunion but a brutal struggle between Herald's pent-up rage and his faith in himself and in God.

August Wilson is a demanding playwright; the fabric of his plays is densely woven and speaks to attentive audiences. In the first scene of *Joe Turner*, Bynum describes a cleansing ritual that preceded his finding his song. That ritual is unwittingly repeated by Herald upon himself, and not only frees him from the past and sends him out to sing his own song, but gives Bynum the sanction of his life, for the last line of the play is 'Herald Loomis, you shining! You shining like new money!' (p. 94). Wilson's language is incantatory, his story at once a spiritual allegory and a social document.

The Piano Lesson, a play still in progress through regional theatre productions and not yet published in a definitive version, is
Wilson's play of the 1930s, agains set in Pittsburgh. It is about
the conflict between a brother and sister over how their joint
legacy – a piano whose legs were carved by their grandfather in
the likeness of family members separated by slavery – should be
used. The brother wants to sell it to buy land, the sister to keep
it as a shrine: she is searching for a sense of self-worth from the
past, he by building a future.

In writing about American blacks, a people whose ancestors
were first torn away from Africa and then dispersed after emancipation, Wilson is seeking to define black identity not in white
but on its own terms:

> From what I've seen of blacks in America, we've run away from
> our African past. You really should know your past, or you don't
> know who you are, it's as simple as that. And if you don't know
> who you are, then you don't know what direction to proceed
> in. . . . Part of the problem in this society is we're not allowed
> our cultural differences.
>
> (Quoted in Brown, 1987)

Wilson's projected cycle of plays and his storytelling characters invite comparison with Eugene O'Neill's, his poetic gifts with
those of Tennessee Williams, his social awareness with that of
Arthur Miller. No contemporary dramatist has excited so much
hope that his body of work may place him among the giants of
American playwrights, and may even raise him to the pinnacle.

Perhaps white critics and audiences have responded to Wilson
partly because the size and shape of his vision remind us of
Shakespeare's, and of the beginnings of western drama in Greece.
The stories dramatised by August Wilson bring to mind Hecuba's
cry towards the end of *The Trojan Women*: 'Had not the very hand
of God gripped and crushed this city deep in the ground we
should have disappeared in darkness, and not given a theme for
music, and the songs of men to come' (ll. 1242–45). Laden with
grief and yet enlarged into a healing vision, these words might
be said about blacks in America. August Wilson is the kind of
praise-singer Hecuba foresaw, transforming individual and racial
tragedies into a universal poetry celebrating life.

BIBLIOGRAPHY

'A Conversation with Bill Moyers', on *A World of Ideas*, WNET-TV, first broadcast 20 October 1987.

Bernstein, R. (1988) 'August Wilson's Voices from the Past', *New York Times*, 27 March.

Brown, J. (1987) 'Staging the Black Experience', *Washington Post*, Oct.

DeVries, H. (1987) 'A Song in Search of Itself', *American Theatre*, Jan.

Dudar, H. (1988) 'When Southern Blacks Went North', *New York Times*, 18 Dec.

Euripides, *The Trojan Women*, trans. by Richmond Lattimore, in David Grene and Richmond Lattimore (eds) (1968) *The Complete Greek Tragedies, Euripides III* (New York: Washington Square Press).

Freedman, S. G. (1987) *New York Times Magazine*, 15 March.

'From Barroom to Broadway', interview with Bob Brown, *20/20*, ABC-TV, first broadcast 9 Dec.

Fuller, C. (1979) *Zooman and the Sign* (New York: Samuel French).

———. (1981) *A Soldier's Play* (New York: Samuel French).

Gussow, M. (1988) *New York Times*, 20 Dec.

Hill, E. (ed.) (1987) *The Theatre of Black Americans* (New York: Applause Theatre Book Publishers).

Hurlburt, D. (1988) *American Theatre*, Oct.

Mortiz, C. (ed.) (1987) 'August Wilson', *Current Biography Yearbook* (New York: H. W. Wilson) pp. 607–10.

New York Times (1988) 3 March.

Sanders, L. C. (1988) *The Development of Black Theater in America* (Baton Rouge: The Louisiana State Press).

Variety (1988) 27 Aug.

Wilkerson, M. B. (ed.) (1986) *9 Plays By Black Women* (New York: New American Library).

Williams, M. (1985) *Black Theatre in the 1960s and 1970s* (Connecticut: Greenwood Press).

Willis, J. (ed.) (1980/81) *Theatre World* (New York: Crown Publishers) vols 35–43.

Wilson, A. (1985) *Ma Rainey's Black Bottom* (New York: New American Library).

———. (1986) *Fences* (New York: New American Library).

———. (1988) *Joe Turner's Come and Gone* (New York: New American Library).

Wolfe, G. C. (1987) *The Colored Museum*, in *American Theatre*, Feb.

Records of the Tony Award nominations and winners 1947–88 courtesy of the League of American Theatres and Producers.

5

The Sound of a Voice: David Hwang

GERALD RABKIN

In 1979, a Stanford University senior, enacting a time-honoured rite of passage, directed a production of his first play in the lounge of his college dormitory. Within a year, the play, *FOB* (Fresh Off the Boat – an ironic acronym for recent immigrants) made a rapid journey from Stanford to the O'Neill Theatre Center in Connecticut to Joseph Papp's Public Theatre in New York, and the fledgling playwright, a young Chinese-American, David Henry Hwang, received national recognition as a vigorous new voice in the American theatre.[1] A year after the impact-making debut of *FOB* at the Public Theatre in 1980, Hwang confirmed his originality there with *The Dance and the Railroad*. Through the ensuing decade, Hwang slowly increased his *oeuvre*, but no new effort achieved the attention of his early work until 1988 when he made a spectacular Broadway debut with *M. Butterfly*, a play which rapidly achieved a dreamed-about level of critical appreciation and commercial success. With the successful London production of the play in 1989, this recognition has been replicated internationally. In an era in which the imaginative authority of drama has clearly waned (on Broadway in particular the playwright is an endangered species), Hwang's artistic ascendancy is one of the few bright spots in contemporary American theatre.

From the very outset, Hwang displayed a maturity that belied his years. *FOB* is a play about young people, but it is far from the familiar *Bildungsroman* in which the trauma of the young author's coming of age is enacted. It is a chamber play about ethnic consciousness centred on three cousins, all in their early twenties, who represent different groups of Chinese in America: Dale is an ABC – American-born Chinese – who is completely committed to effacing his Chinese roots; his dream is one of total assimilation into mainstream white culture. His opposite is Steve, a fresh-off-the-boat immigrant from Hong Kong on whom Dale projects all the greenhorn characteristics that he abhors. The most enigmatic of the trio, Steve enters the play identifying himself with Gwan Gung, the warrior god brought to America by Chinese immigrants as a source of inspiration in a hostile and repressive land. The central action of the play focuses on the competition of the two young men for Grace, Taiwanese-born but American-reared. As the competition proceeds on ascending levels of abstraction, it is, significantly, *her* journey towards identity that powers the play.

It is no surprise that Grace rejects Dale's assimilationism, choosing the tradition embodied by Steve. But Hwang refuses to polemicise her decision by over-simplifying the theme of ethnic choice. The play's originality derives from a more complex dramatic strategy. However attracted to the theme of racial consciousness, so dominant, as he was writing, in emerging black and Hispanic art, Hwang is aesthetically attracted to another contemporary dramatic force: the free-associative, quasi-surreal, mythic dramaturgy of the white experimental tradition, particularly as displayed in the plays of Sam Shepard. While at Stanford, Hwang attended San Francisco's Magic Theatre where Shepard was playwright in residence, and also visited the Padua Hills Playwright's Festival in Claremont, California, where Shepard, Maria Irene Fornes, and other contemporary experimentalists worked with fledgling writers.[2]

But whereas Shepard had to construct a personal mythology out of the heterogenous legends and detritus of America's past and present, Hwang sensed his cultural advantage. He had available in his own ethnic tradition a powerful storehouse of legend and ritual. His dramatic inspiration was to confront the imperative theme of identity *not* in the naturalistic mode of so much contemporary drama, but obliquely, by moving beyond realism into the realm of Chinese myth. On one level, *FOB* is indeed realistic – it places socially and psychologically coherent characters in a concrete environment: the backroom of a small Chinese restaurant in Torrance, California. But it soon explodes beyond realism by boldly moving into the realm of the legendary. The inspiration for this move was provided by two Californian, Chinese-American writers to whom the young playwright is acknowledgedly indebted: Maxine Hong Kingston and Frank Chin.

Hong Kingston's *The Woman Warrior* had recently been published in 1976. It revealed a sensitive, highly original writer who had created a moving memoir by merging the autobiographical and the mythic. In a series of structurally complex and stylistically innovative vignettes, Hong Kingston recounted her 'childhood among ghosts', the struggle, pain and beauty of growing up in America Chinese and female. In the chapter 'White Tigers' she evoked the figure of Fa Mu Lan, the eponymous Woman Warrior who takes her father's place in battle, as a symbol of the need of a people *and* a gender to transcend passivity. 'The swordsman and I are not dissimilar. May my people understand the resemblance so that I may return to them.'[3] This theme of ambivalence regarding one's cultural identity was not lost on young David Hwang.

Frank Chin was the first Chinese-American to have major plays produced in New York (*The Chickencoop Chinaman*, 1972, and *The Year of the Dragon*, 1974 – both done by the American Place Theatre). Directly contemporary with the emergent, militant black theatre, Chin identified intensely with the black urge to challenge a racist society and theatre in which the minority is stereotyped and dehumanised. He claimed a place in the literary and theatrical sun for all Asian-Americans. (In 1974 he co-edited a militant anthology of Asian-American writing called *Aiiieeeee!*) An angry, rhetorically effusive writer ('Damn straight I have hard feelings. I like 'em, they're mine!'[4]), Chin was judged by contemporary critics a playwright too disordered to achieve wide success. But his intersecting of naturalistic detail, experimental non-realism, and Chinese ritual clearly broke new dramatic ground that Hwang was soon to cultivate.

To combat white society's relegation of Asian-Americans – particularly Chinese-Americans – to states of 'self-contempt, self-rejection, and disintegration',[5] Chin evokes in many of his works the legendary figure of Gwan Gung, a revered Chinese folk-hero who fought battles for the Han dynasty. Because of his skill in battle, Gwan was deified as the God of War, and his moral virtues made him the god of writers and scholars whom in legend he protected. A century ago, he travelled to America in the novels and operas brought by the Cantonese immigrants who came to work on the railroad (a subject Hwang was soon to confront in *The Dance and the Railroad*). For Chin, Gwan Gung represents the active, individualistic masculine ideal that his impotent characters cannot achieve.

In *FOB*, Hwang merges the figures of the mythic warriors borrowed from Hong Kingston and Chin with the characters of Grace and Steve. By so doing the young playwright affirms his American roots; he makes a particular point in his preface to the play that it is 'invaded by two figures from American literature'.[6] The roots of his play, he insists, are not Chinese but 'thoroughly American' (p. 10). But the physical conjuration of the legendary Fa Mu Lan and Gwan Gung permits the play to move into a stylised form inimical to realism, Chinese opera – a move affirmed in production by the on-stage presence of musician-stage-managers in the classical Chinese theatrical tradition. The play's audacious shifts from realistic comic banter to confessional monologue to operatic ritual are necessitated by the difficulty of the search for cultural identity. On one hand, like the black militants, Hwang charts a journey to racial pride. He is unambiguous in his rejection of Dale (the one character without a legendary surrogate) with his rage to be accepted by whites at all costs. Hwang clearly accepts the reality of Steve's historic burden of racial discrimination. Like Hong Kingston and Chin before him, Hwang affirms that the warrior spirit must be cultivated if Chinese-American self-respect is to be achieved.

But, like Hong Kingston and Chin, Hwang is aware that Chinese culture carries its own burden of internal conflict. Though both distillations of the warrior spirit, Fa Mu Lan and Gwan Gung are often in conflict. In the play's climactic 'group story', a Chinese opera that the characters improvise, Grace as Fa Mu Lan battles Gwan Gung and reproaches him for not realising that ferocity is not enough, that he can no longer fight the old battles as he did in the old country. Tradition will not suffice: 'You are in a new land' (p. 48). Finally, what divides the warrior spirits is less than what must unite them. In deciding to leave with Steve, Grace/Fa Mu Lan teaches him that 'We are in America. And we have a battle to fight' (p. 48). The darkening stage is left to the rejected Dale who repeats his opening litany of revulsion against the 'clumsy, ugly, greasy FOB' (p. 50).

The figure of Gwan Gung is again evoked in *The Dance and the Railroad*, a play that spins variations on the themes and techniques of *FOB*. Set not in contemporary California, but in 1867 somewhere in the west where the transcontinental railroad is being completed, this is a chamber play for two actors that again confronts the theme of Chinese-American identity in a theatrical style ranging from the realistic to the ritualistic. The protagonists are two immigrant Chinamen – Lone and Ma – working under repressive conditions to fulfil the white man's dream to span the continent. They enter into a complex master–apprentice relationship that forces each re-examine himself. Lone is the old hand; he has been working on the railroad for two years. Ma is the FOB, only in America for four weeks, captivated by the dream of the Gold Mountain where even the snow is warm. Lone is, indeed, the loner – the rebel artist who denigrates his 'dead' compatriots who lack spiritual goals. An actor in the old country until forced abroad, he obsessively, solitarily practices his demanding craft on a secluded mountaintop.

Lone's solitude is breeched by the young, ebullient Ma, who persists until Lone accepts him as an acting disciple. Though newly arrived, Ma completely identifies with his fellow Chinamen who are embarking on a strike against their shameful working conditions. Nonetheless, he sees in the reclusive, disdainful Lone a master who can lead him to higher plane of achievement. After many difficult trials, such as having to spend a night enacting a locust, Ma earns the right to play a major role, the heroic figure of the immigrant's favourite god, Gwan Gung. But once he has earned that cherished right, he rejects it. He does not have to *play* Gwan Gung; he *is* Gwan Gung, because he is a Chinaman who despite the odds has won his strike. As Lone pulls out a gong, master and disciple, like the characters in *FOB*, perform a climactic Chinese opera which this time ends with the triumph of the striking Chinamen.

Hwang then moves his play in an ambiguous direction, however: at the moment of celebration, Lone informs Ma that the men did not get their full demands. Ma is appalled by 'a strike that has gotten us nothing'[7] and declares his independence from his compatriots whom he, too, now sees as 'dead men'. If Ma is now Gwan Gung it is *not* because his identity is subsumed by his group, but because he has come to realise that every journey to identity must be individual. 'I've got to change myself. Count my change. Learn to gamble. Learn to win. Learn to stare. Learn to deny' (p. 41). He will no longer merely accept the values of the group, nor will he any longer study to be an actor. Lone, meanwhile, recognising that the apprenticeship is over, comes to his own realisation: one does not have to dance to proudly prove one's superiority over others. 'Today I am dancing for no reason at all' (pp. 41–2). As Ma departs for good, Lone resumes his dance.

Is Hwang endorsing his characters' final decisions? At a time when Hwang was aggressively affirming his racial militancy ('I write about Asian-Americans', he reported to *The New York Times*, 'to claim our legitimate, but often neglected place in the American experience'[8]), he appears at the end of this play to withdraw from group solidarity. It seems to me not so much a case of contradiction as of painful self-scrutiny. The young playwright indeed makes common cause with his marginalised group's right to find its authentic voice. He proudly sees his plays as part of a burgeoning Asian-American theatre movement which has produced artists such as Winston Tong and Frank Chin and theatre groups such as the East West Players of Los Angeles, San Francisco's Asian American Theatre Company and New York's Pan-Asian Repertory. He acknowledges that his plays would not exist without the energy of this new theatre, and, indeed, in *The Dance and the Railroad*, pays homage to the contributions of Asian-American artists by giving his characters the actual names of their performers, John Lone and Tzi Ma. But Hwang also affirms the American part of his Chinese-American identity in his intense sense of his own individuality. It is this personal dimension that he scrutinises in his next play, set in the very American – and Chinese – arena of the family.

In October 1981, four months after the successful opening of *The Dance and the Railroad*, the Public Theatre produced Hwang's most expansive play to date, *Family Devotions*. A comically scathing composite portrait of several generations of a well-to-do Chinese-American family, it is the most overtly autobiographical of Hwang's plays, and contains what Hwang's first plays avoided: a thinly veiled self-portrait of the introspective young playwright, who here focuses his obsessive search for identity upon the particularities of his own origins and upbringing. It does so initially in a much less experimental manner than before by offering the audience what seems to be a conventional comedy about about the visit of a Chinese Communist to his wealthy Californian in-laws. But, gradually, in an audacious stylistic swerve, the comedy dissipates and the play is darkened, ritualised and solemnised as Hwang painfully examines his divided roots.

David Henry Hwang was born and raised in the middle-class Los Angeles suburb of San Gabriel, the son of Henry and Dorothy

Hwang, an accountant turned bank president born in Shanghai, and a pianist and teacher born in Amoy, China, but reared in the Philippines. From his mother David received a heritage uncommon to Chinese-Americans, a tradition of Protestant fundamentalism. In China, Dorothy's grandparents had been converted by Christian missionaries, her grandmother even becoming an exorcist. The family migrated to the Philippines where they became successful merchants before coming to the United States in the early 1950s, and soon after, at a dance for foreign students at the University of Southern California, Dorothy met Henry Hwang. The couple could not marry, however, until Henry converted to Christianity. In the Land of the Gold Mountain, the couple raised a family (two sisters besides David) and pursued the American Dream. Henry, in particular, never looked back, identifying completely with his adopted culture.[9]

It is a not unfamiliar immigrant tale: the parents rejecting the old country with its old values, their American-born children disturbed by this rejection, determined to retrieve their lost inheritance. What makes David's variation on this story different is the intense disparity between Protestantism and Confucianism, the latter being, as David observed, 'more a code of ethics than a religion'.[10] David's scrutiny of his deeper roots is motivated by his passionate need to escape what he clearly sees as the destructive confluence of Christian hypocrisy and prudery with the most venal aspects of American materialism. It is a debilitating legacy he feels compelled to exorcise. And yet he cannot escape what created him, the consequences of his Christian upbringing. There is in all his work a persistent metaphysical quest, a yearning for spiritual resurrection, that is undeniably Christian.

This double need to reject *and* affirm is the subject of *Family Devotions*. As a family comedy, the play wickedly and hilariously satirises *nouveau-riche* values and empty religiosity. The occasionally farcical plot is driven by the visit of Di-Gou, a doctor who has remained a loyal citizen of the People's Republic of China, to the Bel Air mansion of his long-unseen relatives. Di-Gou's sisters, Ama and Popo, and their respective families gather for the occasion in the high-tech home of Ama's daughter, her Japanese-American husband, and their teenage daughter. Popo's daughter Hannah, her Chinese-American husband, Robert, and their artistic son, Chester, complete the family portrait. It is the latter group that represents David Hwang's acerbic vision of his own family.

The character of Robert draws heavily from actual events in the life of Henry Hwang (particularly a bizarre incident in which he was kidnapped and released). Since Robert's background conforms in essentials to the biographical facts about the elder Hwang, it is not unreasonable to assume that we are being presented with an accurate, if comically stylised, portrait, one which is anything but flattering. Robert unashamedly admits that as an FOB he consciously 'decided to turn my back on China'.[11] He is an unabashed celebrator of a free-enterprise system that has made him a successful banker. He sees himself as even more American than his sister-in-law's nisei husband who has also made it financially. 'What do you know about American ways?', he challenges him. 'You were born here!' (p. 73) But brothers under the skin, the husbands agree that technology and tax shelters are what America's about.

David's self-portrait is not without irony. On one level, he presents himself as culturally ignorant and insensitive. When Robert mischievously shows Chester an article in a local Chinese paper praising him as a brilliant, up-and-coming young violinist (music being Hwang's surrogate metaphor for drama in the play), Chester complains: 'I can't read this, Dad! It's in Chinese!' (p. 61) And anxious to leave for a concert, Chester couldn't care less about meeting his long-lost relative from China; he just wants to get far away from family chaos. But he does meet Di-Gou, to whom he is immediately drawn, and becomes increasingly involved in a developing confrontation that escalates towards a disturbing conclusion.

The confrontation is rooted in the compulsion of the women elders, who remain devout Christians, to bring their recalcitrant atheistic brother back into the fold. At first, Ama and Popo are wonderfully drawn comic characters, throwing off funny put-downs of Japanese treachery – 'Japanese always kill and laugh, kill and laugh!' (p. 54) – and of Communist 'brainwash'. But as the play unfolds they become increasingly the tragic custodians of a faith built upon lies and self-deceit. They insist that their brother as a youth accompanied on journeys of conversion a celebrated ancestor who becomes a famous, influential evangelist. To win the apostate back to the faith the old women initiate a ritual of family devotions before an altar backed by a huge neon cross. Di-Gou counters by trying to prove to his sisters that nothing was the way they claim, that these stories never happened. Their brother's attempt to demystify their faith exacerbates the sisters' fervour, and the devotional ritual intensifies into physical combat. As the women try to throttle their brother, Di-Gou resists and emerges spiritually triumphant – a pyrrhic victory which ends, startlingly, in the deaths of the sisters with whom he has finally been reunited.

As witness to the developing struggle, Chester is at first bemused, then passionately involved, sensing that his own identity is at stake as well. Before the last combat, he is enlightened by the perceptive Di-Gou who warns him against complete denial of his blood: 'Study your face and you will see – the shape of your face is the shape of faces back many generations – across an ocean, in another soil. You must become one with your family before you can hope to live away from it' (p. 77). So, even as he rejects the crass materialism, the false piety from which he springs, Chester realises that he must reclaim the wheat of his cultural inheritance from the chaff. At the end of the play, after the ritual confrontation which symbolises the death of false belief, Chester gets up, picks up his suitcase and stands alone, the lights dimming to a single spot on his changing face.

For all its formal audacity, the energy of *Family Devotions* springs from the vision of a detailed milieu on which the playwright turns a sharp eye. But when, later in the decade, he returns to the idiosyncratic form he calls 'spiritual farce'[12] to reconfront his persistent metaphysical need, he is much less successful. *Rich Relations*, which opened at the Second Stage Theatre in 1986, was Hwang's most resounding flop. It was announced as Hwang's 'cross-over' play, his first containing no Asian characters. But the play's problems do not rest primarily in Hwang's unfamiliarity with an 'alien' culture; as he pointed out, it is culturally condescending to ghettoise him as an 'ethnic writer'.[13] In my judgement, the play fails because Hwang allows his mystical propensities to completely undermine his ironic sensibility.

Rich Relations compels interest, however, because – Caucasian characters notwithstanding – it amplifies the central theme of *Family Devotions*, the attempt to forge one's identity out of the crucible of false family values. The later play is again set amidst the wealthy of Los Angeles. Keith, a disturbed school teacher in spiritual disarray, returns to the expensive high-rise apartment of his materialistic father, Hinson, a real estate baron who reveals a contradictory past in which he was both gangster *and* Christian pastor. His troubled young son has in tow a former student, Jill, a child-woman of sixteen, wise beyond her years. The homecoming is complicated by the intrusion of Hinson's sister, Barbara, who has money on her mind, dragging along her diffident daughter, Marilyn. The strident Barbara had once been a faith healer, which is revealed as a family tradition. The play – which, like *Family Devotions*, starts out as satiric comedy – rapidly escalates into improbability and takes leave of any realistic or comic grounding. The characters never cohere, but become conduits for portentous talk of sin, belief, crucifixion and resurrection. In an unconvincing reach for Shepardian surreality, the action enters a bewildering realm of symbolic action in which characters perch on balcony railings, fall to their apparent deaths, and then are miraculously resurrected.

However out of control, *Rich Relations* counterposes familiar positive and negative themes. Hinton worships the god of technology; his apartment is a forest of TVs, VCRs, stereos and so on. But his is a technological vision that soon reveals itself as dystopic: television sets that are programmed to serve as telephones emit indecipherable sounds, spy-pen walkie-talkies refuse to work at all. At the climax of the play, it is no surprise when the recalcitrant appliances all explode, a symbolic action which is for Hwang uncharacteristically simplistic. That the worship of Mammon is destructive is a truism as obvious as the crass father's cliched articulation of his dog-eat-dog philosophy: 'Sometimes you eat. Sometimes you get eaten.'[14]

Despite his materialism, however, Hinsin shares with the play's other characters an insatiable spiritual hunger. He reveals that a generation ago he had been given up by doctors for dead, but revived to confound their fatal predictions. Indeed, it was his now greedy sister whose prayers resurrected him. As piously narrow-minded as Ama and Popo, Barbara is not unaware that her family is in chaos and that her beliefs have not broughts her peace. The most intense of the play's spiritual crises, however, is suffered by the troubled Keith, who desperately seeks a redemption that can only come from an act of grace. Clinging to the child-woman Jill as a potential saviour, he yearns to be raised from the spiritually dead.

But it is not he who is resurrected, it is Jill, who has apparently been catapulted to her death below by the explosion of the appliances. She mysteriously reappears, having passed beyond her own demons to a new awakening. The increasingly enigmatic play ends with the resurrected Jill rejecting her tortured boyfriend to leave with the also revitalised Marilyn: her mother had sacrificed her, pushing her over the edge, but she refuses to fall. As her body stops miraculously in mid-plunge, she affirms the human need to 'rage against the grave . . . [to] being ourselves back from the dead' (p. 85). This theme of the *necessity* of willing our rebirth is repeated by the departing Jill in as strange a code as any in contemporary drama: 'It shouldn't be that hard', she tells the bereft Keith, 'to bring someone back from the dead. It should be something you could do before dinner and still have energy for dishes' (p. 87). Hwang's self-irony seems to have completely deserted him.

The obsession with resurrection that derails him artistically in *Rich Relations* was perhaps a necessary personal exorcism. In 1986 Hwang was desperate to escape a bad patch of writer's block. After the early burst of dramatic energy culminating in *Family Devotions* in late 1981, he entered a fallow period which saw in the next five years only one public offering, a bill of one-acts titled *Sound and Beauty*. Much of the problem derived from the cultural mantle that had been thrust on him at the tender age of twenty-three. He was anointed *the* Asian-American playwright and asked to be spokesperson on all sorts of public issues. Though flattered by his success, he was creatively disabled. 'Growing up as a person of color, you're always ambivalent to a certain degree about your ethnicity. . . . There is necessarily a certain amount of self-hatred, a confusion at least . . . about which I was ambivalent [that] was being thrust into the forefront.'[15] It is one thing for an individual artist to express his personal contradictions; it is quite another when these conflicts are being read, often hostilely by his own ethnic group, as representative of Chinese-American concerns.

Hwang was not, however, entirely disempowered by his confusion of roles. The two one-act plays offered at the Public Theatre in 1983 under the collective title *Sound and Beauty* were, in general, critically welcomed as mature achievements. Spare and compressed two-character dramas, *The Sound of a Voice* and *The House of Sleeping Beauties* represent the playwright's first journey away from Chinese-American subject matter. They are derived from Japanese sources ancient and modern: the first play based on an archetypal folk legend, the second weaving variations on modern novelist Yasunari Kawabata's haunting novella, the title of which Hwang appropriates. In different ways both plays strive for the ritualised simplicity of classical Japanese theatre, a tradition more reticent that Chinese opera with its gongs and acrobatics. The confrontation with Japanese material also consciously affirms the Pan-Asian strain in Hwang's search for identity, the need he shared with other Asian-American theatre artists to forge a popular front of racial consciousness.

The Sound of a Voice, the more classical of the duo, follows the simple legendary plot of many Noh plays. In a remote corner of a forest a traveling *samurai* encounters a mysterious woman recluse. As he falls under her spell, she seems to reveal witch-like, supernatural powers. The liaison that develops between the couple is finally destroyed by the *samurai*'s growing fear of the power the woman has over him. As he breaks free, the abandoned woman kills herself.

In a Noh play there would be no doubt that the woman is indeed a demon who must be resisted and exorcised. As an exclusively male art form, then and now saturated with Buddhist asceticism, Noh theatre can be intensely misogynistic. Time and again in Noh plays, women – particularly isolated or independent women – transform themselves into evil, vengeful spirits. Hwang's inspiration in *The Sound of a Voice* was to write a modern Noh play that challenges this traditional demonology. In his play, the dramatic evidence reveals no supernatural power at work; the woman is aware that the man has most probably come to kill her because he considers her a witch, but this is because 'there are boundaries outside of which visitors do not want to see me step.'[16] Inevitably, the slightest deviation from her prescribed subordinate role makes the woman dangerous: 'Right from birth, I didn't cry. My mother and father . . . thought they'd given birth to a ghost, a demon' (p. 16).

Hwang subverts and naturalises his traditional material to advance a feminist theme: that man's fear of woman diminishes his own humanity. The *samurai* may have come to kill, but he stays to love. The woman opens up a world outside his rigid masculine realm. When he arrived his world was clear, purposeful, but now the woman has 'rearranged everything', 'changed the face' of his heart. He has indeed found in her presence the 'simplest thing, the sound of a human voice' (p. 22), but he will not accept the gift. He cannot surrender his supremacist values, his restlessness, his love of danger. He will not be domesticated. And how could a woman who bested him in martial arts by anything but a demon?

Abandoned once again, her last hope of escaping her demonised isolation gone, the woman hangs herself. Hwang leaves us not with despair, however, but with a final affirmative image of beauty: around the woman's hanging body thousands of flower petals swirl in a blizzard of colour – a rainbow of beauty that proud man does not see.

The second of the Japanese plays, *The House of Sleeping Beauties*, is more than an adaptation; it is a meditation on Kawabata's novella not fully accessible without knowledge of the original. In Kawabata's work, an old man named Egeuchi visits a mysterious demi-brothel where men near the ends of their lives literally sleep with young virgins who are rendered comatose by sleeping potions. Written when Kawabata was in his sixties, it is suffused with a sense of imminent mortality. Obsessed with both the joys and betrayals of memory, it ambiguously celebrates the vitalising power of female sexuality. In Yukio Mishima's perceptive words, it is 'an esoteric masterpiece . . . dominated by a strangling tightness . . . [in which] urged on by the approach of death, lust inevitably attaches itself to fragments.'[17]

David Hwang was in his early twenties when he wrote his version, and Kawabata's obsessions are not his. If he adheres to the essential plot of his source (without dramatising the actual encounters with the sleeping beauties), Hwang shifts to different themes: instead of death from physical decay his is the theme of death through choice. Fascinated by the dual suicides of Kawabata and his friend and commentator, Mishima, Hwang offers here a dramatic speculation upon these acts of extremity. To do so he strategically replaces old Eqeuchi with the character of Kawabata himself, a dramatic decision that offers Hwang the opportunity to speculate articulately on related themes: the loss of artistic creativity, *thanatos'* claim on *eros*. The story's climax is the sudden death of one of the sleeping beauties; the play climaxes with the character Kawabata conquering his literary impotence to produce the story from which the play springs, and then deciding it is time to end his life's journey.

The play's self-referentiality allows a direct critique of the story. In the play's last scene, the old woman peruses her guest's manuscript and complains that she has been hardened and coarsened, turned into 'an old woman who serves tea and takes your money' (p. 76). Kawabata responds that art is not reportage, but does not deny the charge. In the original story, the woman is 'perhaps in her mid-forties', the laconic gate-keeper to the mysterious chambers where the sleeping beauties lie. In the play the woman is deepened and humanised, given a past and a name, Michiko, and carries equivalent dramatic weight to Kawabata; she is even made the same age (seventies). The essential action of the play takes place *not* in the sleeping chambers but in the ante-room where old man and old woman intertwine their fates.

That *The Sound of a Voice*'s feminist theme is reiterated is obvious in this (condensed) exchange:

Kawabata: If I were to commit *hara-kiri*, would you chop off my head?

Woman: You're so self-centered, all you men, every last one of you. . . . If *I* wanted to commit *hara-kiri*, would you chop off *my* head?

Kawabata: Woman don't commit *hara-kiri*.

Woman: What if I did? What if I were the first? What if I wanted to do it like a man? Completely. Powerfully.

Kawabata: That's a foolish question.

Woman: I'd be braver than you or your friend.[18]

Finally, she does indeed join him in a ritual of self-destruction less violent than disemboweling: a poisoned tea ceremony. As always, Hwang favours an ambiguous ending. Since Michiko retains the original woman's instinct for pragmatic survival, why accompany Kawabata? For love? Because her game is up? Both? Neither? In any case, Hwang's *The House of Sleeping Beauties* accepts an equal claim of women's desires nowhere credited in Kawabata's haunting novella.

During his fallow years in the mid-1980s, Hwang involved himself with film and television projects which either never were realised or made little mark.[19] Then, as his star waned, a number of forces conjoined fortuitously, leading to his first Broadway production and his greatest success. Jack Viertel, then a dramaturg at the Mark Taper Forum in Los Angeles, read in the newspapers of a bizarre case that suggested dramatic possibilities: under the headline 'France Jails 2 in Odd Case of Espionage' a dispatch in *The New York Times* (11 May 1986) recounted how one Bernard Boursicot, a former French diplomat, and his lover, a Beijing Opera performer named Shi Peipu, had each been sentenced to six years in jail for spying for China. Their affair had begun twenty years previously when Boursicot was stationed in Beijing. The article's really incredible disclosure was that at the trial the opera star was revealed to be a man, a fact that the Frenchman was as shocked to discover as everyone else.

Viertel suggested to Hwang that this strange case might be a perfect subject for him; Hwang replied that he was indeed intrigued. A script soon followed, and the wheels of production really started to turn when director John Dexter read it enthusiastically and Viertel was appointed to the board of the Jujamcyn Organization which owns five Broadway houses. And so, in March 1988, *M. Butterfly* opened at the Eugene O'Neill Theatre, the only new American play of the season to arrive without the benefit of non-commercial development. Its enthusiastic reception was capped by the Tony Award for the Best New Play of 1988.[20]

M. Butterfly's curious subject matter permitted Hwang to take a major artistic step. Apart from *Family Devotions*, his previous major plays were short chamber works that made their points sparely, laconically. But since this bizarre real-life personal drama was played out against major historical events – France and America's involvement in Vietnam and the Chinese Cultural Revolution – a minimalist aesthetic would no longer suffice. With a Broadway production a distinct possibility, Hwang could express himself on a grander scale the before. Themes that had always preoccupied Hwang were inherent in the narrative: the cultural symbiosis of East and West, Asian passive victimisation, male fear and idealisation (mirror tendencies) of woman's otherness. The fact that one of the major players in the tale was a Beijing Opera performer immediately offered a formal strategy for dramatising the case. Could there be a more suggestive contrast than the styles of western and eastern opera? And so Puccini's triumph of sentimental 'Japonisme', *Madame Butterfly*, becomes one half of a cultural dialectic that sets against it the 'alien' creative vocabulary of classic Chinese theatre.

M. Butterfly represents, then, Hwang's most ambitious attempt to bridge his cultural inheritances. Stylistically, it aims for the broad theatricality of Beijing Opera, a form that eradicates our traditional western generic boundaries between music, dance and drama, and draws power from a startling contrast between bold effects – percussive music, acrobatics, the bright and gorgeous costumes of the actors – and the bare stage on which a few pieces of furniture stand unrepentantly as symbols. For the first time Hwang could strive for the complete spectacular visual/aural ambience of Chinese classical theatre rather than appropriate its rituals selectively. Hence, *M. Butterfly's* coups of theatrical transformation, its sequences of traditional Chinese performance *and* western grand opera.

But a specific Asian theatre convention is at the heart of Hwang's dramatic vision – one now marginalised in western theatre but which remains dominant in the theatre of the East: the art of female impersonation. In the classical theatre of both China and Japan – as in ancient Greek and Elizabethan theatre – women were prohibited from the stage. In traditional Beijing opera, as in Noh and Kabuki to this day, female roles were played by male actors: the Chinese *dan*, the Japanese *onnagata*. The Chinese have proven more willing than the Japanese to break tradition, and on the twentieth-century stage actresses have increasingly assumed the *dan* roles of its classic theatre, which partially explains why a supposed China expert like Bernard Boursicot (called René Gallimard in the play) could well have believed his beloved was a woman performer.[21]

The art of female impersonation is Hwang's brilliant strategic means of linking western social and psychological specificity with Asian stylisation. As he literalises the convention of impersonation through the facts of sexual duplicity, he simultaneously propels historical reality toward the symbolic. This impulse, as we have seen, has always characterised Hwang's work, which has consistently aimed to infuse western dramatic forms with an Asian sensibility. But as he seeks the ceremonial dimension that is the legacy of Asian theatre, Hwang always acknowledges that he is working in the theatre of the West. And so, while he works with traditional narrative material, he does so in a dramatic shorthand that veers beyond realism.

That realistic logic is not his major concern in *M. Butterfly* is revealed by his omitting one salient detail surrounding the actual case: when Shi Peipu followed Boursicot to Paris and moved in with him, Shi was accompanied by a child, purportedly the fruit of their long liaison. But when Song Liling (Hwang's incarnation of Shi) appears in Paris to re-seduce Gallimard, no child is in sight, despite the dramatic mileage the playwright had extracted from the previous scene in which Song announced his/her pregnancy to the rapturous father-to-be.

Hwang could well have enhanced his play's narrative credibility, and diminished his protagonist's derisive anatomical ignorance, by either eliminating the question of paternity altogether, or, alternately, pursuing more aggressively the mystery of the child, surely a crucial piece in the intricate puzzle. But to have followed the latter path would have blurred the inverted yin/yang symmetry of his enmeshed lovers. Hwang seizes the duplicitous announcement, however, as a vital expression of a theme that has perennially fascinated him: potency, real and imagined. It is indeed the theme of power that is at the heart of two interrelated myths that the play scrutinises: femininity and Orientalism. It's hard to imagine a more precise expression of the radical feminist definition of the feminine as 'the woman defined by male gaze, construct, and desire'[22] than the passionate ideal Gallimard has constructed, an ideal all the more powerful because it fuses with the parallel myth of the submissive Orient symbolised by Puccini's tragic heroine.

As the play's title tells us, however, *this* butterfly is finally a *monsieur*, an image incarnated at the play's conclusion. Hwang consciously undercuts Gallimard's absorption of Puccini's romantic fable by interjecting the cynical voice of Song, who notes, for example, that 'if a blond homecoming queen fell in love with a short Japanese businessman' and killed herself because he treated her cruelly, westerners 'would consider the girl to be a deranged idiot.'[23] That the personal drama between the odd couple should take place against the historic loss of Vietnam is for Hwang the global consequence of the West's delusionary assumption of Asian submissiveness. But, as always, Hwang does not retreat behind political pieties: Song's last turn toward the self-sacrificed Gallimard (who has been transformed into Butterfly) is saturated with customary ambiguity; is it an ironic contemplation of a literal suicide or a plaintive image of shared immolation? As Song had told Gallimard after the sexual revelation: 'Maybe – I want you . . . Then again, maybe I'm playing with you. How can you tell?' (p. 15). Once again Hwang demonstrates that the search for identity is elusive. As the inheritor of dual cultures, he cannot accept a taxonomy of rigid separation, however insistent its claims. To do so would deny part of himself. In a society – indeed, a world – in which we have just begun to recognise our repressed intercultural dependency, the sound of David Hwang's distinctive dramatic voice has become increasingly resonant.

NOTES

1. 1981 Obie Award for Best Play; 1981 Drama-Logue Award.
2. Jeremy Gerard, 'David Hwang: Riding on the Hyphen', *New York Times Magazine*, 13 March 1988, p. 88.
3. Maxine Hong Kingston, *The Woman Warrior* (New York: Vintage, 1977) p. 62.
4. Frank Chin, *The Chickencoop Chinaman* and *The Year of the Dragon* (Seattle: University of Washington Press, 1981) pp. 63–4.
5. Frank Chin, J. P. Chan, L. F. Inada and S. H. Wong (eds), *Aiiieeeee!: An Anthology of Asian-American Writers* (Washington, DC: Howard University Press, 1974) p. viii.
6. David Henry Hwang, *FOB* and *The House of Sleeping Beauties* (New York: Dramatists Play Service, 1983) p. 10.
7. David Henry Hwang, *The Dance and the Railroad* and *Family Devotions* (New York: Dramatists Play Service, 1983) p. 41.
8. David Henry Hwang, '"I Write Plays to Claim a Place for Asian-Americans"', *New York Times* (Arts and Leisure section) 12 July 1981, p. 4.
9. Ibid., and Gerard article.
10. Gerard, p. 89.
11. Hwang, *Family Devotions*, p. 71.
12. Gerard, p. 89.
13. Ibid.
14. David Henry Hwang, *Rich Relations*, unpublished typescript, 1985, p. 14.
15. Gerard, p. 89.
16. David Henry Hwang, *The Sound of a Voice* (New York: Dramatists Play Service, 1984) p. 16.
17. Yukio Mishima, 'Introduction' to Yasunari Kawabata's *House of Sleeping Beauties* (Tokyo: Kodansha International, 1980) pp. 7–8.
18. Hwang, *The House of Sleeping Beauties*, pp. 72–3.
19. *My American Son*, about the Iran–Contra affair for Home Box Office TV; *Seven Years in Tibet*, a film script set in India during the Second World War.
20. Also the Outer Critics' Award, the John Gassner Award and The Drama Desk Award – all the Best New Play.
21. Ironically, however, when actresses first appeared they copied the artful conventions invented by men to represent femininity on stage, even simulating walking on crippled, bound feet. And many learned their art from the greatest Chinese actor of this century, the *dan* master, Mei Lanfang.
22. Rosemary Curb, 'Re/cognition, Re/presentation, Re/creation in Woman-Conscious Drama', *Theatre Journal*, October 1985, p. 303.
23. David Henry Hwang, *M. Butterfly*, in *American Theatre*, August 1988, p. 4.

PART II

Theatre Collectives
in the 1980s

6

Elizabeth LeCompte and the Wooster Group

ALEXIS GREENE

The Wooster Group is one of the pre-eminent avant-garde theatre companies working in America. Its headquarters are the Performing Garage, a spacious former garage on Wooster Street, in what is usually referred to as the 'SoHo' district of New York City. There, under the artistic leadership of Elizabeth LeCompte, a permanent company of theatre artists create pieces that explore the realms of post-modern theatre: its aesthetics; deconstructive approaches to text; and relationships to post-modern American culture.

The origin of the Wooster Group is found in the evolution of the Performance Group, an iconoclastic collective of theatre artists that was founded in 1967 by Richard Schechner, editor of *The Drama Review* and professor at New York University's School of the Arts. Schechner aimed to experiment with environmental theatre, the process of group creation, non-traditional performance techniques that demanded an unusual amount of physicality and psychological vulnerability, and direct performer–audience contact. He outlined his concept of theatre in an essay entitled 'Six Axioms for Environmental Theatre', published originally in *Tulane Drama Review*: '1. The Theatrical Event Is A Set of Related Transactions', or, in other words, the elements of performance include audience, the environment, technicians, the paraphernalia of production, as well as performers and text; '2. All the Space Is Used for Performance; All the Space Is Used for Audience; 3. The Theatrical Event Can Take Place Either in a Totally Transformed Space or in "Found Space"; 4. Focus is Flexible and Variable; 5. All Production Elements Speak in Their Own Language', or, put another way, no element, whether performer or text, is more important than any other element – 'one element is not submerged for the sake of others'; '6. The Text Need Be Neither the Starting

117

Point Nor the Goal of a Production. There May Be No Text at All'
(Schechner, 1968, pp. 160–4).

Schechner's axioms were best expressed in the Performance
Group's first three productions: *Dionysus in 69* (1968); *Makbeth*
(1969); and *Commune* (1970). *Dionysus in 69*, for instance, focused
on the *Bacchae* of Euripides, yet the majority of the lines were
improvised by the performers during workshop rehearsals and
the performances themselves. The actors played themselves more
than any roles that Euripides had devised, often using variations
on encounter exercises during performance, to increase openness
to their emotions and to each other. Physical nakedness was also
encouraged as a tool to aid vulnerability. The physicalisation
of actions mentioned in the text received significant attention,
notably in the collective physicalisation of the birth of the god
Dionysus, during which the actors lay on the floor and straddled
each other to create an image of the birth canal through which
Dionysus was brought into the world. The audience, for its
part, sat on scaffolding that towered above the open space of
the garage, and the performers often clambered among them
or urged members of the audience to join the actors in the
performance space.

It was this production that attracted Elizabeth LeCompte and
her colleague Spalding Gray to the Performance Group, and in
1970 the two joined Schechner's collective, LeCompte as assistant
director on *Commune*, and Gray as an actor. LeCompte, who was
born in 1944 in Summit, New Jersey, had studied fine arts at
Skidmore College and had become enamoured of theatre while
waitressing at a local restaurant that also presented plays. She had
come to New York in 1967 and, as she recounted in an interview
for *The Drama Review*, thought that her stint on *Commune* would
be only a summer job. However, both she and Gray remained
with the Performance Group, and when Schechner left for a
trip to India in 1971, he put LeCompte in charge of directing
Commune with a new cast for an extended tour, and he also
gave her responsibility for managing the Performance Group in
his absence. Slowly, LeCompte and Spalding Gray would become
the focus for the work of other artists in Schechner's collective.

LeCompte describes the years with Schechner as formative in
terms of her ideas about performance and text even though,
by around 1974, LeCompte had come to conclusions that set
her apart form Schechner. For instance, Schechner wanted to

explore performance by using some of the techniques of sensitivity training, which had become popular as a therapeutic tool during the 1960s. In an interview with LeCompte, critic Lenora Champagne writes that, largely as a result of intense stage fright, LeCompte found Schechner's approach personally unworkable. On the occasions when she was required to perform, LeCompte sought to manipulate her fear by distancing herself from the performance experience by the use of masks, both literal and figurative: wigs; costumes; elaborate make-up; gestures and actions that were set beforehand. As LeCompte explained, 'I did the same things every night in *Cops* (1978), with hardly any variation. Performing was a sort of meditation. I went through a set of actions. . . . It was as though the audience was watching me through glass. They couldn't touch me. I couldn't touch them' (Champagne, p. 20). Critic David Savran writes that LeCompte also came to believe that Schechner's performance methods were 'dangerously psychoanalytical, urging the performer really to feel – at least in rehearsal – what he was experiencing on stage' (Savran, 1986, p. 3). More and more, LeCompte was drawn to the work of theatre artists such as Richard Foreman and Robert Wilson, whose approaches to performance were cooler than Schechner's: more abstract; more controlled; visual rather than verbal.

From her experience with Schechner, and from observing and working with other theatre artists, LeCompte began a process of culling that continues today. The development of a piece is really a lengthy exploration of objects and materials, improvisational in approach but not undirected. 'In this process', says LeCompte, 'I think of myself as the leader of a children's gang. I revert to six, seven, eight. I try to come up with situations [that have] a certain structure wherein we can play; where the structure is not so rigid that we can't reinvent it all the time, but not so loose that I don't have control. . . . Later, I edit' (Greene, 1989).

To this process of selection, LeCompte brings her perceptions as a visual artist and her bias toward spatial organisation and the potential contrasts that can be elicited in performance from the manipulation of colour, shape and texture. She also brings a post-modernist attitude toward text and performance. Although she claims not to be well-versed in post-modern deconstructive theory, her approach (and that of the Wooster Group as a whole) is akin in particular to the theories propounded by Jacques Derrida and Roland Barthes. With Derrida and Barthes, LeCompte operates as though textuality includes any material in the environment, any element in the world. Textuality extends to the whole world. Following hard upon this premise is the further concept, stated by Barthes in 'From Work to Text', that, constructed as it is of 'intertextual citations, references, echoes, and cultural languages – which are anonymous and untraceable – the text accomplishes the irreducible plural of meaning, answering not to truth but to dissemination' (Leich, 1986, p. 106). For LeCompte, there is no one meaning to any element of text; there are instead ambiguities and ambivalence. Indeed, along with Barthes, she has denied the power of the one author who assigns the one meaning to his/her work. As LeCompte and the Wooster Group have demonstated more than once, to unfavouable public response, they deny the traditional assumption that the text belongs to the 'author', but see a signed work as one more element of extended textuality that offers a freeplay of meaning. This freeplay of meaning is 'produced', as Barthes writes, 'by the reader in an act of collaboration, not consumption' (Leitch, 1986).

In Wooster Group performances, this post-modern view of text translates into a multiplicity of signs (literary text, physical objects, gesture, dance, song, music, film) that audiences do indeed often find ambivalent if not completely contradictory. The impact on the reader/viewer in the theatre is one of focus that is split and split again, in a disjoining that nevertheless urges the viewer to respond to the multiplicity all at once:

> I don't think that anyone who grew up in the fifties, experiencing TV, could possibly work in terms of one linear text. We learned a different way of collecting information, of editing and arranging it. I'm washing dishes; I have a dish in my hand and I turn around, and somebody is weeping in a soap opera. Or I hear that in the background; I turn around again and see a dishwashing ad. I'm washing dishes, we're doing the same gesture. The visual imagery is on one track, while you continue on your track, doing things at the same time. There's a discontinuity right away.
>
> (LeCompte, to Green, 1989)

At times, LeCompte's assumptions about meaning manifest themselves by taking a theatrical icon such as Thornton Wilder's

Our Town (1938) and destroying the meaning for herself. 'A play like *Our Town'*, says LeCompte,

> is the kind of thing that has been defined clearly for many years, until there is a kind of coating around it, of one meaning. We know now what Emily represents. There is no ambivalence about it any more, at least in literary circles writing about it. So I tend to be attracted to the kind of thing that is stable and then to destabilize it.
>
> (Greene, 1989)

The first piece that LeCompte created with actors from the Performance Group was *Sakonnet Point* (1975), later to be the first movement in what was subsequently titled *Three Places in Rhode Island* and known as the *Rhode Island Trilogy – Sakonnet Point*, *Rumstick Road* (1975) and *Nayatt School* (1977). *Sakonnet Point* is on record as being composed and directed by both Spalding Gray and LeCompte, although at some points in the piece's development, LeCompte stepped into the role of director, while Gray and the others worked associatively and improvisationally with found objects the brought to rehearsal. Gray reports that there was no theme to start, yet with Gray as the focus, what emerged eventually were images connected to the Rhode Island town where Gray spent summers as a boy: images of lost childhood and innocence.

For *Sakonnet Point*, the space at the Performing Garage was arranged so that the audience could sit on levelled platforms on three sides of the expansive playing space. On the fourth side, on top of a fourteen-foot platform, LeCompte placed a large domed red tent, which was lit from within. Inside the tent, two women played Tchaikovsky's First Piano Concerto on a phonograph and talked to each other inaudibly. A black tarpaulin stretched diagonally from the platform to the floor of the pit-like rectangular space, and three clotheslines ran from the tent platform to the platform opposite. The images of childhood unfold in this space like snatches of dreams, emerging with no rational organisation, sometimes experienced through the dreamer's distorted perspective, as for instance in the sequence entitled 'Spalding and the Woman with the Fan'.

As Savran describes in *Breaking the Rules*:

> At the beginning of the scene, she enters the playing space, slamming the door behind her. She then takes a black ball out

of her pocket and proceeds to bowl down the plastic tree forest. She fans herself with a Japanese paper fan while Spalding whips the air by spinning a length of zip cord. She puts on a record of children's song, goes around the space piling up objects on a green towel and drinks a glass of milk, letting the milk drool from the sides of her mouth. Both performers then take off their shoes and socks while Spalding spins the laces.

(p. 67)

'For me', LeCompte told Savran, '*Sakonnet Point* was the primordial mud out of which the rest of the work arose. . . . I was thinking of Cézanne and trying to find a form analogous to his painting, but in another language' (Savran, 1986a, p. 59). Savran likens the piece to

a still life, fixing a seemingly casual grouping of objects into a rigorous and highly formal composition. Just as the late paintings of Cézanne dissolve three-dimensional space into a shimmer of surfaces and planes, *Sakonnet Point* fragments action, space, and characters. It suggests, by juxtaposing multiple vanishing points, that the spectator's ever-changing perceptions fabricate a world of objects and people, and that form is less an intrinsic property than the onlooker's projection.

(Savran, 1986a, p. 59)

In terms of the *Trilogy*'s organisation, *Sakonnet Point* can be likened to the first movement of a concerto, an allegro that sets out certain visual and structural themes that are then taken up with more complexity in *Rumstick Road* and *Nayatt School*. For instance, *Sakonnet Point* is only incidentally referential to Gray's boyhood, but *Rumstick Road* evolved consciously out of Gray's distress about the suicide of his mother, and the verbal text is largely composed of interviews that Gray taped with his father and grandmothers. Certain objects from *Sakonnet Point* reappear in *Rumstic Road* (the red tent, the miniature house). And the disjunction in the action and use of objects is even more highly formalised in *Rumstick Road* than in *Sakonnet Point*.

Rumstick Road is constructed in four parts, each of which begins with a direct address to the audience from Gray/sound engineer, who reads letters while seated in a sound booth upstage centre. During these sequences the audience is bathed in white light, and Gray is in silhouette downstage of the booth. The lights come up to reveal an area stage left, in which is placed the red tent and behind that a window through which the audience sees the miniature house, seeming to float in darkness. Images shift abruptly. Gray and a woman emerge suddenly from a door in the third area, stage right, and they chase each other through doors behind the sound booth, around the red tent and back again, until the woman disappears suddenly behind scenery. A man appears stage right, and he and Gray wrestle with a gun in an image evocative of television detective series from the 1960s. The two *segue* into a tango, then the music of the popular song 'Volare' rises in volume as the image changes again, this time to reveal Gray stage left, draped in a white bedsheet. He places himself under a physician's examination table downstage of the sound booth, while the man, now in the role of doctor, examines the woman, sending her into paroxysms of giggles and a final scream, as Gray, like a voyeur or a child witnessing a primal scene, crouches below the table.

Such sequences are intercut with others that utilize the verbal text: Gray's recorded interviews, staged so that he seems to interview his father as the audience watches, or seems to telephone his mother's therapist from the playing space at the Performing Garage; the quoted letters, apparently recited by Gray, but on occasion actually read by the sound engineer. Such displacement techniques, in addition to the juxtaposition of ironic images and aesthetically exquisite images, or sentimental verbal text with jarring visual and aural images, distance the audience from the piece. As a result, neither the verbal text not any image offers a 'meaning' that is fixed, for most potentially recognisable signs, whether of father–son affection, or of the dead mother's words about herself, are almost immediately contradicted by sounds, gestures, actions, or music that render the first sign ambivalent.

A year after presenting *Rumstick Road*, Gray, LeCompte, and the actors working with them performed *Nayatt School* (1978). This third movement recapitulates some of the strains of the earlier two: the piece has a connection to Gray's life, and there is the Group's signature of action that is disjointed yet organised. *Nayatt School* is particularly notable, however, as the first piece in which LeCompte used an established text, T S Eliot's verse drama *The Cocktail Party* (1950), as a starting place for theatrical exploration. *Nayatt School* is essentially a deconstruction of Eliot's play, involving

'Examinations of the Text' that finally reveal the underside to both the traditional form and the ordered world projected by Eliot's script. At the end, as the performers smash recordings of the play to which they have been listening throughout, and masturbate over them, *Nayatt Schoo* '[exposes] the madness that has been repressed, the chaos that lurks behind the restraint of Eliot's play-world . . . and which is always threatening its decorum' (Savran, 1986a, p. 130).

Nayatt School is also notable fo a shift in Gray's role as performer. In this piece, he became for the first time 'lecturer', sitting or standing at the long narrow table that was the focal point of the setting and, divorced from the action, explaining *The Coctail Party* through an extended monologue. It was a role he repeated in the *Trilogy's* coda, *Point Judith* (1979), where again he was a speaker of monologues, a role that would eventually take him out of the Group.

In *Point Judith*, LeCompte again used an established text, this time a thirteen-minute version of Eugene O'Neill's *Long Day's Journey Into Night* performed at top speed in farce chase style (Gray played James Tyrone). Savran suggests *'Point Judith* uses *Long Day's Journey Into Night* as a hinge, around which swing two myths, two dreams (or nightmares) of isolation, one male and the other female' (Savran, 1986a, pp. 137–8). Part I, entitled 'Rig' (by associate member Jim Strahs) is a sexually obsessive colloquy among men who work on an oil rig at sea, while Part III, 'By the Sea', a film by Ken Kobland, follows the daily routine of a group of nuns, all but one of whom are played by men. '"Rig" plays off the scenes of male bondage in *Long Day's Journey Into Night*. . . . "By the Sea" elaborates on Mary Tyrone's experiences as a girl, her education in a convent, and her dream of becoming a nun' (Savran, 1986a, p. 138). Even more than the use of *The Cocktail Party*, the deconstruction of O'Neill's drama seeks to find what Barthes calls the 'plurality of its systems' (Leitch, 1983, p. 203), its aggression, brutalisation of women, sexual repression and symbolisation of a playwright's guilt.

Critics generally responded favourably to the *Trilogy* and its epilogue. Writing about *Three Places in Rhode Island* in the *Soho Weekly News*, James Leverett praised what he saw as the work's image of a 'spiritual sickness' invading the 'material world'. 'Every part reinforces the terrifying growth of the whole. . . . What began in *Sakonnet Point* as a pastoral idyll ends [in *Nayatt School*] in a

plague of the most urban of all diseases' (1978, p. 71). Arthur
Sainer, in *The Village Voice*, wrote that *Sakonnet Point* 'suggests
both memory and immediate reality. It is attenuated and distant,
blatant and near. . . . And this simultaneity is hard to account for
and it's one of the triumphs of the piece'. Richard Eder, in *The
New York Times*, called *Rumstick Road* 'a brilliant and engrossing
work; one whose abstraction and complexity are at the service of
genuine emotions, and whose artistry and execution is such that
even its conceptual misfirings are splendidly theatrical' (1978).
About *Point Judith*, however, James Leverett wrote that

> LeCompte, always brilliant at creating visual imagery, brings
> the work to a formal climax by having the actors build a metal
> skeleton of a house and repeating yet again a structure used
> in all four plays. . . . But this piece asks for some resolution
> beyond a mere formal one, or at least some new perspective
> concerning the themes of sexuality and family.
>
> (1980)

Point Judith signified both an end and a beginning for the Wooster
Group. It was the last piece Gray created with LeCompte (although
he would appear in others), for he left to work as an actor and
monologuist on his own. His departure allowed LeCompte to
assume the artistic centre of the Group in addition to her role as
director of individual pieces. In 1980, Richard Schechner left the
Performance Group, which disbanded. LeCompte and the artists
who had been working with her (Ron Vawter, Libby Howes, Jim
Clayburgh, Willem Dafoe, Kate Valk and Peyton Smith) retained
the Performing Group's non-profit status, and LeCompte became
artistic director of what had always been the Performance Group's
corporate name, the Wooster Group.

Three Places in Rhode Island and *Point Judith* also established
a Wooster Group style. The pieces are notable for the small
amount of original verbal text they contain; the verbal text is
largely a conglomeration of recorded interviews, letters, recordings of other performances, and previously scripted material.
Throughout, there is the recognition that popular culture is part
and parcel of the American way of life, and these early pieces mark
the Wooster Group's commitment to drawing on both the content
and technology of the popular media. Physical objects such as
record players, microphones, tape recorders and film, as well

as popular songs and dances make up the texts. Indeed, under Le-
Compte's guidance, the early work shows the predilection for util-
ising every element of culture as text, the infinite text of Barthes's
definition. In terms of performance, these first pieces also reveal
LeCompte's determination to distance the audience from the performer, llargely through what critic James Bierman calls 'the proliferation of spatial options and perspectives . . . events occurring
in two or three locations simultaneously' (1979, p. 28).

The first significant creation of the newly formed Wooster Group
was *Route 1 and 9 (The Last Act)*(1981), a deconstruction of Thorton
Wilder's Pulitzer Prize-winning drama of small-town America, *Our
Town*. 'We began doing *Our Town* as a reading', LeCompte told
Savran, 'but excluding the part of the Stage Manager, that voice
that connects, so that it would stand as a number of scenes,
placed next to each other' (Savran, 1986a, p. 9). Gradually, other
materials were introduced, so that by its last performance at
the Performing Garage, *Route 1 and 9* was composed of four
parts:

PART IA THE LESSON: In which A man Delivers a Lecture on the
         Structure and Meaning of *Our Town*
PART IB THE LESSON: In which the Stage Hands Arrange the
         Stage for the Last Act of *Our Town*
PART II THE PARTY: In Which the Stage Hands Call It a Day
         and a Telegram Is Sent
PART III THE LAST ACT: In Which Four Chairs are Placed on the
         Stage Facing the Audience to Represent Graves
PART IV ROUTE 1 & 9: In Which a Van Picks Up Two Hitchhikers
         and Heads South

The rational outline belies the humour and the occasional
grotesquerie of the piece. In PART IA, the audience at the Performing
Garage gathered in an upstairs gallery, from which they watched
four black and white television monitors suspended from the
ceiling, on all of which actor Ron Vawter was shown giving a
lecture that explicated the 'meaning' of Wilder's play. Abruptly the
monitors were turned off, and the audience moved downstairs. In
the intervening blackout, the audience overheard a conversation in
which two men talked about building a 'skeletal house'; the lights
came on, and two 'stagehands' entered, made up in grotesquely
exaggerated blackface, and in burlesque fashion assembled a

skeletal house stage right according to instructions given to them over a loudspeaker. In PART II, the men were joined by two women in blackface, and the group soon staged a chaotic party replete with vaudeville routines. Chief among these gags was a scatalogical Pigmeat Markham routine, in which all the revellers had to 'send a telegram' (defecate), because Pigmeat poured castor oil into the punch. While the party grew increasingly farcical, scenes from *Our Town* were played on the television monitors above the audience's heads.

In PART III, the monitors were lowered and became the sole focus, replaying tapes of the third and last act of *Our Town*, while the live party continued quietly in the background. By the end of the sequence, the party-goers had removed most of their blackface, and just as the character George burst into tears on the videotape, the song 'Jump on the Line' began, the actors approached the audience, dancing wildly, 'blood' streaming down their faces. In PART IV, two videotapes were played simultaneously: the four monitors carried colour film of a van moving quietly out of New York City and on to the highway, past gas stations and other emblems of roadside Americana; and at the same time, an ancient black and white television set was rolled out of the skeletal house, and a black and white tape of a man and woman having sexual intercourse was played. Throughout this sequence, the live actors sat quietly around the playing space.

Route 1 & 9 catapulted LeCompte and the Wooster Group into the public eye. The New York State Council on the Arts, charging racism, cut its funding of the Wooster Group by 40 per cent, and the Wooster Group arranged a number of public forums that debated both the work's possible racism and the issue of what some considered the Council's censorship. Critics who had confidently assessed *Three Places in Rhode Island* in terms of conventional themes were sometimes angry and confused by sequences they viewed as 'pointless' and 'predictable' (Gussow, 1981). 'Watching the performance, I turned red with titillation and embarrassment', wrote John Howell in *Soho News*. 'I both enjoyed and was put off by *Route's* willfully perverse black and white ideas. Although this performance means to offend (and it does), its bullets seem larger than its targets' (Howell, 1981). Others praised what they saw as the Wooster Group's politically and aesthetically radical stance. 'This work ruthlessly depicts the disintegration of white American society', wrote Bonnie Marranca. 'It's been a long time since any avant-garde theater in New York presented a politically controversial work of such emotional ferocity' (Marranca, 1982).

LeCompte has denied that the initial impulse for the work was political. 'I came upon some Pigmeat Markham records a year or so before I started working on the piece', she told Savran. 'The routines interested me because of their performance tone and because of the idea of blackface. . . . It was a visual idea, an exercise in performance, a device to give the performance distance. Blackface offered a physical mask. . . . The jokes offered a cultural mask' (Savran, 1986a, pp. 26–7).

Indeed, in the context of deconstructing *Our Town*, the blackface sequences serve as a cultural mask that has several potential (and ambiguous) meanings. It can be viewed as a mask that black America adopts for its own protection, or one that was forced on them unwillingly, or as the other side of the white American insular small town world that Wilder is depicting. The blackface sequences become both the image of what bigoted America has created and also an image of raucous, uninhibited freedom that the Emily Webbs and the George Gibbses can never allow themselves to experience. The sequences are neither racist nor unracist, neither 'bad' nor 'good', but both 'bad' and 'good', depending on who is perceiving them. LeCompte herself has admitted that the Markham routines were consciously ambiguous as performance material: 'The blackface is both a . . . painful representation of blacks and also wild, joyous, and nihilistic and, therefore, freeing' (Savran, 1986a, p. 31).

The withdrawal of funding by the New York State Council on the Arts forced the Wooster Group to mount a retrospective of its work in 1982, and in 1983 the company travelled to Holland at the invitation of the Globe Theatre in Eindhoven, to work as artists in residence. In the meantime, the Wooster Group worked on *L.S.D. (. . . Just the High Points . . .)*, which opened officially to New York audiences in the fall of 1984.

As LeCompte has related it, the Wooster Group's experiences with *Route 1 & 9* led them to explore Arthur Miller's drama *The Crucible*, which was written in 1954 as an allegory paralleling the Salem witch-hunts of the seventeenth-century with the communist witch-hunts of Senator Joseph McCarthy in the early 1950s. The intent, as with *Route 1 & 9*, was to use a well-known text as a referential object. But where that piece had investigated the contradictions and repressions in America's cultural psyche, *L.S.D* sought to deconstruct a history play and in so doing examine an actual period in America's cultural history, the world of the counter-cultural movement of the 1960s.

As with *Route 1 & 9, L.S.D.* is divided into four parts:

PART I   NEWTON CENTRE: In Which The Men Read From Great Books and the Babysitter Remembers the Leary House-hold

PART II   SALEM: In Which the Men are joined at The Table by Women in Costume and Excerpts from a Play are Performed

PART III   MILLBROOK: In Which The Reading Continues and a Man in Miami Arranges a Gig in One Of The Local Hotels

PART IV   MIAMI: In Which The Men Debate and a Troupe of Dancers Impersonates Donna Sierra and the Del Fuegos

Despite the four-part structure, organisationally *L.S.D.* is one of the most complex works the Wooster Group has created. The piece includes numerous intertextual citations: the taped memories of Ann Rower, who babysat for Timothy Leary in Cambridge, Massachusetts, while Leary was at Harvard and conducting experiments with LSD; texts selected at random by the performers during rehearsal, excerpts from the writings of such counter-cultural myth-makers as Jack Kerouac, Arthur Koestler, William Burroughs, Alan Watts and Allen Ginsburg; and excerpts from *The Crucible*. Originally the *Crucible* excerpts were to be fifty minutes long, then LeCompte cut them to twenty-five minutes in an effort to appease Miller and his lawyers, who had not given the Wooster Group permission to perform any part of Miller's play. LeCompte finally eliminated Miller's dialogue, and the segment was performed in pantomime. However, Miller still threatened legal action, and in November 1984, LeCompte closed the production. In subsequent performances of *L.S.D.* a piece by Michael Kirby called *The Hearing* has been used in PART II.

'The way I attack this idea that there is no one meaning [is that] there is no one history, either', says LeCompte. 'There is a moment, and in that moment, everything is contained' (Greene, 1989). *L.S.D.* is complex because it is a memory work that cuts back and forth between texts, points of view, and periods of time with such randomness as to make history seem all of a piece. What is history? What is fact? What is the past that is not now and vice versa? Savran is right in calling *L.S.D.* an 'hallucinatory chronicle' (1986a, p. 174), made up as it is of such uncertain perspectives as hearsay and memory and the often delusional constructs of its soothsayers.

In terms of representing one meaning, *L.S.D.* is impossible to pin down. Visually, however, the piece was almost static. Le-Compte focused the setting on a twenty-foot long steel grey table, a table first seen in *Nayatt School*, behind which the actors sat on a five-foot high platform and took turns reading their various texts. The performers rarely moved from behind the table which was strewn with microphones, papers, books, a television monitor, pitchers of water – all the accoutrements of a hearing room. The main action is this reading of texts, although that is interrupted periodically by various dances and by a Ken Kobland film about Miami. 'The whole piece is a reading that breaks down', LeCompte told Savran. 'The performers, the authors, are still ten years later, trying to continue this reading' (1986a, p. 196).

As with *Route 1 & 9*, a public furor surrounding *L.S.D.* threatened to obscure the artistic and intellectual achievements of the work itself. Yet, as with the charges of racism in regard to *Route 1 & 9*, the question of who owns a text eventually lent additional dimensions to the Wooster Group's work. As originally conceived, the excerpts from *The Crucible* could be viewed as one side of the 1950s, a side judged by Miller as politically dangerous, a side also judged negatively by Kerouac and some of his contemporaries, who experienced the 1950s as sexually and spiritually repressive. Yet, as Miller apparently perceived on the one occasion when he attended a performance, *The Crucible* was an icon being used against itself: Tituba was played in blackface; a fourteen-year-old boy played Deputy Governor Danforth; three elderly women played the young girls; Ron Vawter as the Reverend Hale delivered his speeches at breakneck speed. Miller's drama was turned into an object, like *Our Town*, whose meaning existed to be destroyed, in order to expose what lay beneath. The play may have been morally 'good', because of the intent with which it was written, but because of its cultural status and supposed inviolability, it had become morally suspect. Indeed, although Miller was within his legal right to challenge the Wooster Group's unauthorised use of his material, this refusal took on the cast of that same censorship and control that *The Crucible* had purportedly been written to protest. Once again, a public furor seemed to accentuate the underside of American culture. As in *L.S.D.*'s presentation of history, past and present appeared to occur simultaneously.

Despite the premature closing of *L.S.D.*, 1984 heralded years of new organisational strength for the Wooster Group. While working so feverishly on *L.S.D.*, the Wooster Group had also presented *North Atlantic* (1984), a piece by Jim Strahs that had been in development since 1983 as PART II of *L.S.D.* and then was later developed separately. *North Atlantic* (the title is a play on the Rodgers and Hammerstein musical *South Pacific*) is a blackly farcical impression of the relationships between men and women, here depicted as based on a yearning for sexual power. While critics were divided as to the merits of the text, most agreed that the setting was startling. The piece takes place on an American military ship, and the 'stage' at the Performing Garage was one enormous plane of metal, set at a forty-five degree rake, across which the performers scrambled. The long metal table that was by now frequent to Wooster Group productions slid up and down this expanse, usually coming to rest at the foot of the rake, where the actors could patrol a narrow shelf and sit or stand at the table. 'LeCompte's staging', wrote Michael Feinglod, 'applies all the standard techniques of stage deconstruction, ignoring the fact that nothing in the script is strongly enough built up to be worth such dismantling' (1984). Greg Leaming suggested 'the production is so technically accomplished that LeCompte's bleak vision nags at us long after we leave the theatre' (1984).

In 1985, the Wooster Group was one of eight American companies to receive a five-year grant from the National Endowment for the Arts, an allotment that helped buttress the Wooster Group's position in the arts community. Also in 1985, the company (LeCompte included) performed in *Miss Universal Happiness*, written and directed by Richard Foreman. That same year they were in residence at the Kennedy Center in Washington, DC, where they gave previews of a new work in progress, *Frank Dell's Saint Anthony*. In 1986, while still developing *Saint Anthony*, the Wooster Group toured Australia, performing at the Adelaide Festival, and then toured Europe with a revised *L.S.D.*, now retitled *The Road to Immortality: Part Two (. . . Just the High Points . . .)*. During the 1986–7 season, the company presented *(. . . Just the High Points . . .)* in New York as the second part of a new trilogy, the first part being *Route 1 & 9*, the third part to be *Frank Dell's Saint Anthony* (1987).

As critic Elinor Fuchs has noted, 'the title alone is virtually an archaeological dig' (1988). *The Road to Immortality* is the title of a spiritual guide written in 1932 by the Irish spiritualist Geraldine Cummins and apparently much prized by the comedian Lenny Bruce in the last months of his life. Frank Dell was a name that Bruce assumed early in his career as a stand-up comic; a figure named Frank Dell also appeared in *L.S.D.* as a leader of a down-at-heel dance troupe, Donna Sierra and the Dell Fuegos. In *Saint Anthony*, Dell is the suicidal leader of a down-at-heel theatrical troupe which, as in Ingmar Bergman's film *The Magician* (1958), must perform for the local powers-that-be to prove they are bona fide. *The Temptation of Saint Anthony* is a lengthy dramatic poem by Gustave Flaubert, about a fifth-century Egyptian saint who lived in the desert. Peter Sellars, while artistic director of the Boston Shakespeare Company, approached LeCompte in 1983 with the idea of collaborating on a deconstruction of the Flaubert work. After choreographing several dances for the proposed piece, Sellars dropped out of the collaboration. LeCompte later added other materials: film footage of a pornographic cable television programme; a Ken Kobland film of an elderly woman (Irma St Paule) lying on a bathroom floor while Ron Vawter as Dell jabs at her inert body with a stick. *The Road to Immortality, Part Three: Frank Dell's The Temptation of Saint Anthony* was the final title of the piece when it formally opened to the reviews of New York critics in October 1988. It is, in the opinion of several critics, a self-reflective piece, as much about the Wooster Group itself as about temptations or Lenny Bruce. 'A theater troupe on the lam performing mystery plays about temptation: that's the Wooster Group', wrote Fuchs. Indeed, on one level, the piece seemed to be a celebration of all that was theatrical: 'Walls rise and descend, doors with actors strapped to them fly dangerously open and slam shut. There are also trashy costumes, wigs, beards, sensational lighting . . .' At another level, Fuchs found the piece to be a sad contemplation of mortality, both 'human and artistic. . . . It is as if LeCompte and her group, in their exacting struggle to force the oddest "bits of culture" into relation on the stage, had come to the end of a certain line of thought and been pushed to consider their relation to theater itself' (1988).

In their journey from *Sakonnet Point* to *Frank Dell's The Temptation of Saint Anthony*, the Wooster Group has striven to establish the vitality of the American theatrical avant-garde in a political and economic environment that has generally not been conducive to such experiments. Some of the experiments have been too radical for the times, specifically the sometimes blithe assumption by LeCompte and her company that text is the property of a culture rather than an individual.

Yet in pushing at the bounds of performance, LeCompte and the Wooster Group have established a unique aesthetic that places the materials of contemporary American culture in sometimes ugly, sometimes electric, always provocative juxtaposition. Refusing to provide an accessible aesthetic, or easily digestible ideas or sentiments, LeCompte and the Wooster Group have preferred instead to provoke and to anger their audiences, to provide a range of possibilities and perspectives, rather than one easy answer. Indeed, LeCompte insists 'My function on this earth is to question' (Greene, 1989).

BIBLIOGRAPHY

Aronson, A. (1985) 'The Wooster Group's *L.S.D.* (. . . *Just the High Points* . . .)', *The Drama Review*, summer, vol. 29.

Auslander, P. (1987) 'Toward a Concept of the Political in Postmodern Theatre', *Theatre Journal*, March, vol. 39.

Bierman, J. (1979) 'Three Places In Rhode Island', *The Drama Review*, March, vol. 23.

Champagne, L. (1981) 'Always Starting New: Elizabeth LeCompte', *The Drama Review*, fall, vol. 25.

Eder, R. (1978) 'Stage: Spalding Gray's Youth', *The New York Times*, 19 Dec.

Feingold, M. (1984) 'North Pedantic', *The Village Voice*, 7 Feb.

Fuchs, E. (1988) 'End of the Road?', *The Village Voice*, 25 Oct.

Greene, A. (1989) Interview with Elizabeth LeCompte, 13 March.

Gussow, M. (1981) 'The Stage: *Route 1 & 9*', *The New York Times*, 29 Oct.

Howell, J. (1981) 'Black and white all over', *Soho News*, 10 Nov.

Leaming, G. (1984) 'Wooster Group's *North Atlantic*', *Villager*, 16 Feb.

Leitch, V. B. (1983) *Deconstructive Criticism* (New York: Columbia University Press).

Leverett, J. (1978) 'Mapping Rhode Island', *Soho Weekly News*, 21 Dec.

———. (1980) 'Point Counterpoint', *Soho Weekly News*, 10 Jan.

———. (1982) 'The Wooster Group's "Mean Theatre" Sparks a Hot Debate', *Theatre Communications*, July/Aug. .

Marranca, B. (1982) 'Our Town, Our Country', *LIVE*, vols 6/7.

Patterson, J. (1982) 'Reaction Grows to Cuts in State Arts Funding to Theatre Group', *Villager*, 21 Jan.

Rabkin, G. (1985) 'Is There a Text on This Stage?', *Performing Arts Journal*, vol. IX (2/3).

Sainer, A. (n.d.) 'Hurrying to Nowhere to Go', *The Village Voice*.

Savran, D. (1986a) *Breaking the Rules* (New York: Theatre Communications Group).

———. (1986b) 'Terrorists of the Text', *American Theatre*, Dec.

Schechner, R. (1968) 'Six Axioms for Environmental Theatre', *Tulane Drama Review*, vol. XII, no. 3, pp. 160–64.

Shank, T. (1982) *American Alternative Theater* (New York: Grove Press).

Shewey, D. (1982) 'The Wooster Group Stirs Controversy', *The New York Times*, 16 May.

7

Lee Breuer and Mabou Mines

S E GONTARSKI

For many artists of the 1960s and 1970s, interiority, that post-Enlightenment fetish explored darkly by Romantic poets, painters and musicians, and the symbolist poets, flaunted in a radical theory of colour by the Fauves and in terms of cubist distortions by the German expressionists, squeezed into a Freudian paradigm by Andre Breton and the surrealists to give shape to Dada's nihilism, plunged into its pre-ideational realm, into its inchoate, universally mythic sphere by the abstract expressionists and some fluxus performers, had run its course. At least with the embrace of popular culture by the American cubist Stuart Davis, who in 1950 proclaimed 'I like popular art, topical ideas, and not high culture or modernistic formalism' (Hughes, p. 330), art began its fascination with the surface texture of its culture, with popular signs, popular media and popular myths.

The theoretician for this resurfacing was an unlikely disciple of St Thomas Aquinas, Marshall McLuhan, who, in *The Mechanical Bride* (1951), began his exploration of 'the folklore of industrial man', and with *The Gutenberg Galaxy* (1962) and *Understanding Media* (1964) procalimed the utopian possibilities of the 'global village', an electronic replacement for (or at least adjunct to) the human nervous system. In the visual arts Robert Rauschenberg, in a Dada revival of the late 1950s, used found objects – street junk which harkened back to Marshal Duchamp's 'ready-mades' and Man Ray's surrealist objects – in his *combine-paintings*, not as keys to unlock the secret and censored recesses of interior life, as they were with the surrealists, but as emblems of the phantasmagoria, fragmentation and dross of contemporary culture – like the 'Merz pictures' of Kurt Switters. In literature William Burroughs and poet Brion Gysin (the latter perhaps better known for his recipe for brownies in the Alice B Toklas Cookbook than for his poetry), developed their 'cut-up' method of composition, slicing into the daily newspaper with the rapacity of Tristan Tzara attacking a Shakespearean sonnet.

The embrace of popular culture was, at least by implication, deeply ideological, an assault on the privilege and elitism of art, an extended democratisation begun by the futurists, Dadaists and extended in a burst of romantic Marxism by the surrealists. With icons like a Campbell's soup can or boxes of Brillo scouring pads, Andy Warhol could embrace (and for a time ironised) the age of mechanical reproduction (in both senses, like Francis Picabia). Rather than revivify mythic heroes from antiquity, Warhol could embrace and proliferate, in a parody of fecundity, Marilyn Monroes or Elvis Presleys to suggest that our heroes are little more than their images, which could be stamped out with all the sterility of soup cans. In the theatre Michael McClure and Sam Shepard staged those Merz-heroes: McClure brought together Jean Harlow and Billie the Kid in the erotic seduction of *The Beard* (1967), and Shepard offered us a series of American pop/mythic heroes like Marlene Dietrich, Mae West, Captain Kidd, Paul Bunyan and Jesse James in *The Mad Dog Blues* (1971).

It was not so much that artists were rejecting interiority wholesale, that the principal discovery (or invention) of modernity, although for many artists the *terra incognita* had become *terra cognita*, but rather they found irresistible the glitz of the protean culture of mass production and conspicuous consumption, the superstimulating neon-lit world of post-modernity. The psychological romanticism of surrealism (and the interior monologue in fiction, or confessional poetry, for that matter), that is, interiority itself, had been if not replaced by those devaluations of form broadly called 'conceptual art' and 'performance art' (via Robert Rauschenberg's *combines* and Allan Kaprow's *Happenings*), then at least substantially modified by them.

In the summer of 1981, Lee Breuer took a few trial steps into the mainstream of literary/theatrical culture and brought his pop iconography with him, staging his first Shakespearean production, *The Tempest*, for Joseph Papp's 'Shakespeare in the Park as Pop' collage (as he would in 1988 bring his pop version of Sophocles to Broadway as *The Gospel at Colonus*, with music by 'Clarence Fountain and the Five Blind Boys of Alabama'). In Breuer's staging, Shakespeare's opening tempest was not dramatised on stage but radioed in, crackling and distorted, through loudspeakers in an echo of Mabou Mines' earlier collaborative piece, *Send Receive Send* (1973). Ariel was fragmented into a multitude of forms. Trinculo was played by a woman who spoke like Mae West. Stephano spoke with a W C Fields accent. Antonio, Sebastian and others were dressed like gangsters and arrived (in Breuer's stretching theatre towards cinema) via helicopter. Caliban was a punk rocker, an image that Breuer had used that spring for the title character in his American Repertory Theater production of Frank Wedekind's *Lulu* (1981).

Breuer's *Tempest* was Shakespeare as Merz-theatre. But in this assault on both Shakespeare and the bourgeoise sensibility, the text of Shakespeare remained intact, unlike, say, Charles Marowitz's assaults on the bard in *The Marowitz Hamlet* (1965) or *A Macbeth* (1969). In fundamental respects, however, Marowitz's theatrical methods of coupling contraries, blending method acting with the anti-realistic techniques of Artaud, which Marowitz developed working with Peter Brook's Season of Cruelty (1964), for instance, came very close to Lee Breuer's aesthetics. Reviewing Breuer's *Tempest* in *The New York Times*, however, Frank Rich complained that 'These ideas [the plethora of pop images] are never reconciled with each other and rarely with the play' (10 July 1981). But Rich's call for an aesthetics of reconciliation, which is finally an aesthetics of reconciliation, which is finally an aesthetics of allegory, the Shakespearean hand fitted snugly into the post-modern glove, may miss the point. The object of Merz-Shakespeare (or 'ontological/hysterical' Shakespeare, if such existed) may not be to hold Shakespeare together, but to take him apart, to dismantle, disperse or deconstruct his work, in a diaspora of meanings. In Breuer's case, however, and this is what separates his work from that of many of his fellow post-literate, imagistic theatricians, the deconstruction retains respect – if not reverence – for the literary tradition, the historical text.

From the beginning, Lee Breuer has tried to reconcile an iconoclastic theatre of images (theatre as plastic art) with a devotion for the literature of theatre (theatre as literature). In her anthology of new theatre, *The Theatre of Images*, Bonnie Marranca calls attention to the crucial non-literary sources of Breuer's theatre, even as she misses connections between this new conceptual theatre and futurist and Dadaist performances and the surrealist soiree: 'Just as Happenings had no immediate theatrical antecedents [an arguable assumption, at best], the Theatre of Images, though not quite so renegade, had developed aesthetically from numerous non-theatrical roots' (Marranca, 1977, p. ix). Mel Gussow, writing for *The New York Times*, put the matter a bit more concretely, suggesting that the 'multidimensional experience' of Mabou Mines theatre 'is indebted to painting, sculpture, and to dance, music and theater'. The attempt to assimilate a variety of artistic genres and to reconcile high and popular culture was, of course, as much part of the surrealist agenda as it was that of the experimental theatre of America in the 1960s and 1970s. After all, the most influential work for theatre during the post Second World War period was not a work written directly for the stage but for what Andre Breton called 'the theatre of the mind', Antonin Artaud's *The Theatre and its Double*, and that work is best understood seen against the tradition that nourished it, surrealism. For Breuer theatre is both literature and plastic art, particularly that visual art that embraced post-war American kitsch, pop art. In the 'Preface' to his *The Red Horse Animation* (1970, 1972) he acknowledges his attraction to comic books:

> . . . COMICS TALK TO ME . MORE PERTINENTLY NOW . EVEN . THAN THEN . WHEN I WAS THE GREEN ARROW . (WINNER NORTH HOLLYWOOD PARK HALLOWEEN COSTUME COMPETITION 9 P.M. IN FRONT OF THE BONFIRE OCTOBER 31, 1948) . THEY TALK TO ME AT ALL HOURS . ON THE PHONE . LONG DISTANCE.

In fact, what 'text' exists for *The Red Horse Animations* is not only post-scripted, that is, born of the collaboration of rehearsal and performance, but it is published as a comic book with drawings by Ann Elizabeth Horton. Even in publication the text is inseparable from its visual imagery and is presented through that visual imagery, not as in traditional publication where a script, a sketch for performance, is at best augmented, adorned by one or two production photos.

And yet Breuer's training was literary as well as cinematic. A literature major at UCLA, Breuer was attracted to the work of Bertholt Brecht, Frank Wedekind and, most importantly, Samuel Beckett. It was to see Beckett's *Waiting for Godot* performed by the San Francisco Actor's Workshop that Breuer hitchhiked to San Francisco in 1958, and his first assignment for that group was to direct Beckett's *Happy Days* – Breuer has retained that attraction to and respect for Beckett's texts, which he has subsequently staged with stunning theatrical images. Writing in *The New York Times*, Roger Copland noted, 'Mabou Mines has always placed words and visual imagery on an equal footing. This is especially evident in their Beckett work – theatre pieces based on texts which Beckett never originally intended to be staged' (1977). What the group found appealing in Beckett's texts was not a psychological depth of characterisation, but its opposite, the multiplicity and fragmentation of character, of the modernist ego (hence, the proliferation of Ariels in *The Tempest*). Despite his early interest in Stanislavskian method and his directorial focus on 'private moments', Breuer and the company rejected the trappings of illusionistic theatre and psychological characterisation (although retaining an interest in the psychological machinery of acting as developed by Stanislavski and Grotowski) in favour of a more Brechtian alienated performance. In Beckett's texts the group found man as motor, a conception which helped shatter the illusions of realistic theatre.

The two Beckett 'plays' the group performed, *Play* and *Come and Go* (begun in 1971 but the group's major success with the works was in New York at the Theater for The New City in the fall of 1975), are characterised by repeated, mechanical behaviour. *Play* is a post-mortem dram in which members of a love triangle, interred to their necks in funerary urns, their faces splattered with mud of decomposition, recount yet again the clichés of their banal passion at the insistence of an inhuman, inquisitorial beam of light to which they apparently speak. In *Come and Go* the formal patterning of action of a trio of former schoolmates exchanging intimacies about the missing third anticipates much of Beckett's late, formalist theatre. The piece premiered in May of 1971 at the Brooklyn Bridge festival with the three women performing on a pier with cordless microphones and the audience on another pier with speakers in their midst. When Breuer subsequently adapted the work for the stage, the image of the three women, clucking like pigeons, faces veiled, seated with hands crossed in a pattern of mystic symbolism, was as alienated, distanced and dehumanised within the theatre as it was on the piers thanks to a huge mirror through which, the audience finally discover, it has been viewing the action. The women were actually situated behind and above the audience, in the balcony, and their image reflected to the stage via mirrors. The result was finally dissociative, an assault on perception with voices and visual images reaching the spectator from opposite ends of the theatre, and the spectral image allowed the women simply to vanish into shimmering darkness while the other two discuss her affliction.

The third work on this ninety-minute programme of 'Mabou Mines Performs Samuel Beckett', was the group's adaptation of Beckett's novella, *The Lost Ones*, which began as a reading–demonstration by David Warrilow. In Beckett's text his characters, some 205 barely distinguishable creatures, live in a 'flattened cylinder fifty metres round and eighteen high for the sake of harmony'. The principal occupation of these 205 creatures, divided into four groups, the vanquished or non-searchers, the watchers, the sedentary searchers, and the climbers of ladders, is to search for its lost one. Their principal physical business, however, is to discover an exit and so free themselves from the cylinder through one of the tunnels accessible by faulty ladders or through the ceiling. Warrilow, at first holding the text, began demonstrating the world of the cylinder and its inhabitants with the aid of a miniature cross-section of a cylinder and tiny, half-inch images of the naked inhabitants, only one of whom, one of the vanquished, is ever named; she is the North. Warrilow then manipulated these figures with tweezers or forceps. As Ruby Cohn recounts in her *Just Play*, 'After Warrilow decided to abandon the book, Mabou Mines designer Thom Cathcart, having scraped the paint off 205 toy German railroad dolls, conceived the decisively brilliant idea of seating the live theater audience in a rubber cylinder environment' (1980, p. 224). The shoeless audience entered the cylinder to Philip Glass's minimalist sounds, which emulated Beckett's 'faint stridulence of insects', and was provided with binoculars to watch, to spy on the miniature creatures. As Bonnie Marranca noted, 'Breuer has theatrically conceived *The Lost Ones* with at least four perspectives in mind: that of the narrator; the narrator in the role of a "lost one"; the model of the cylindrical world; the experience of the audience living through time in an environment that approximates the cylinder' (1978).

The Mabou Mines Company has retained its interest in Beckett's work throughout its existence, adopting him almost as company playwright, but the group has not always been able to maintain the same propitious balance between author's text and company visualisation that marked the group's original Beckett evening. In the spring of 1976 JoAnne Akalaitis adapted *Cascando*, Beckett's twenty-minute radio play, into a sixty-minute stage work set in a fisherman's cottage in Nova Scotia. The cottage, which could have been decorated by Red Grooms, was cluttered with objects: photos, a used tyre, a goldfish bowl, a tortoise shell, a polar bear and an assortment of rusty kitchenware. Four men and a woman sat around a table, and in a corner another male sat in a rocking chair. Akalaitis divided Beckett's narrative of the journey of Woburn and Beckett's three characters, Opener, Voice and Music, among six players. The group around the table was Voice, speaking at times in unison, at times separately, and each of the characters performed an activity, shaving, knitting, carving wood, playing cards, building houses of cards and painting. While visually stunning, the adaptation was more often than not chaotic, as stage business distracted from and finally eroded Beckett's narrative.

Much of the group's subsequent creative energy was devoted to adapting Beckett's prose works to the stage. In 1979 Frederick Neumann adapted and directed Beckett's 1946 novel *Mercier and Camier* on a high-tech set made of plexiglass. The audience was separated from the actors by a trough, Beckett's canal, and the narrator (David Warrilow) was seen on television via video tape. Some seven years later (1983), Neumann (in collaboration with Honora Fergusson) turned his attention to Beckett's 1980 novella, *Company*, and staged it, disregarding Beckett's injunction to 'Keep it simple, Freddie' (Cohn, 1987, p. 178), complete with laser beams, satellite dishes and video. Mel Gussow's reservations about the production would be equally applicable to much of the group's later work with Beckett: 'Mr Neumann was unable to devise a metaphor sizable enough to encompass the various personae within Beckett's single character' (1986). Undaunted, Neumann tackled *Westward Ho* in 1986, playing it knee-deep in a grave. His performance was augmented by three silent, dimly lit creatures: a solitary woman and a man and a boy, both with white hair. The man and boy, at times holding hands, finally walk away on an endless ramp. In one of the group's more imaginative and austere adaptations, Ruth Maleczech, with collaborator Linda Hartinian, staged a fourteen-minute version of Beckett's story 'Imagination Dead Imagine' (1984) with the central character as a catafalque. The group's relations with Beckett have not always been harmonious, however. In December of 1984 JoAnne Akalaitis, acting as an independent director and not as part of the Mabou Mines Company, staged *Endgame* in New Haven, and prompted Beckett to take action to halt the performance at the American Repertory Theater. As opening night approached lawyers for both sides were still negotiating. In question were Akalaitis's alterations of Beckett's text. She set her production in a subway station with an abandoned subway car as backdrop. She added music composed by her ex-husband, Philip Glass, a practice which was part of every production of Beckett's work performed by Mabou Mines with the exception of David Warrilow's *A Piece of Monologue* in 1980, by which time Warrilow was no longer part of the company. Beckett had further objected to the increasingly common American practice of non-traditional casting, black actors in two of the four roles, as he had in the past objected to the casting of *Waiting for Godot* with women. An eleventh hour compromise allowed the piece to open but the theatre was forced to include Beckett's harsh disclaimer in the playbill: 'A complete parody of the play. Anybody who cares for the work couldn't fail to be disgusted'. Beckett, who had allowed the group wide latitude in interepreting his prose works for the stage insisted yet again that his theatre pieces were meant to be performed as written.

In retrospect the conflict was inevitable. No one who knew her work, and Samuel Beckett certainly did, could have expected JoAnne Akalaitis simply to stage a traditional production of *Endgame*, as no one who knows Beckett's attitude toward his theatre, and Akalaitis does full well, could have expected Beckett to accept what he saw as substantial textual alterations. Akalaitis, on the other hand, felt that she had maintained textual integrity since the play's dialogue remained intact; only the visual imagery – also specified in the text, of course – was altered. As Akalaitis moved the play into a new aesthetic space, however, she certainly altered Beckett's precise conception of the play. Whether or not her alterations enriched or eroded Beckett's play is a question that still divides critics. In general, however, none of the Mabou Mines' later work on Beckett managed to capture the visual vitality and the creative balance between Beckett's script and the company's conception of the work that was evident in the group's original Beckett evening. Assessing their Beckett adaptations, Ruby Cohn speaks with an enthusiasm about the early triptych that she cannot muster for the later work: 'The Beckett evening was to coalesce the three strands of their esthetic:

1) the Stanislavskian legacy of motivational acting, 2) estrange-ment–narrative performance deriving from Brecht and Oriental theater, 3) the conceptual formalism of the visual arts of the 1960s' (1980, p. 225).

The group has continued adapting non-theatrical writing to the stage as well. In 1977 JoAnne Akalaitis turned her attention to the work of Colette. Working with sculptor Ree Morton and painter Nancy Graves, Akalaitis devised *Dressed like an Egg*, which opened at the Public Theater in May of 1977. And Bill Raymond conceived a show based on the life of Ulysses S Grant. Written by Dale Worsley, *Cold Harbor* began life as a reading, much like David Warrilow's early versions of Beckett's *Company*, but Raymond's work also developed into a full theatrical piece. As he was searching for a theatrical point of view for his reading, he seized on the idea of having a model of the former president on display in a museum. Encased in glass, seated at a table with the skull of a horse at his feet, Mr Raymond was brought up on stage like a blow-up of a Joseph Cornell box, and amid period photographs, dioramas and *tableau vivant* he contemplated his life, including the stigma of being called 'Lincoln's butcher' and being credited with 'the first use of annihilation as a tactic or war' aat the battle of Vicksburg.

Always foregrounded in the work of the Mabou Mines Company is the collaborative nature of theatre art. Conceptually, then, the group finds it difficult approaching theatre as a matter of following the precise instructions of a power external to the group, even that of an author, and so Mabou Mines seems more comfortable adapting non-dramatic texts to the stage or generating their own material than mounting work written expressly for the stage. Closer to the theoretical centre of their work is the series of collaborations with visual artists like Ruth Maleczech's staging, with Linda Hartinian, of Beckett's 'Imagination Dead Imagine' as a visual poem. In the early 1970s the group worked on a series of performances that devalued literary content. In 1972 the group performed two pieces at New York's Pauula Cooper Gallery, *Music for Voices* and *Arc Welding Piece*. With music by Philip Glass, *Music for Voices* was performed by eight singers seated in a circle on television monitors. The singers faced inward, the monitors outward, and the audience saw the actors faces electronically in extreme close-ups while it heard their voices live. With *Arc Welding Piece* sculptor Jene Highstein cut into a seven foot steel cylinder with his arc torch as a group of performers, their faces distorted with Fresnel lenses, mimed emotional states. In 1973 the group performed *The Saint and the Football Players* at New York University's Loeb Student Center and in 1976 at Pratt Institute in Brooklyn. Based on Jack Thibeau's 'The Saint and the Football Player – a Xerox Poem', the work was Lee Breuer's first attempt to shape a theatrical work around a popular art form, in this case football as a performance spectacle. In its most spectacular version the cast included over 100 participants, a marching band and a fleet of fork-lift trucks. As the ball passed along the field, the apex of its trajectory was marked by a picture of St Theresa. In *Send Receive Send*, a collaboration with Keith Sonnier, the audience had a series of high, lighted speakers to look at. One group of actors transmitted from hiding in a nearby room, while another group transmitted from across town. For forty-five minutes, the audience listened to wordless messages, broadcast by the actors, mixed with randomly received CB transmissions.

But perhaps the group's most far-reaching experiments were its attempts to blend film, comics (particularly as combined in the animated film) and live theatre in a series of theatrical 'animations', written and directed by Lee Breuer: *The Red Horse Animation*, *The B-Beaver Animation* and *The Shaggy Dog Animation*. *The Red Horse Animation* was first presented in 1970 at the Paula Cooper Gallery and the Guggenheim Museum, and the main character, the Red Horse, is more a composite of characteristics than a traditional literary character. As Breuer himself puts it, the Red Horse, itself composed of three performers, embodies

> psyches – for a while I thought I was talking about metaphors of states of mind, but that was too removed. I now think of the psyches as actual animals, in the sense that you can be in the human world and the animal world – or the world of ghosts – at the same time. [The animations are] sort of choral monologues, each one dealing with a different psychological personality.
>
> (Goldman, 1978, p. 46)

And so the character invents itself as the work progresses. The audience, viewing the action from above at a forty-five degree angle, witnesses both vertical and horizontal images. Much of the percussion music is supplied by the specially amplified floor played by the performers' moving across its surface. In *The B-Beaver Animation*, an exploration of impediments and blockages, the central character is a beaver and the action is played on a sculpture of boards, poles and planks constructed by Tina Girouard.

The Shaggy Dog Animation opened at the Public Theater in New York in the fall of 1977 (after an earlier version at the Open Space in SoHo), and featured a three-foot high puppet, Rose (actually a dog but in human form), which was created by Linda Wolfe and at times took as many as four people to manipulate, and a form of musical synthesizer, the Eden Harmonizer, controlled by Robin Thomas. The actors, aligned with their backs to the audience, were separated from the spectators by a net full of helium-filled balloons or pillows which hid both the set, a miniature bathroom and kitchen (all in 'super realistic' style with quality kitchenware, stainless steel fixtures and ceramic tiles) and the star, Rose. The stage was also dominated by a twenty-three-foot long radio dial on which Rose tuned in rock and roll music in Act I, country and western and latin music in Act II, and jazz in Act III. The performers' rock dialogue was filtered through the Eden Harmonizer to produce an almost incomprehensible montage of sound. When the pillows were released, the set broke into as many as seven distinct units, and Rose gradually became an extension of the performers. At one point JoAnne Akalaitis strapped the puppet onto her body and Rose became 'human' as she baked cream puffs. In each of the animations, the group was experimenting not so much with the multimedia approach of some 1960s theatre, that is, the mixing of media, but with shifting media especially into the electronic age, moving variously from music to words, from words as music to music as words, producing finally a layering of sound and a montage of shifting means of communication. For Breuer the plurality of media reflects his idea that 'Advertising in America is a serious art form'.

In 1980 Breuer used material from the four hour long *Shaggy Dog Animation* to create a *tour de force* for actor Bill Raymond. The result was *Prelude to Death in Venice*, which takes place not in Venice, Italy, as did Thomas Mann's tale of the ageing artist, but in the seedy seaside town of Venice, California, where would-be artist, Bill, who carries his alter ego with him in the form of a life-sized doll named John, holds a series of telephone conversations, often two at a time, at a brace of telephone booths.

For Breuer the piece suggests part of the mid-life crisis, when one realises

> that you will never quite realize your dreams. . . . Bill, the artist who carries John, the artist-hustler, around with him, is falling apart because he realizes he's not going to be the perfect man, the perfect lover, the perfect artist, the perfect film-maker. At the same time he is still in love with the image of himself as a perfect 16 year old.
>
> (Quoted in Holden, 1986)

When the piece was reprised at the Dance Theater Workshop in May of 1986, it ran in repertory with another Breuer piece, an electronic *tour de force*, *Hajj*, which opened originally at the Public Theater in 1983. Sitting before a make-up table Ruth Maleczech delivers her monologue, during which her mirrors become a trio of video monitors showing her youthful and aged as well as in her current image. 'The video was designed', says Maleczech,

> so that there would be no technology visible. At the same time the audience sees all the changes that are normally hidden in the theatre – the make-up table, the mirrors, and the process of transforming one face into another. Though the piece is both a woman's journey into her life and her past, it is also an artist's journey into his or her sources.
>
> (Holden, 1986)

The masks and make-up for the production were, moreover, designed by Linda Hartinian who worked with Miss Maleczech on Beckett's *Imagination Dead Imagine*.

Categorising the work of the Mabou Mines Company is finally something of a self-defeating enterprise since so much of the group's effort is directed to resisting classification, and so Mabou Mines Company is several companies, a harmonious group and a loose and volatile collection of singular and independent artistic talents. At times their work embraces the arid formalism of minimalist art and at times the rejection of form as suggested by the surrealists and visual artists like Kurt Switters, Robert Rauschenberg, Allan Kaprow and a host of conceptual artists. Fascinated by the poetic precision of the Beckettian text, the group has also filtered what text exists in some production through machines that produce the audio equivalent of junk collage. Influenced by principles of alienated acting and narrative acting (although Mabou Mines has actually staged no Brecht), they are as deeply committed to the personally psychological which generates theatrical images. As Lee Breuer has observed,

> The difference between Mabou Mines and other theater groups is that we're interested in the values of motivational acting as well as those of the "art" world. Robert Wilson and Richard Foreman attract the art gallery audience too; but their work makes less use of psychological acting.
>
> (Copland, 1977, p. 12)

These attempts to blend contrasting aesthetics – motivational acting and alienated acting, literature and the plastic arts, respect for classic texts and disdain for textual theatre, respect for a writer's vision and hostility toward external authority, the disregard of content in favour of form as in minimalist art and the disregard of form in favour of a direct and often subliminal thematic statement as in much conceptual art – has characterised most of the theatrical experiments of the group. Rather than becoming self-cancelling, however, these experiments in opposition, both within and between works, capture the polarities of our art and culture without necessarily reconciling or resolving them. In our current age of fragmented egos Mabou Mines Company has devised extraordinary images of self, alienated even from itself (and hence the attraction to Samuel Beckett's texts). Little wonder that Mel Gussow, theatre critic for *The New York Times*, has called Mabou Mines Company 'America's foremost experimental ensemble' (1986), an opinion echoed by colleague Jeremy Gerard, again in *The New York Times*: 'indisputably among the most influential experimental ensembles of our time' (1987).

BIBLIOGRAPHY

Cohn, R. (1980) *Just Play: Beckett's Theater* (Princeton University Press).
——. (1987) 'Mabou Mines Translations of Beckett', in Alan Warren Friedman, et al. (eds) *Beckett Translating/Translating Beckett* (University Park: Pennsylvania State University Press).
Copland, R. (1977) *The New York Times*, 1 May.
Gerard, J. (1987) *The New York Times*, 20 March.

Goldman, H. M. (1978) 'Where Conceptual and Performance Art Meet', *Theatre Crafts*, vol. XII, no. 3, pp. 20–23, 43–9.
Gussow, M. (1986) *The New York Times*, 21 Sept.
Holden, S. (1986) 'Complex, Probing Portraits in Mabou Mines Revivals', *The New York Times*, 16 May, C1, C4.
Hughes, R. (1981) *The Shock of the Future* (New York: Knopf).
Marranca, B. (1977) *The Theatre of Images* (New York: The Drama Book Specialists).
———. (1978) *The Soho Weekly News*, 23 Oct.
Spector, S. (1978) 'Ensemble Design', *Theatre Crafts*, vol. XII, no. 3, pp. 24, 56–7.

1. Contraband. *Religare* (1986).

3. Martha Clarke. *The Garden of Earthly Delights* (1984).

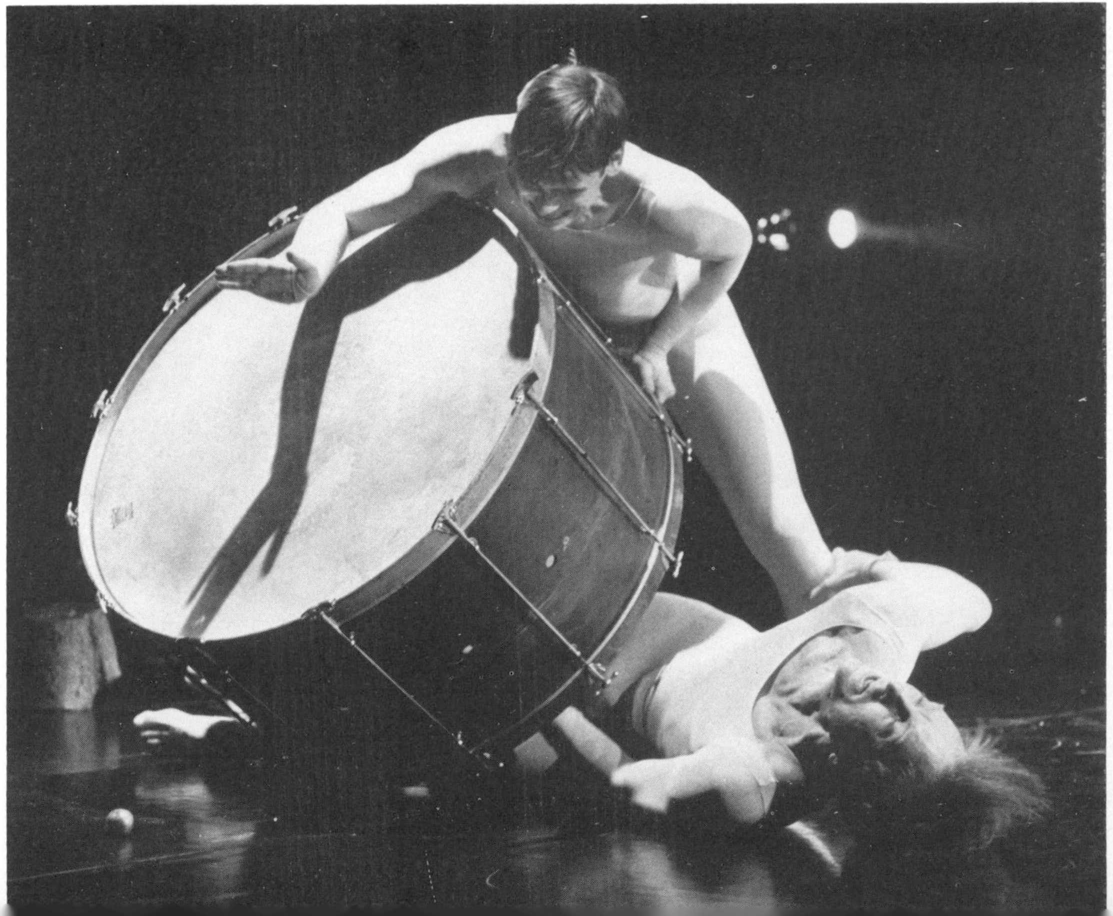

4. Martha Clarke. *The Garden of Earthly Delights* (1984).

5. Martha Clarke. *Vienna: Lusthaus* (1986).

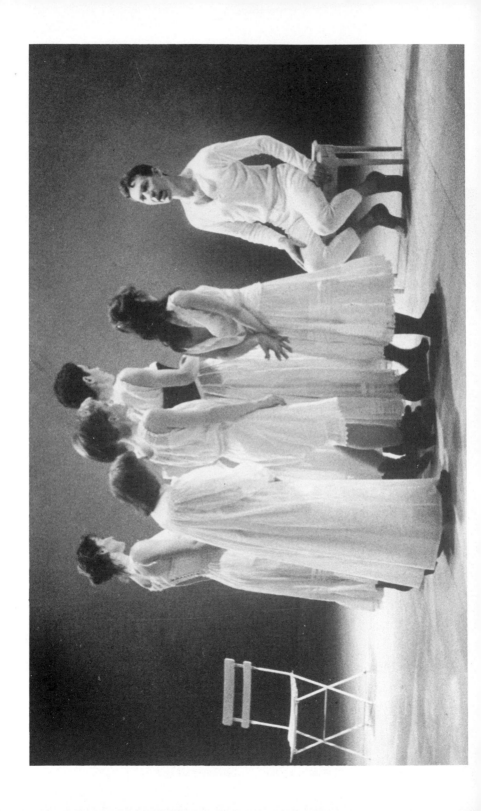

7. Martha Clarke. *Vienna: Lusthaus* (1986).

8. Martha Clarke. *The Hunger Artist* (1987).

9. Martha Clarke. *The Hunger Artist* (1987).

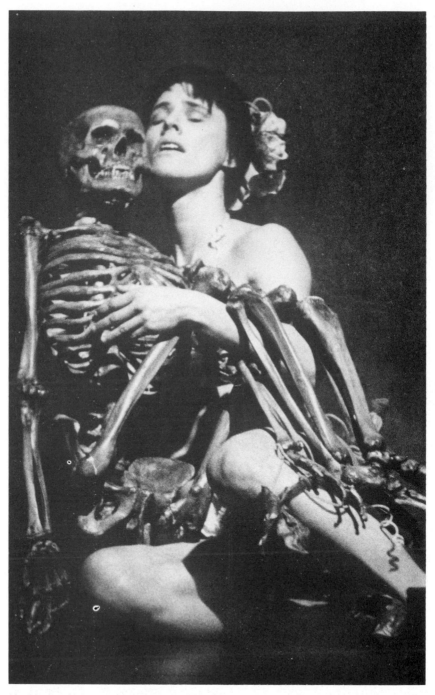

10. Martha Clarke. *Miracolo d'Amore* (1988).

11. Martha Clarke. *Miracolo d'Amore* (1988).

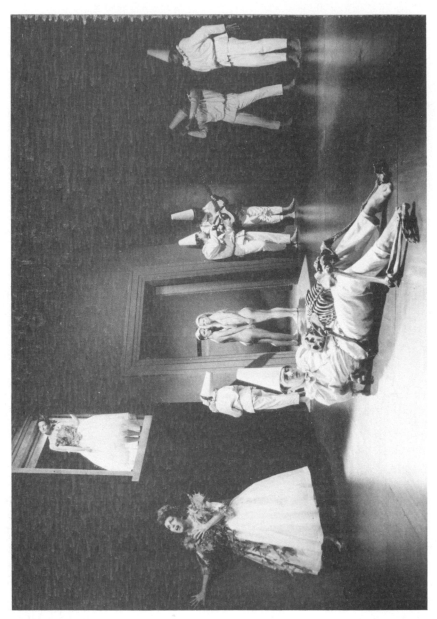

12. Martha Clarke. *Miracolo d'Amore* (1988).

PART III

Other Forms
of Theatre

8

Beyond the Broadway Musical: Crossovers, Confusions and Crisis

GLENN LONEY

Americans like to think of themselves as innovative, be it in industry or the arts. In the theatre, the American Minstrel Show was long designated as the nation's distinctive contribution to dramatic art, until the offensive, racist nature of such entertainments became a major embarrassment. The laurels for innovation then passed to the American musical, specifically as produced on Broadway, the most demanding critical and popular commercial arena. Analysis of the evolution of the Broadway musical will show, however, that it has borrowed heavily from popular entertainments of the past, such as burlesque, extravaganza, comic opera, operetta, music hall, vaudeville, and even the now despised Minstrel Show. One blood-line of the American musical flows from the world of Parisian and Viennese operetta, with *My Fair Lady* (1966) and *A Little Night Music* (1973) as attractive descendants. Another stems from the world of variety and vaudeville, often verging on revue and incorporating a range of performing specialities, with few serious musical demands being made on its popular stars. Even with the supposedly innovative Rodgers and Hammerstein musical *Oklahoma!* (1943), hailed as a break with musical formulas of the past, however, many of the elements were merely reshuffled or refocused. In fact, *Oklahoma!* established yet another musical theatre formula, avidly copied, from which its creators were themselves ultimately unable to escape, despite some brave experiments.

In recent years, successive imitations have proved largely pallid echoes of another era. Nostalgia of course always has its claims, but even successful revivals of the 'classics' of the 1940s and 1950s generally have not earned long runs on Broadway. And, despite determined efforts by some composers and librettists to move with the times, adapting newly popular musical forms and social concerns to the Broadway stage, not least inspired by the practical desire to win new young audiences and previously ignored ethnic spectators, no important body of innovative musicals has developed in the commercial arena, save the challenging musicals of Stephen Sondheim. The reasons for this erosion are complex, and one of the most compelling is economic, not artistic. The cost of mounting a new Broadway musical is now in the millions, and it is increasingly possible that the investment will be a total loss in only a night or two, if the major New York critics are not emphatic in their admiration. This not only has discouraged innovation but even imitation of past popular musical formulas.

It's also possible to posit a 'generation gap' between a much older audience – a dying breed – which once thrilled to the scores of Jerome Kern, George Gershwin or Irving Berlin, and younger potential theatre-goers who frankly live in quite another world, whose musical developments do not easily lend themselves to narrating a plot or etching a character. An amusing irony was the ascendency in the American musical theatre of Briton Andrew Lloyd Webber, who repeatedly demonstrated an impressive ability to synthesise elements of the past – including even classical modes – with rock, pop, and other more contemporary forms, while native American composers and their varied collaborators strove largely in vain to preserve the popularity of the stage musical.

STEPHEN SONDHEIM

Were it not for the wide-ranging talent and the continuing creativity of Stephen Sondheim, there would be little hope for the future of the American musical, although there are newer, younger voices emerging in New York in non-Broadway venues, as well as in regional theatres and opera groups around the United States. Sondheim has repeatedly demonstrated his courage in challenging audiences in the commercial arena with daring devices, intricate intrigues and fascinating characters, revealed in ingenious lyrics and richly evocative, inventive and complex scores. He is the proven surviving professional of the American musical theatre, although some critics and admirers are less enthusiastic about *Into the Woods* (1987), say, than earlier works such as *Company* (1970) and *Sweeney Todd* (1979).

Sondheim has been justly praised for breaking the patterns, avoiding the formulas of successful Broadway musicals of the 1940s and 1950s. Yet his initial mentor was none other than Oscar Hammerstein II, from whom he learned a great deal about the craft of creating a musical. This in fact remains the foundation of his work, which, while impressively innovative, is often rather a brilliant development of music and theatre traditions, rather than a renunciation. Certainly his astringent wit has prevented him from emulating Hammerstein's pervasive, if sincere, sentimentalism. His first professional achievements were as a lyricist, rather than a composer: *West Side Story* (1957), with a book by Arthur Laurents and a dynamic score by Leonard Bernstein, and *Gypsy* (1959), again with a Laurents book, but this time with a Jule Styne score.

Lehman Engel and other experts on the musical, while expressing admiration for Sondheim's talents, have on occasion deplored his seeming lack of interest in generating 'hit' songs in his scores. Working with Bernstein and Styne, however, Sondheim devised ingenious lyrics that brilliantly articulated the thoughts and feelings of the characters, as projected in the respective books and scores. Songs such as 'Tonight', 'Maria', 'America', 'Somewhere', and 'You'll Never Get Away From Me' have become classics. At the same time, they are effectively integrated into the two shows, especially in *Gypsy*, where Styne and Sondheim's songs reinforce the narrative about lives in a species of musical theatre, notably Gypsy Rose Lee's in burlesque, as she fought to be free of the dominance of her protective mother, Rose.

Some fans of musical theatre, nostalgic for shows with a long string of hits, such as *The Pyjama Game* (1954) or *Brigadoon* (1947), complain that Sondheim and his colleagues simply don't write – or try to write – popular songs anymore. 'Send in the Clowns' is frequently cited as one of the few Sondheim songs that has won wide popularity and recognition, divorced from the score of the show. And yet it was written specifically to take advantage of the severe vocal limitations of one of *Night Music*'s stars, rather than to seek a place in the 'top ten'. In fact, there are several reasons why Broadway musicals do not seem to generate as many popular songs as they once did. A major one, especially in Sondheim's case, is the change in scoring. In the heyday of Kern, Berlin and Porter, audiences became very familiar with the best songs in a show during the few hours they were watching it. A ballad would be heard initially in the overture, followed by a first-act performance with the lyrics, with a possible reprise and certainly an inclusion in the finale. As the audience returned from intermission, that and other infectious themes were played by the orchestra, and the ballad was apt to re-emerge in Act II, followed by another repetition in the show's finale. Small wonder audiences, as the phrase has it, 'walked out of the theatre, whistling the hit tunes'. Even before a new musical opened, 'singles' from the score might already be promoted on radio broadcasts and recordings. If a show did become a hit, a cast album – after *Oklahoma!'* – was a must, and sheet-music of the score's hits sold widely, as many people still played the piano and sang at home among family and friends.

It is argued by some cynics that most composers still struggling for recognition in the American musical theatre don't know how to write real tunes or melodies people would want to remember anymore. That's open to debate, but the lack of opportunity for repetition of a song in a score, as well as the changing tastes in musical modes, suggest that some show songs could become widely popular if they were more aggressively programmed and presented on radio and television. This also has less to do with art than with economics, as does the survival of the Broadway theatre arena. It would appear, in many Sondheim musicals at least, that not only the composer-lyricist, but also the others on the creative team – notably the director Harold Prince – have been far more intent on an artistic achievement than on commercial success. As Sondheim's career has developed, a number of admiring critics have suggested that successive musicals were well ahead of their time, certainly ahead of the popular audience.

In addition to Sondheim's varied talents, the musicals on which he has collaborated have generally been distinguished by the quality of their books or plots. Most post-war Broadway musicals, despite their celebrity, have books of staggering simplicity and characters of appalling shallowness. Often in such shows, the songs are the only moments of genuine illumination of a character's thoughts, feelings, desires. In Sondheim's shows, however, there is usually a subject of substance, characters with dimension, and a narrative conflict that really engages the attention.

It's more than mere custom that both operas and musicals are identified most frequently – and catalogued that way – with their composers, rather than with their librettists. This acknowledges the primacy of the music in such works of music theatre. In the past, composers have often been the driving force or the prime movers in developing new operas and musicals, changing librettists to suit their needs or whims. On Broadway, books of shows have customarily been the least valued of the production elements, subject to all kinds of last-minute revisions, not least to accommodate repositioning of a potential hit song, or to insert a new musical number. For many producers, song-hits, dynamic dance-numbers and stunning spectacle are far more important than the narrative framework that binds them together.

From the first, Sondheim has been aware of this and the often lost potential of a book worthy of its score. His music and lyrics for *A Funny Thing Happened on the Way to the Forum* (1962) were wonderful energisers of a saucy but ramshackle plot, plucked from Plautus. In *Sondheim & Co* (1974) he told Craig Zadan, 'One of the biggest problems I've found over the years is that good bookwriting is the most undeveloped part of the musical theatre and the part there is most to be learned about'. After his experience with *West Side Story* and *Gypsy*, his confidence in the talents of book author and stage-director Arthur Laurents led to his next collaboration, *Anyone Can Whistle* (1976), but this time, he provided both lyrics and score. This charming, if short-lived, fantasy starred Angela Lansbury, who was later to become a definitive Rose in a West End *Gypsy* and an indomitable Mrs Lovett in the Broadway *Sweeney Todd* (1979). Not only did Sondheim strive to serve and strengthen the books of shows on which he worked, but he was also adept at adapting projected musical numbers to the special talents – or shortcomings – of performers themselves.

With the death of Oscar Hammerstein II, Richard Rodgers was searching for a new lyricist. Sondheim and Laurents joined him for *Do I Hear a Waltz* (1965), a musical version of *Time of the Cuckoo* (1952). But Sondheim's gifts as a creator of songs in service of a musical with meaning had still not found an effective outlet. Given the chaotic nature of the commercial musical theatre, he could well have continued to function as yet another composer's talented young lyricist, as long as he could not find a producer for a project of his own.

Sondheim's good fortune – and that of audiences as well – was the vision of Hal Prince, who had worked with him as a producer on *West Side Story* and *Funny Thing*. Sondheim rightly gets full credit for the impressive scores and lyrics which were to follow, in collaboration with Prince, but Prince, now also a director, deserves equal honour for 'conceptualising' the musicals they created. Prince had begun his Broadway career as a producer, with George Abbott as his mentor. Later, he was to learn much from choreographer-director Jerome Robbins, which encouraged him to try directing musicals. *She Loves Me* (1963) was Prince's first staging, with *Cabaret* (1966) his first resounding success.

Although Prince has since renounced the role of producer in favour of directing exclusively, at that time his dual roles put him in a unique position to bring together the best possible production elements for a new musical. With *Company*, in 1970, Prince and Sondheim began their now historic – and possibly classic – series of 'concept musicals'. Definitions of that term vary. Martin Gottfried, in *Broadway Musicals* (1979), insists that such works are primarily are primarily based on a scheme of staging, rather than a narrative. While this may be true of some experimental non-Sondheim Broadway musicals such as *Runaways* (1980) and *Working* (1978) – which Gottfried sees as Prince–Sondheim-inspired – they are both effectively collages of characters and experiences. In contrast, *Company* (based on some short plays by George Furth about modern marital problems), as developed by the collaborators, proved to have one of the oldest of narrative structures, episodes held together by the picaresque figure of Bobby, the bachelor besieged by his married friends. *Company* won six Tony Awards, including Boris Aronson's for his ultra-modern skeletal stage-design. It was in fact very chic, very sophisticated, very satirical; not at all the comfortable, sentimental, rambunctious or colourful musical Broadway audiences had come to expect. The incisive, yet subtle, satires of Sondheim's lyrics were enhanced by his musical inventions, making such songs as 'Company', 'You Could Drive a Person Crazy', 'Barcelona', and 'Getting Married Today' memorable even outside the framework of the show. There were 690 performances, an encouraging run for so innovative a work.

This was followed the next year by *Follies* (1971), which had only 522 performances, far fewer than its admirers thought it deserved. Its detractors were surprised it didn't close the opening week. Some didn't understand what *Follies* was all about; others did, but insisted it was not a compelling idea, nor did they respond to the central characters. It became a truism that Sondheim and Prince were on the cutting-edge of innovation, possibly a decade ahead of public taste. In the commercial musical theatre, however, this is indeed faint praise and not encouraging to Broadway investors. Fortunately, there were enough who did want to support these new musical adventures.

For *Follies*, Aronson created a set of platforms and steps, surrounded by the rubble of a recently demolished theatre, to which some of its former performers had returned – joining the theatre's ghosts and memories – for a final reunion (and a stock-taking of their lives by two married couples for whom the show's title was emblematic). The starkness of the setting – echoing the starvation in the lives of the core characters – alienated some Broadway musical fans, who left before the fantastic and almost psyche-delic 'Loveland' scenery descended from the flies. Once again, Sondheim's potent songs were admired in the show's context, even if they didn't become instant national hits. The show album, however, has since won for them a host of fans, suggesting that issuing a show album *prior* to a Broadway opening – if that were feasible – and broadcasting it widely before the premiere might help ensure its survival, even with lukeward reviews. Television ads now do that in part, but costs are prohibitive.

In 1973, Ingmar Bergman's film, *Smiles of a Summer Night*, became the basis for a new concept musical, *A Little Night Music*, with its titular nod to Mozart. About a love lost and recovered, set in a Swedish manor-house at the turn of the century, the book was by Hugh Wheeler, who also worked with the team on *Sweeney Todd*. Among the musical novelties were setting all the songs in three-quarter time and providing and narrating chorus of five singers. Sondheim's first big commercial song success, 'Send in the Clowns', was specially written to capitalise on Glynis Johns' vocal limitations. It had 601 Broadway performances, as well as a London run. It also became a film, directed by Prince.

Sondheim was quick to share the plaudits with his orchestra-tor, Jonathan Tunick, who he has said enhanced his songs with the way in which the instruments of the orchestra are used. Sondheim's fondness for experiment, for dissonant harmonies, for unusual phrases, make his music extremely difficult to orches-trate. Tunick told Craig Zadan that every song in *Company*, for example, had to have a new style of orchestration created for it (Zadan, 1974). Gimmicks used to orchestrate conventional Broadway musical scores, with the set-pieces so admired by Lehman Engel and others, simply do not work with Sondheim's complex music and lyrics.

Pacific Overtures (1976), with a book by John Weidman, chronicled the opening of feudal Japan by Commodore Perry and its aftermath, as shown in individual lives and in Japanese culture. Prince adopted the devices of the Kabuki theatre for this sharply satiric vision, seen through Japanese – not Western – eyes. Opening January 1976, it was not a commercial success, lasting only some six months. Nor did many critics appreciate the brilliance and pathos of this achievement in musical theatre – as much Prince's as Sondheim's. In a subsequent off off Broadway revival – *not* staged by Prince – there was an increased critical understanding, but even with an off Broadway transfer, this too did not last long. Only with the production of this impressive musical by the English National Opera in London – and a subsequent recording of the entire libretto, not merely the songs, as in a Broadway cast album – did *Pacific Overtures* begin to gain the recognition it deserves. David Patrick Stearns notes that Sondheim's music suits operatic voices – although Sondheim had told him he's not fond of 'pushed' voices – and is also a welcome challenge to audiences jaded with the standard operatic fare (Stearns, 1988). Unlike Bernstein, who seems to have had both pop and classical yearnings – with attendant incipient musical schizophrenia – Sondheim's catholic taste and love of experimentation have not trapped him in any style or mode.

Sweeney Todd, though produced with typical Prince panache at the Drury Lane Theatre following a relatively warm New York reception, was an almost immediate London failure, possibly because it was based on a popular English melodrama. Some who still remembered Todd Slaughter in the role even resented the Americans' tinkering with this demi-classic. On Broadway, however, it had a run of 558 performances and an extended tour thereafter. With Bernstein's *Candide* (1956), it entered the repertory of the New York City Opera; both works were staged by Hal Prince, who described these migrations from the musical stage to the opera as 'crossovers'. Stearns' contention that Sondheim's music is gratifying to opera singers is borne out, but then some of the leading interpreters of the roles in these shows are also heard on Broadway – more crossovers. There

have been problems with the expanded production scale needed
for a much larger stage than is the Broadway rule; with 'miking'
which is an opera taboo; with lack of choral clarity – essential in
both *Candide* and *Todd* – the possible result of singing so often
in foreign tongues to largely uncomprehending audiences, and
with loss of pace and tone when performed in repertory rather
than in an extended run. Despite the squeamishness of some
Broadway audiences about Sweeney Todd's murderous revenge
and Mrs Lovett's meat-pies stuffed with ground-up victims, the
opera public seems to have taken such monstrosities in its stride,
especially as Sondheim has presented them. Invoking the *Dies irae*
at the opening is only another instance of Sondheim's musical
intelligence and ingenuity; here, it is the wrath of Todd, not the
wrath of God.

Unfortunately, *Merrily We Roll Along* was not well received
in 1981, neither by critics nor audiences. It rapidly closed with
a loss reported at some $5 million. A subsequent production
in London at the Guildhall School convinced British critics and
Sondheim fans that this exercise in looking backward by some
sourly successful professionals – echoes of *Follies* – had much
to commend it, even if the book was problematic. This failure brought the Sondheim–Prince collaboration to a close, with
Sondheim discovering a different kind of co-creator in the imaginative James Lapine, who provided him with both the book and
the staging for *Sunday in the Park with George* (1984) and *Into
the Woods* (1987). Visually, *Sunday in the Park* was fascinating as
the *pointillist* painter Georges Seurat composed his masterpiece,
Sunday Afternoon on the Island of La Grande Jatte, with a giant
version of the painting demonstrating the artist's choices and
changes. Just as Seurat built up his canvas into a landscape
with figures, from myriad tiny specks of oil colours, so also does
Sondheim's intriguing score echo the dot-motif. *Into the Woods*,
beginning in a fanciful fairytale mode, soon discovers the darker
shadows in the mythic forests of childhood imaginings, project-
ing daunting metaphors for human disappointments and natural
disasters, culminating in the almost too convenient reassurance
of 'No One Is Alone'. It's interesting to speculate how much
more challenging – and forbidding – such a work could have
been, had Sondheim collaborated with Bruno Bettelheim, whose
psychological interpretations of familiar fairytales make Lapine's
imaginings seem trivial.

OPERA CROSSOVERS

Those who see opera as an elitist treat and the musical stage as a truly popular venue – not so popular in fact with current high ticket-prices – have forgotten, if they ever knew, that opera was once a very popular entertainment. It is still that in Italy, of course, but there was a time in London when Handelian Italian operas were the entertainments of choice, until mocked by John Gay's ribald spoof, with English folk-tunes, *The Beggar's Opera* (1728). Today, only the tremendous costs of production, with the obligatory increase in the cost of seats, prevents opera from becoming a much more popular form of music theatre, even with young audiences, who have responded enthusiastically to opera experiments when they have been heavily subsidised, both in production and at the box-office. Impressarios of the past, those with touring companies or commercially based opera-houses, had to fill their seats, so there is a long tradition of borrowing from the legitimate stage – adding music to such popular plays as *Camille* – as well as from operetta stages and other musical theatres. If Offenbach, Johann Strauss and Gilbert & Sullivan provide much lighter fare than Wagner, Verdi, Puccini and Richard Strauss, at least they are at ease beside Rossini.

In a time of crossovers, the fundamental problem, both in Britain and America, has been that opera has long been regarded as the domain of great voices, to the detriment of dramatic and theatrical values. The truth is that opera's greatest composers were pre-eminently men of theatre, the music theatre. Verdi and Puccini found their most powerful subjects on the dramatic stages of their day. Verdi ranged from Shakespeare to Schiller to Dumas. In *Madame Butterfly* (1904) and *The Girl of the Golden West* (1910), Puccini elevated the dramatic contrivances of Broadway impressario David Belasco to the level of passionate music theatre. Richard Wagner, after his initial imitations of Italian opera, conceived a consummate form, music drama as *Gesamtkunstwerk*, in which all the arts would be appropriately involved.

Today, Wagner's drama is being realised, but in ways he could not have imagined – even in his own Bayreuth *Festspielhaus*. As great voices are being replaced by many not-so-great voices, theatrical values are finally coming to the fore and with impressive results. Although some major European talents, such as Franco Zeffirelli and Jean-Pierre Ponnelle, have been pioneers of this new vision in American opera-houses, native stage-directors, choreographers and designers have been conducting a quiet revolution since the 1960s. Frank Corsaro's emphasis on theatre values was crucial to the critical and popular success of the New York City Opera, which now also has Hal prince stagings in its repertoire. In fact, this trend has reached the point where some drama critics grudgingly admit that to see really good musical theatre now, one has to go to the opera.

One of the most controversial of this new breed of opera-director is Peter Sellars, noted for his modernisations of Mozart: *Cosi* in a diner, *Don Giovanni* in Spanish Harlem and *Figaro* in jet-set Manhattan. Even Wagnerian masterpieces such as *Tannhäuser* have received the Sellars treatment, translated to a motel in the fundamentalist red-neck American southland. In such transformations, opera of necessity becomes music theatre. Nor does Sellars confine himself to finding contemporary 'relevance' in operatic 'warhorses'. His epic staging of John Adams's minimalist opera, *Nixon in China* (1987), with libretto by Alice Goodman, was visually memorable – even if the score was eminently forgettable – especially in the way that techniques of the Peking Opera were employed and images suggestive of the theatre of Robert Wilson were deployed. Fortunately, the episodic libretto has some genuinely satiric moments while treating the Nixons with an odd compassion. The very minimality of Adams's score prevents any powerful characterisation or dramatic comment, raising the uneasy question of whether the composer, by yielding to the musical fashions of the moment, is avoiding the potential challenges of creating a truly dramatic score or is not competent of providing anything more complex, demanding, moving or dramatic.

In an interview for *The New York Times* Adams declared that minimalism's 'classic period is now past' (Crutchfield, 1987), which was good news to those who are easily bored in the theatre. Distinguished often for its hypnotic repetitiveness – made more effective for some youthful listeners with generous inhalations of controlled substances – minimalism as practiced by Philip Glass and Steve Reich has enjoyed a tremendous vogue. Adams admitted that it was, however, 'obviously a movement of very limited potential' (Crutchfield, 1987). What was curious was that both mature sophisticated audiences and the raffish, untutored young, including punk rockers, flocked to productions of Glass operas and Reich concerts. In discussing his own maturation, John Adams mused – in a manner of reinventing the wheel – that he might be encompassing the evolution of western music until he might some day find himself transformed into another Menotti, who it may be remembered in his own prime was hailed as the genius who brought opera to Broadway, with *The Medium* (1947) and *The Saint of Bleecker Street* (1954). Like Wagner, Menotti was his own librettist, but with rather less majestic results. But, with scores already minimal, one does not long for more composer-created librettos, especially from artists who either have no sense of dramatic structure or who are indifferent to any kind of effective, intelligent sung text.

Surely modern, but hardly minimal, are the works of Dominick Argento, who has profited by long association with the Minnesota Opera and its capable stage-director, H Wesley Balk, and outstanding American exponent of opera-as-theatre. Not only has Balk staged old and new operas with a wonderful theatricality, but he has devoted much thought and experiment to the training of singer-actors, as well as creating librettos himself. Argento, who had also composed incidental music for the theatre, is eclectic and inventive. *Casanova* (1985), now in the New York City Opera repertoire, makes dramatic and comedic use of the traditions of eighteenth-century Italian opera, but *Postcards from Morocco* (1971), *The Voyage of Edgar Allan Poe* (1975) and *Miss Havisham's Fire* (1979) explore different modalities. Argento seems one of America's few current avant-garde composers whose works are likely to remain in circulation because of their musical interest and theatricality, although none so far has the mark of a repertory standard on it.

ROBERT WILSON'S THEATRE OF IMAGES

Stefan Brecht, son of Bertolt and a long-time admirer and co-worker of Wilson's, titled his own analysis of Robert Wilson *The Theatre of Visions* (1979). That is really a more potent description of the works than mere 'images', for however startling or arresting individual stage-images may be in a Wilson production, they are never entirely static. Even in slow-motion, they are often changing into something different. *Einstein on the Beach* (1976), with a score by Philip Glass, brought Wilson his first big burst of media attention, especially in New York, where a 'one-night-stand-only' performance at the Metropolitan Opera was 'standing-room-only' as well.

Actually, his initial efforts in New York began with *The King of Spain* (1969), followed that same year by *The Life and Times of Sigmund Freud* at the Brooklyn Academy of Music (BAM). Next came *Deafman Glance*, in 1971, shown both in Brooklyn and in Europe. In 1972, Wilson created *KA MOUNTAIN AND GUARDenia TERRACE* – he is fond of such abrupt shifts of type-case – a seven-day epic at the Shiraz Festival in Persepolis, well before the return from exile of the Ayatollah Khomeini, who surely would have put a stop to such western excesses. By 1973, Wilson was ready with his twelve-hour epic, *The Life and Times of Joseph Stalin*, which began at BAM at 7pm and concluded, with a greatly diminished audience, at 7am the following day. The scale of these productions – one might even say the audacity of them – the impressiveness of their settings, the size of their casts, the detail involved in their articulation and animation, the precision required in their lighting, and the costs to mount them – generated largely from subsidies, rather than from the box-office – despite the dedicated assistance of an army of volunteers, made them impossible to play in an extended run, to tour widely or to preserve in a regular repertory.

Although Wilson's work does indeed attract young audiences, not often to be seen at either Broadway musicals or opera performances, this is not a broad popular following nor could it be, given the circumstances of production. Wilson's audiences, whether mature sophisticates or younger seekers of novelty, are hardly mainstream, so the work almost by definition becomes elitist. And his penchant for recycling various arresting images in later works, since they generally have no objective points of reference in the experiences of most viewers – though they may well trigger some deep, troubling memory – sometimes seem self-indulgent exercises in aesthetic onanism. And repetition in successive works also runs the risk of exhausting their provocation or stimulus potential with Wilson fans.

My first impression, on seeing *King of Spain* and *Sigmund Freud*, was of revisiting the landscape of my nightmares. How had Wilson known of those surreal locales and bizarre activities? Dadaism and surrealism were mingled with the fantastic and futuristic. The almost dream-like quality of the movement in some scenes had initially been inspired by his work with handicapped children; it proved hypnotic, especially when accompanied by musical fragments. Because these productions required large groups of performers as conceived, most of them untrained with little time available for on-stage rehearsals, Wilson carefully plotted all the movement in advance. This led some of his colleagues to characterise the work as 'choreographies', and in a sense they were. But Wilson seemed to prefer to identify them as operas, though there was seldom any extended sung text or vocals. The fact that Wilson had been a painted in his native Texas served him well, as his visions expanded to three dimensions, with detailed drawings – virtual storyboards – leaving nothing to chance in the preparation of a major event.

Adolph Appia and Gordon Craig are often invoked as spiritual and theoretical progenitors of a heroic modernist vision of staging, rejecting a routine realism for a theatre of suggestion and symbols, of light and shade and darkness. Robert Wilson's work seems a fulfilment of some of their dreams. John Rockwell, a *New York Times* music critic, noted his reactions to *Joseph Stalin*:

> The *religious* intensity of those stage-pictures will remain in my mind forever, as in the scene in which shadowy apes emerged through a forest of trees carrying apples, then watched in awe as the apples mysteriously ascended into the flies . . . just as an elegant human couple in 18th century formal dress emerged from the wings, the woman carrying a white parasol that was on fire.
>
> (Nelson, 1984)

Robert Stearns also observes:

> As in dreams, shapes and actions present themselves, disappear and return in other forms. We as the dreamers may be delighted, surprised, or terrified, but the dream is independent and cannot be controlled. Awake we analyze, interpret, and try to find meaning. But Wilson art is as elusive as the stuff of dreams . . .
>
> (Nelson, 1984)

A Letter for Queen Victoria was presented on Broadway at the American National Theatre and Academy Theatre (ANTA) in 1974, as Wilson sought to introduce his work to the mainstream theatre audience, as well as to major critics who hadn't been to BAM. The images and their possible intent were too baffling for most reviewers and too alien from conventional Broadway musical theatre fare. Back at BAM and away from his customary proscenium-frame, Wilson offered *$ Value of Man* in 1975, but images in an open arena were not so forceful. His important and germinal collaboration with minimalist composer Philip Glass followed, with the summer 1976 production of *Einstein on the Beach* in Avignon and on European tour. Singers in the orchestra pit intoned numbers and *solfegio* to hypnotic, intricate patterns of a few musical notes. Its later critical success at the Met required a second performance, but it was never designed for the repertory of the Met or any other opera, nor did its form or substance commend it to the routine of opera production. In fact, it produced a severe deficit, from which Wilson and his Byrd Hoffmann Foundation recovered with difficulty.

Having already enjoyed the largess of European patronage, Wilson was encouraged to work largely in western Europe until 1984, creating *Death Destruction and Detroit* in West Berlin at Peter Stein's *Schaubuhne* in 1979, followed by *Edison* – another evocation of Wilson's obsession with light – in Lyon, Paris and Milan, also in 1979. In 1977, however, he devised an intimate chamber work with the collaboration of minimalist choreographer-dancer Lucinda Childs: *I Was Sitting on My Patio This Guy Appeared I Thought I Was Hallucinating*. Childs' contributions were minimal in the extreme, when not outright boring from repetition of banal fragments of movement. In 1982, another small work, *The Golden Windows*, was created for Munich's *Kammerspiele* and seen several years later at BAM. *Great Day in the Morning*, shown that year in Paris, featured soprano Jessye Norman in a staged concert of spirituals; this never made the trip to BAM.

Meanwhile, Wilson was preparing his epic-of-epics, *the CIVIL warS: a tree is best measured when it is down*, designed for a 1984 gala in Los Angeles as part of the Arts Olympics. Six nations would help Wilson produce six evening-length sections – all related in some way to images of war and conflict – which would then be brought together in Los Angeles. The sections would be linked by 'Knee Plays', for which David Byrne of Talking Heads composed some fascinating music for Wilson's surprising kinetic choreography. Parts of *the CIVIL warS* have been produced, but the totality has not yet been achieved. Continuing the collaboration with rock composer-performer Byrne in 1988, Wilson conceived *The Forest* – roughly based on the ancient Sumerian Gilgamesh epic – as a four-hours-plus visual commentary on nineteenth-century industrialism, contrasted with the world of nature, including of course the trees of the title. Byrne's eclectic score, sometimes suggestive of the easy ebb and flow of 'new age' music, often seemed merely a pleasant background, but it occasionally did provide forceful aural emphasis for images and actions. Wilson noted that he liked to stage *against* the music now and then, but in *The Forest* there was not really all that much connection anyway. First shown in West Berlin at the *Freie Volksbühne*, it was later seen at BAM, which was by this time well known for its 'Next Wave Festival' each fall, spotlighting the most avant-garde of American and foreign works of dance and music theatre.

OTHER VOICES, OTHER VENUES

Having learned more than a thing or two from his collaboration with Wilson, Philip Glass struck out on his own with *Satyagraha*, premiered in Rotterdam in 1980. This was a celebration of the life of Gandhi and his campaign of civil disobedience in India. With Sanskrit *Bhagavad-Gita* texts adapted by Constance De Jong, major moments were visualised with designer Robert Israel's large props, such as a huge printing-press and a schoolhouse. Glass's minimalist repetitions, combined with the arcane language, provided an oddly appropriate effect of Hindu chanting and invocation. Owing to its elemental production demands – really more of a choral concert with props – it was successively shown at New York State's Artpark, at BAM, at the Chicago Lyric Opera and then the Seattle Opera. It was also produced abroad, and the San Fransisco Opera revived it at the close of the decade.

Negative critics have argued that such works cannot be easily replicated, at least not by other than the original creative teams. That's not the case with Glass's post-Wilson work, where specific images are not essential. But one can hardly imagine a Richard Foreman staging, a Meredith Monk invention or a Martha Clarke pastiche being effectively revived or re-created by any but those eccentric artists. If a structured dramatic text were the core – or the inspiration – of such productions, replication might be easier or new images could be devised for new stagings of the basic substance. Where images and actions or movements are central, however, it is more problematic: rather like recent dedicated but somewhat academic efforts to recreate the dances of Isadora Duncan and Denishawn. Wilson's visions are so uniquely personal that, even with the storyboards in hand, they would seem to defy an effective re-creation.

Fortunately, videotape provides the possibility of a permanent record, if the artists choose to use it. Glass's *Einstein on the Beach* score has been recorded, as has *Satyagraha*, indications that the music won't soon be forgotten. But survival in sound-recordings omits the images and movement, and filmed and taped audio-visual records are certainly not the same thing as live performance. If they are taped with a video camera or two in restricted positions, they are little more than archival. The problem about such visions of music theatre – especially those with texts in dead languages and with unusual instrumentation – is that they present immense practical difficulties for inclusion in a normal opera repertory. The Bavarian composer, Carl Orff, to whom Glass has paid musical homage, often spoke of his own majestic *Prometheus* as a 'festival opera', since its libretto was in classic Greek and had to be learned phonetically, something better suited to festival-time with all performances in only a few weeks.

Joining Glass's treatments of Einstein and Gandhi in 1984 was the monotheistic Egyptian pharaoh, Akhnaten, in the opera of the same name, commissioned by the Stuttgart Opera. Achim Freyer staged the premiere, having also mounted *Satyagraha* for Stuttgart. That same year *Akhnaten* was seen at the Houston Grand Opera and at the New York City Opera, but not in Freyer's manic staging. Some ancient pharaonic texts were integrated, even less accessible than *Satyagraha*'s Sanskrit. Glass also contributed music for Wilson's Rome and Cologne sections of *the CIVIL warS* in 1984, but before that, he'd devised a score for a chamber-opera, *The Photographer/Far from the Truth*, inspired by the action-photos of Eadweard Muybridge. This had both a Dutch subsidy and premiere, followed in 1983 by performances at BAM and five other American cities, hungry for avant-garde experiences. In addition to composing minimalist music for concerts and films, Glass also found time in 1985 to devise music with co-composer Robert Moran for *The Juniper Tree*, based on a (truly) Grimm fairytale.

The year 1988 was a very busy one, with Glass opera premieres of *The Fall of the House of Usher*, at Robert Brustein's Harvard-based

American Repertory Theatre; *The Making of the Representative for Planet 8*, based on a Doris Lessing novel for a Houston debut; and *1000 Airplanes on the Roof*, performed initially in Hangar No. 3 at Vienna's International Airport. *1000 Airplanes* is essentially a 90-minute sci-fi mono-melodrama, with an actor speaking – not singing – David Henry Hwang's fantastic monologue of a New York nebbish kidnapped by alien spacemen and returned to earth with diminished memory. *Time*'s Michael Walsh praised the score and Glass's direction, noting the composer's determination 'to invent a way for English to be used as a viable music-theatre language' (Walsh, 1988). For many who saw it at New York's Beacon Theatre, prior to a thirty-nine city American and Canadian tour, the real star of the show was Jerome Sirlin, who created the ingenious two-dimensional projections on three-dimensional surfaces, skills he had learned working with music theatre conceptualist George Coates in San Francisco. Glass's three works in one year make Verdi seem slightly less prolific, but at least Verdi's operas have largely found and held a place in the popular repertoire.

George Coates' *Actual Shō*, after its 1987 Stuttgart premiere, was the first performance of an American work in Poland – as distinguished from American plays in translation – since the repeal of martial law. Yugoslavia was also among the seven European nations it visited. Computer-generated graphics and photographic projections were blown up to achieve unusual effects on Levelor blinds, a huge top-like toggle-revolve and a three-dimensional set of stage-framings. The impact of real images – such as projected manholes, from which performers popped up from apertures in the revolve, or railroad tracks, or a giant frying-pan – was by turns comic and frightening. The amusing narrative thread of *Actual Shō* was a hungry parson's reverie, suspendedd between life and death, after choking on a chicken bone at a wedding feast. It sounds grim, but it was not. Coates' animated singers vocalised to the dynamic score of Mark Ream, which mingled rock, jazz, gospel, reggae and 'new age' music with nonsense syllables. Some of them sounded very much like an endless repetition of 'Deo', and considering the circumstances, that invocation was in order. Notable was the tenor of Rinde Eckert. Movement was devised by Hitomi Ikuma. Coates believes his 'Performance Works' are related to opera, which he perceives as sung in phrases that audiences cannot understand. So in his works verbal communication is often displaced by visual and musical impressions. Effectually, performers and audiences are enveloped in a collective dream – different to each who experiences it.

Beginning as a member of Berkeley's Blake Street Hawkeyes – spawned by Rick Zank's Iowa Theatre Lab – Coates showed early impulses for non-linear, wryly comic, and highly kinetic theatre, sometimes defined as 'Actualism'. In 1977, he offered *2019 Blake*, with mime artist Leonard Pitt, followed in 1979 by *Duykers the First* with tenor John Duykers. This toured the United States and abroad, encouraging Coates to expand with such talents as Eckert, composer Paul Dresher and projection-designer Ted Heimerdinger. In 1981, they created *The Way of How*, a trilogy including *Are Are* and *SeeHear*, briefly seen at BAM in 1983. Relating the metaphysical to the details of daily life was a thrust of the work. Even more impressive visually was *Rare Area*, commissioned for Belgium's Kaai Festival. Coates stresses the collaborative and interactive nature of these works, with input of performers, designers, composers, movement artists, technicians and production staff equally valued. The *San Fransisco Examiner* critic, Richard Stayton, notes the ensemble's growth toward a revolutionary style, merging all theatre arts into a new form. It's interesting, however, that Coates himself chose to describe *Rare Area* as 'A New Music Theatre Spectacle'. He and Robert Wilson are the two most interesting talents in the theatre of images, though Wilson's visions are more intensely personal, best evoked in three-dimensional stage-settings, whereas Coates encourages shared visions, invoked both from the realms of reality and imagination and projected – literally – with a dazzling technology that is really not very complex.

Richard Foreman first came to the fore with *Dr. Selavy's Magic Theatre* (1972), in which he unveiled some of his distinctive visual and movement mannerisms as a counterpoint to a selection of songs composer Stanley Silverman may have found in his trunk. They also collaborated on *Elephant Steps* (1971), but Foreman's Ontological-Hysteric Theatre did not thereafter develop into a form of music theatre. He has, however, consistently shown an affinity for music and movement that relates to musical modes. He has also staged operas, drawing on his unique perceptions.

Peter Schumann's Bread and Puppet Theatre, on the other hand, owes some of its justly won celebrity to its joyously raucous brass band. Angels on stilts playing trumpets and trombones in front of Judson Memorial Church in Greenwich Village, as a 'pre-show' to entice potential audiences into the main event, is surely a kind of street music theatre. The use of music in Schumann's actual performances is even more effective and theatrical. Blaring brasses are often the only appropriate accompaniment to a passionate passage of frankly political theatre.

If the Bread and Puppeteers can evoke New Orleans jazz bands on occasion, composer Bob Telson has proved himself able to work with a wide variety of black and Caribbean styles – gospel, jazz, calypso, reggae, mambo, samba – and nowhere more successfully than in the 1983 *Gospel at Colonus*, a collaboration with Mabou Mines founder Lee Breuer. Wildly acclaimed at Philadelphia's American Music Theatre Festival, at BAM and on tours, *Gospel* was finally brought to Broadway, but in a period of empty theatres. Even without much competition, its retelling of the Oedipus legend with a black gospel choir and various soloists and its sheer energy and joy didn't seem sufficient bait for audiences who had been flocking to *A Chorus Line* for fourteen years. But there was also the confusion caused by fracturing the Oedipus saga, with various singers and actors taking turns as Oedipus, Jocasta and Creon. Those who didn't already know Sophocles' version could hardly have intuited it from *Gospel*. But, as in much modern experimentation in music theatre, a coherent dramatic text is almost the least of the artistic concerns, as though it were some outmoded relic of an ever-changing theatre art.

Another major Telson–Breuer collaboration, *The Warrior Ant*, initially was projected as a twelve-part piece. Shown at Yale and BAM, early segments raised serious questions about the project's viability. Breuer's concept was recounting the life-saga of a giant soldier ant as a metaphor for modern life, with the heroic ant seen as a mythic saviour. As reported in advance,, Breuer's thoughts and Telson's observations about the work indicated they were in different realms, Telson being far more realistic about the popular appeal of his music than Breuer about his woolly philosophising, far more suited to non-linear works where logic is a distinct disadvantage. In the event, it was something of a Next Wave disaster at BAM, where even the most enthusiastic, hardened veterans of the avant-garde were fleeing for the exits. The eulogy came from Frank Rich of *The New York Times*:

If the Brooklyn Academy of Music's Next Wave Festival is a serious portent of cultural things to come, the term avant-garde can finally be retired from New York's vocabulary. . . . "The Warrior Ant" is nothing if not a throwback to the smorgasbord esthestics of that totemic artistic happening of the 1950s, the Ed Sullivan Show.

(Rich, 1988)

He was referring to Breuer's odd melange of Bunraku, belly-dancers and Caribbean musicians. Rich found Breuer's lackluster script 'alternately pretentious and facetious', with asides including excretory and baseball jokes. He pondered, '. . . one wonders if there has ever been so much droning in the service of one man's castration fantasies'.

The career of the multifaceted composer Elizabeth Swados could be a chapter in itself, as her interests dart everywhere and her energies encourage her to generate new projects constantly. A 1951 Bennington graduate, Swados had the good fortune to be 'adopted' by Ellen Stewart, who gave her an important showcase at La Mama Experimental Theatre Club (E.T.C.). As often happens in that part of Manhattan, Joseph Papp was quick to spot this new talent at La Mama and lure Swados to the New York Public Theatre, which subsequently gave her entrée to Broadway, where she has been represented by *Runaways* (1978) and *Doonesbury* (1983). Considering Stewart's longtime interest in Third World performance, it was opportune that Swados was also very much attracted to folk-music and native instruments. Her fascination with the sounds of a more primitive nature – especially birdsong – also found its way into her instrumental music and vocals. At the same time, the pounding sounds of urban life, the rhythms of the ghetto, obsessed her.

Swados' first critical notice was won for the exciting, primal score she developed for Andrei Serban's La Mama *Trilogy*, initially in the *Medea* (1972), with a textual melange of the Greek and Latin tragedies of Euripedes and Seneca, neither of them understood by the performers – nor by the audiences, for that matter. *Electra* (1974) and *The Trojan Women* (1974) completed the trilogy, which toured widely abroad to great acclaim. Peter Brook also admired her work and invited her to join his Paris International Center for Theatre Research. She became resident composer, collaborating on *The Conference of the Birds* (1973) and travelling with it and the troupe to Africa. In 1977, Ellen Stewart made Swados composer-in-residence at La Mama, beginning a very busy period. In 1978, *Nightclub Cantata* earned her one of several Obie Awards. *Runaways*, developed from experiences of street-children, transferred to Broadway from Papp's Public Theatre. It didn't stay long, but it did get five Tony Award nominations in a season with little competition. That same season her *Alice in Wonderland*, with Meryl Streep as Alice, should have opened at Papp's Public Theatre, but he decided it needed more work, so it was shown only in concert. He did premiere *Dispatches*, based on Michael Herr's Vietnam journal – with passages set by Swados as songs – a few months later.

Although Swados prefers non-western music, she did draw on mazurkas and polkas for the Serban-staged and Papp-produced *Cherry Orchard* (1976) in Lincoln Center's Vivian Beaumont Theatre. She also created a score for Papp's *Agamemnon* (1977) in the same venue. She works with a guitar, rather than a piano, when composing. After attempting to capture Garry Trudeau's comic caricatures in *Doonesbury*, she joined him again in the satirical off Broadway revue, *Rap Master Ronnie* (1984). Working with the gifted maskmaker and puppeteer, Julie Taymor, Swado composed a compelling *Haggadah* (1981), followed some years later by *Swing*, devised as a clash between 1940s popular music and modern MTV 'rock-videos'. Swados has been criticised for not being more analytical about her own work and spreading her talents too broadly. She did tell a reporter in 1980, however, 'I'm not such a good musician'.

Some observers are not sure there is a proper critical pigeon-hole for either Meredith Monk or Martha Clarke. Music critics are obsessed; dance critics are fascinated; theatre critics are often baffled – if delighted. Monk's earliest work in New York – *Duet with Cat's Scream and Locomotive* (1966), *16-Millimeter Earrings* (1966), *Untidal: Movement Period* (1969) and *Needle-Brain Lloyd and the System Kid* (1970) – was often arresting, bizarre, but it lacked the scope, the ambition, of the 1971 trilogy, *Vessel*, which Monk characterised as 'an opera epic'. Inspired by Shaw's *Saint Joan*, it began in a tiny loft, after which the audience was bused to The Performing Garage on Wooster Street for the second section, 'Handmade Mountain', then filing out in a light drizzle, well past midnight, to savour a symbolic execution of Joan in a parking-lot, on which lighted bridge-lamps were moving about. Then as now,

Monk surrounded herself – as does Robert Wilson – with dedicated collaborators and assistants, since a profit or even a real living was not to be made from such performances. Lighting-designer Beverly Emmons and artist Ping Chong – with whom she continues to devise challenging works – were among the earliest.

In *Vessel*, as Monk presided at her keyboard, shrieking, yelping and gurgling all kinds of odd sounds, her fingers seemed to be hitting the keys at random, much in the aleatory fashion of a clever child exploring pianistic possibilities. Some years later, a Monk press-release quoted John Rockwell of *The New York Times*:

> She has perfected her own technique to emit amazing varieties of sounds rarely heard from a western throat, full of wordless cries and moans, a lexicon of vocal coloration, glottal attacks, and microtonal waverings that lie at the base of all musical cultures.

Vessel's instrumentation included kazoo, jew's harp, dulcimer, accordian and electric organ, to help Monk and her troupe in their 'exploration of the relationship between the aural and the visual experience'.

Then came *Paris, Education of the Girlchild* (1973) and *Chacon* (1974). By the time she presented *Quarry* (1976) at La Mama, she had generated some forty works of various lengths and merits. She and her ensemble were now well known abroad as well. *Quarry*, suggesting the fantasies of a sick child about war and oppression, excited a lot of praise. *The New Yorker*'s Arlene Croce dissented, disliking the generality of the images, verging on *The Diary of Anne Frank*. Croce granted Monk her incorporation of 'a large element of personal mythology', but she decided it was not a dance piece, or any other kind of piece either (Croce, 1977). Later works include *Recent Ruins* (1979), inspired by archaeology; *Specimen Days* (1981), suggested by the American Civil War; *The Games* (1984) – with Ping Chong – opportunely activated by the Los Angeles Olympics, as well as *Acts from Under and Above* (1986) and *Turtle Dreams* (1986).

There are cynics who insist that the most creative thing about many of these avant-garde works of music theatre is the selection of titles. The truth is that music theatre has become a convenient generic for a variety of performance forms and works, as Broadway musicals diminish in number, quality and inventiveness, and opera-houses adopt Broadway's more recent hits to give artificial respiration to an almost moribund and predominantly nineteenth-century repertory, which is itself periodically given spurious electric shock-therapy with trendy, 'relevant' modernised productions, as in the unfortunate Shakespeare, with no agent to protect him.

Escalating production costs, matched by steeply rising ticket-prices, conspire to restrict both conventional and experimental musical productions on Broadway in the last decades of the twentieth century. But economics wasn't the only factory that made the musical less and less a truly popular entertainment. There was also a real cultural and age gap between the admirers of lively but formulaic musicals of the post-war era and potential younger show audiences, who preferred newer musical modes which did not lend themselves to narration, characterisation or projection of emotional subtleties. Momentarily, some musicals such as *Hair* (1967) managed to synthesise new attitudes, fads and music, but they as yet have not spawned a new form or genre, nor did they themselves have staying-power in repertory or revival.

And, while it's encouraging that some effective musicals are being kept alive at American opera-houses, where production costs are enormous, though not as ruinous as Broadway's, these are subsidised performances, as are virtually all the avant-garde experiments in music theatre. Without such support, most of this work wouldn't be possible. For various reasons, including the limited appeal of some creations, broad commercial popularity doesn't seem likely, even though young audiences – themselves limited – have been attracted.

It can be argued that such artists as Monk and Wilson have indeed retained basic scenarios – rather like the *commedia dell-arte* ensembles – for orchestrating their moving images, but at least in *commedia*, the audience had rather clear perceptions of what was going on and why. The determined critics and the sedulous semiotician can, of course, dig deep – in their own psyches and core courses in western civilisation – to find metaphoric meanings in the images offered, but they may be working too hard, harder even than the original creators, who have largely drawn on their own hermetic memories and imaginings. It may be wasted effort to deconstruct what has already been deconstructed. Considering the potency of image – especially colourful, moving images on television, where the frequent intrusion of a spate of commercials has programmed many Americans of all ages to a subconscious attention-span of some seven minutes – it is small wonder that many actual and potential theatre-goers no longer care much about written, spoken or sung texts, preferring the uncritical pleasure of a wash of music and imagery which does not require attention or analysis.

BIBLIOGRAPHY

Bordman, G. (1978) *American Musical Theatre: A Chronicle* (New York: Oxford University Press).
———. (1982) *American Musical Comedy* (New York: Oxford University Press).
Brecht, S. (1979) *The Theater of Visions: Robert Wilson* (Frankfurt: Suhrkamp).
Croce, A. (1977) *The New Yorker* 24 Jan., pp. 79–80.
Crutchfield, W. (1987) 'Recording "Nixon in China"', *New York Times* 15 Dec.
Engel, L. (1979) *The Making of a Musical* (New York: Macmillan).
Feingold, M. (1988) 'The New (And All-Inclusive) American Musical Theatre', 1988 Festival Program (Spoleto/Charleston).
Goldberg, R. (1988) *Performance Art* (London: Thames and Hudson).
Gottfried, M. (1979) *Broadway Musicals* (New York: Harry N. Abrams).
Hoyle, M. (1988) 'The Opera Swap' *Plays and Players*, Sep.
Leverett, J. (1988) 'Knee-deep in Reality: Lee Breuer and His Trouble', *Next Wave Journal*, fall (New York: Brooklyn Academy of Music).
Loney, G. (1983) 'Quick, What Rhymes with Engel?', *Dramatics*, Sep.
———. (1984) *Musical Theatre in America* (Westport, Conn.: Greenwood Press).
Marranca, B. (1977) *The Theatre of Images* (New York: Drama Books).
Mates, J. (1985) *America's Musical Stage* (Westport, Conn.: Greenwood Press).
Mordden, E. (1976) *Better Foot Forward: History of the American Musical Theatre* (New York: Grossman).
Nelson, C. (ed.) (1984) *Robert Wilson: The Theatre of Images* (New York: Harper & Row).
Osborn, M. (1988) 'The Terror and the Dream: Death and Resurrection on the Contemporary Stage', *Next Wave Journal*, fall (New York: Brooklyn Academy of Music).
Prince, H. (1974) *Contradictions* (New York: Dodd, Mead).
Rich, F. (1988) 'Seeking the Truth in an Age of Considerable Boredom', *New York Times*, 24 Oct.
Richards, S. (1980) *Great Rock Musicals* (New York: Stein & Day).
Sondheim, S., et al. (1962) *A Funny Thing Happened on the Way to the Forum* (New York: Dodd, Mead).
———. (1970) *Company* (New York: Random House).
———. (1973) *A Little Night Music* (New York: Dodd, Mead).
———. (1975) *The Frogs* (New York: Dodd, Mead).

———. (1976) *Anyone Can Whistle* (New York: Leon Amiel).
———. (1976) *Pacific Overtures* (New York: Dodd, Mead).
———. (1979) *Sweeney Todd* (New York: Dodd, Mead).
Stearns, D. P. (1988) 'Making Overtures: Stephen Sondheim', *Gramophone*, Aug.
Sutcliffe, J. H. (1988) 'The Argento Papers', *Opera News*, Nov.
Swados, E. (1980) *Runaways* (New York: Samuel French).
———. (1982) *Haggadah* (New York: Samuel French).
———. (1984) *Doonesbury* (New York: Holt, Rinehart and Winston).
Walsh, M. (1988) 'The Opera as Science Fiction', *Time*, 1 Aug.
Wilson, R., et al. (1976) *Einstein on the Beach* (New York: EDS Enterprises).
Zadan, C. (1974) *Sondheim & Co* (New York: Avon).

9

Once Upon a Time in Performance Art

LENORA CHAMPAGNE

A man masturbates under floorboards as the audience walks overhead. A woman extracts a text from her vagina. A man in a red dress looks into his mother's purse. A woman talks about menstrual blood as she pours kidney beans over her forearm. An understated man seated at a table reads a clipping about a woman who saw the face of Christ in a tortilla. A bald-headed woman in her sixties describes the human brain while chopping a cauliflower with a sharp knife.

Ranging from raucous and raunchy comedy to cool irony, from exposing vulnerability to offending the audience, from true story to imagined fictions, from sophisticated intellectual strategy to simple physical tasks or complicated physical tricks, performance art has both borrowed from and revitalised a variety of art forms and styles.

Performance art's roots are not in theatre, but in the art world and in dissent. Contemporary performance has precedents in the Italian futurists, in the Russian constructivists, and in Dada and the Cabaret Voltaire – avant-garde movements that challenged established standards and definitions of art and sought to 'epater le bourgeois' by tolerating and encouraging shocking, outrageous behaviour in live performances or public appearances.

Performance art is a hybrid from that includes one or more live performers. While not purely sculpture, or painting, or poetry, or dance, performance art pieces may incorporate elements from all of these forms. Often, in keeping with the experimental, interdisciplinary nature of the form, mixed media or technology, such as slides, film and video, is incorporated into the work. Objects, movement and language are layered in an abstract or associative collage structure. A story may be suggested or alluded to, but information is generally presented in fragments rather than in the linear narrative form typical of conventional plots.

Rather than being an expert or specialist in the art form he or she appropriates, a performance artist may use movement without being a trained dancer, sing without benefit of lessons, write his or her own material, and most likely has not attended acting class. An artist with skill or technique in one field will explore possibilities in another. While stage presence is an asset, performance often relies on a naïve vitality and directness, and the communicative power of strong visual images.

Performance attracts diverse artists: both those whose concerns are primarily aesthetic, and those who want to address personal/political issues in a public forum, as is the case in work associated with the feminist or gay movements. Whether the artist is exploring and clarifying self-definition or aesthetic issues, performance art is often autobiographical or self-referential. In the wake of the upheavals of the 1960s, artists tore away traditional boundaries and limitations to self-presentation and focused on the self as subject matter or performance site.[1]

Certainly the 'happenings' of the 1960s, which often featured nudity and sometimes played with 'sacred' symbols (such as the American flag) in irreverent ways, challenged both aesthetic and social conventions. During the 1970s, performance became a major form for artistic expression: the form of choice for artists who eschewed more traditional means, such as painting and sculpture, or who challenged the then-prevalent minimalist fashion in art, and performers from the theatre, dance or music worlds whose experimental, conceptual orientation found a place in the art world.

In the spirit of John Cage, Merce Cunningham, and 'happenings', early performance artists celebrated chance structures and experimented with duration and materials. Impermanence was a strategy used to protest the commodity status of artwork.[2] Performances were often unrepeatable or, in the case of certain site-specific or private works, available only in the form of documentation.

In the 1970s art context for performance, the focus was on the integrity of the concept or idea, or on the intimate sharing of a private ritual with the audience, In the 1980s, as performance moves from art galleries to nightclubs, the emphasis is on showmanship and compelling performance style, which tends to favour those artists with theatrical flair.

Tracing trends in performance from the 1970s to the 1990s, several factors stand out: the contribution of the feminist and gay movements, with their focus on self-definition and exploration of stereotypes, to the development of the persona device used in performance; the revitalising effect on theatre of the personal and formal explorations by performance artists; and the shift in performance from an esoteric form of expression to a more accessible and popular one.

I

Someone's in the kitchen, I know.
– a popular song

The emergence of autobiographically oriented performance art in the 1970s coincides with a major social movement: feminism. The women's movement, with its consciousness-raising groups, contributed to the public expression of personal material.

In *The Survivor and the Translator* (1980), a powerful solo work by Leeny Sack about her family's survival of concentration camps, she becomes an adolescent girl and speaks in a saccharine voice about her 'sweet secret'. Gradually, it becomes clear that the words are Anne Frank's, and that she is talking about her first menstrual period.

Along with suicide and death, menstruation and mothers were hot topics in the 1970s, when one of the radical aspects of performance art was talking about subjects that had previously been taboo. Women's place before feminism was pretty well defined, and one can be sure that the 'I' in the line, 'Someone's in the kitchen, I know', is a man, the speaking subject, while the 'someone' is a silent (and spoken about) woman.

In the wake of the feminist movement, some women in the art world had had enough of this silence and its repressive consequences, enough of normative feminine behaviour, enough of staying home. The began talking about and doing the unspeakable, articulating what had been repressed, leaving the kitchen to express their interior lives and explore the outside world.

In her explorations of space, Joan Jonas set mirrors into remote Canadian landscapes; in New York performances, she split her persona among various actors, themselves masked and mirrored on video monitors. Carolee Schneeman used film, slides and nudity in her challenging work, which included *Interior Scroll*, a 1975 performance in which she read a text about discrimination in the art world as she extracted it from her vagina. About her films, filled with 'clutter' and 'the persistence of feelings', a colleague said 'We think of you as a dancer'.

Other women put on personalities like clothes and went around in them. In California, Eleanor Antin donned a beard and called herself the King of Spain, while Linda Montano, a former nun, made daily expeditions as the Chicken Woman. Lynn Hershman created an alternate self, Roberta Breitmore, who had her own driver's licence and social security number and who answered personal ads. Martha Wilson created various personas, including herself as a man in a leather jacket, and, much later, herself as Nancy Reagan.

Persona explorations are a way of challenging and fracturing stereotypes. Trying out personas, especially male personas or images of women different from oneself, is a way to take power by inhabiting images of it, and was part of the social and personal research by women who sought alternatives to the traditional roles they'd inherited.

Many performers today still use the persona device, with its possibilities for different voices and emotional variety, within a solo work to express a multiplicity of aspects of their own character or imagination.[3] While in persona, performers make shocking and explicit personal revelations or images, address political and personal issues, and attack social injustice and cultural stereotypes or taboos.

Karen Finley, creating a panoply of repulsive yet compelling lower-depth characters, pours a can of kidney beans over her forearm as she talks about menstrual blood. A weird bald-headed scientist, Rachael Rosenthal, cuts up a cauliflower while talking about dissecting the human brain. An awed young girl, Holly Hughes, watches her mother's panty hose slither out of the bathroom as she teaches her to masturbate. As her Aunt Sally, Robbie McCauley rages about racial injustice, testifying to a black woman's rape by a black man.

The persona device is used by a number of women who've targeted the sex industry in their work. In *Go-Go World* (1981), researched during her stint as a topless dancer in New Jersey,

Dianne Torr compares the system's use of the dancer who learns tricks to seduce the gazer (for his money), to the expansionist policy and exploitative practices of the United States, which dangles various carrots before developing Third World nations without coming through with anything substantial. Nancy Reilly gets down into grit and mire in her belligerent, highly controlled, ranting solo, *The Gangster and the Barmaid* (1987), playing out a repellent low-life scenario of the desperation and degradation of a topless barmaid, all for 'an inch of pennies'. Her delivery is dry, rapid-fire, physical, no-holds barred, totally lacking in sentimentality. Eileen Myles, a performance poet, tells of being phoned about posing for nude photos. This insinuating phone call is a wry, ironic commentary on the difficulty – near impossibility – for the artist to make a living from her work, and a reminder that, as a woman, one is worth more in this culture as an object than as a creating subject.

In the 1980s, as much subversive energy comes from gays as from women. Now gay men are using persona to explore ideas of gender, to play with stylised images of femininity and mas-culinity, and to create disturbing, complicated self-expressions. Bradley Wester, wearing an elegant red ball gown, dreams he's a pregnant Japanese woman and looks in his mother's purse. James Adlesic, wearing a blue velvet dress, becomes his pregnant alcoholic mother. Brandishing scissors, he knocks back liquor and lifts the dress, revealing his genitals. John Kelly, wearing an elegant man's suit, startles as he sings in an opera diva's voice. All of these men (Kelly, who now stages large works, used to perform solo pieces in drag) look beautiful dressed as women, which can have an eerie or unsettling effect on the spectator. In their work the genders (male, female, and a polymorphous something in between) clash chaotically together in a suggestion that gender shifting in performance may be the equivalent of transformation of materials in other art forms.

Other artists who play with gender are David Cale, Kevin Duffy and Richard Elovich. In the trilogy *Redthroats* (1986) British-born Cale performs all the parts in an epic journey from a small boy's hellish childhood to his adult experiences as a hustler who 'inadvertently' wanders into the gay scene. In *The Blackmouths at Home* (1989) Duffy plays an entire family: Mr and Mrs Blackmouth and Baby Blackmouth. In this family, whose characteristic trait is that they have no teeth, Duffy depicts a nightmarish underclass in which the homeless mother wanders with a suitcase of potatoes after the father kills the baby in a fit of senseless rage. And in his solo performance, *A Man Cannot Jump Over His Own Shadow* (1989), Richard Elovich uses the persona device to get at sexual obsession, shifting from a benefactor named Sal to a manic mad-man picked up in a gay bar, to a terrifying vision of his mother, performed in drag, a stocking over his head.

Who are the women playing dress-up? First, there are the girls at the W.O.W. Cafe, a women's experimental theatre/performance club that has been the spawning ground for a wild and wacky strain in performance, exemplified by Holly Hughes, Carmelita Tropicana, Lisa Kron and Reno (although the latter's work tends toward stand-up comedy).

Hughes, a particularly outstanding writer – her play, *Dress Suits for Hire* (1987) won an Obie for actress Peggy Shaw – is also a compelling performer. In her solo work, *World without End* (1989), she popped out of a pink plaster pig clad in girdle and corset to deliver a monologue charged with desire. Hughes, like Liz Prince (who designs and constructs provocative costumes to complement the themes of the torch songs she sings), has reappropriated the image of the *femme fatale*, the sexually powerful and potent woman. While Hughes has experienced her share of pain and disappoint-ment, she never plays the victim – she transforms her experience into myths she can use, presenting the possibility of power and pleasure in polymorphous sexuality.

Carmelita Tropicana, who came to this country as a child from her native Cuba, also reflects the generally fun and pleasure-loving, gender-bending style typical of W.O.W.-based work. In her per-sona as *emigrée* entertainer, a refugee from the revolution, Carmelita plays out a glamorous star fantasy and ironically explores nostalgia for a retrograde way of life lost to progress.

Irony mixed with nostalgia and a strong sense of humour are part of the pleasure in dressing-up. While differences in focus and strategy are apparent in the costume creations by Pat Olezsko, who attained notoriety in the 1970s, and Liz Prince, a relative newcomer, the sense of fun predominates in both. Olezsko's witty designs (such as her famous coat of arms, with dozens of gloved arms attached) are often based on puns; her sensibility is anarchic, surrealistic. It will always be hard to top the audacity of Olezsko's wildest work, as when she frames various body parts to transform them: drawing a face on her belly so that her pubic hair becomes a beard, and alternately contracting and releasing her stomach muscles to make this 'man' talk. In a short film of hers, two fingers, with little doll shoes on the ends to make them look like legs, go for a walk. The audience responds by rolling in the aisles.

While Prince also plays with puns (her dress for 'Smoke Rings' has a cigarette fringe; the rosette decorations on her 'Soap Song' dress are made of scouring pads), her costumes above all conjure up images of ditsy sex queens from a bygone era. In ironic lyrics and choice of materials (such as tuna fish cans as breast plates on her bottle cap dress), Prince simultaneously personifies and deconstructs the image of the Hollywood glamour goddess, showing how the persona device lends itself to post-feminist self-expression.

From the kitchen, from the bedroom, from inside women's heads, from inside their bodies new expressions emerged and were given shape and definition. Personal history was turned into art by decisions about structure and form; new structures and forms arose with the expression of this personal material. In the best work, the performer creates distance through formal rigour, by framing the material, by structuring it and selecting metaphor.

II

What were the crossovers between theatre and performance art? What is the difference between performance and theatre? Between performing and acting? Why do people want to hear true stories?

The term 'performance art' applies to work ranging from highly personal solo monologues to comedy routines, to large multimedia collaborations between artists from different disciplines. Confusion about the form and variations in quality and style has often led theatre professionals to dismiss performance art, which tends to favour presentation rather than representation. Traditionally, theatre is wedded to representation, with its well-established traditions and formulas. But artists using performance to explore and clarify self-definition and aesthetic issues have made significant contributions to revitalising theatre.

Enhanced, revitalised formal possibilities

In the 1970s, experimental theatre was a place where developments in the visual arts, dance, performance and theatre converged and

merged. Experimental theatre artists who utilised the interdisciplinary approach and associative style of structuring work typical of
performance art include Robert Wilson, Richard Foreman, Meredith Monk and Elizabeth LeCompte. A section from *Rumstick Road*
(1977), created by the Wooster Group and directed by LeCompte,
indicates how the strategy of superimposing devices and forms
from different mediums can create an elegant, poetic, non-linear
image.

A slide of Spalding Gray's boyhood home is projected onto the
back wall of the performance space. Directly in front of it, the
performer Libby Howes begins a repetitive dance-in-place to a violin
concerto while a cassette tape of Gray's grandmother discussing
his mother's madness is played. Layered together are the dry New
England voice, matter-of-factly discussing the mental breakdown,
the emotional intensity of the music, the obsessive dance, with
Libby's hair flying back and forth, her hand extended for support
to the roof of the house in the slide.

The cumulative effect of these superimpositions of information
was the creation of a physical metaphor operating on many levels
and lending itself to multiple interpretations. For me, it was a metaphor for ecstasy in the everyday, and the impossibility of sustaining
life at that pitch; it conjured up associations with a particular state of
being during artistic creation, and the parallel track of the practical
self who inhabits the real world. For someone else, it could have
operated simply as a stunning visual design or a complex sound
track. In the Wooster Group's work, scored movement is more
choreography than blocking. Elizabeth LeCompte, whose training
is in the visual arts, structures the pieces like music, adjusting
rhythm, creating complex images, using video and film as integral
elements.

Autobiography and Catharsis

In 1978 Linda Montano gave a performance/exorcism called *Mitchell's
Death*, in which she inserted acupuncture needles into her face
while relating the events around her ex-husband's death and burial.
After seeing the performance, Ted Shank wrote that

> The impact of the work results almost entirely from the audi-
> ence's knowledge that the events described actually took place
> and that . . . the performers were involved in them. . . . The

performance also gains strength because it seems to be more than a theatrical performance.[4]

While autobiography has long been a source of material for artists, in the 1970s there was particular interest in the authenticity of the conflict at the base of the work. There was a focus on the integrity of the artist's self-exploration and an emphasis on intimate sharing of a private ritual with the audience. Since the artist usually performed the work themselves, and spoke to the audience in the first person, the subject of the work was identical with the subject (the acting, thinking, feeling person) before the spectator.

Not surprisingly, sometimes this work, which created an intimate relationship with the audience because of both the nature of the material revealed and the style of performance, was criticised for being 'confessional'.[5] But it seems to me there is a difference between confession and revelation. When a performer transforms personal pain into something that reveals larger vision, the role of the spectator is not that of pardoner, but of witness. In successful performances, where one acknowledges that what is performed is art, the performer has no need of solace from the group, because the personal experience has been transformed into a metaphor for something that resonates in a larger field. While the process of making the artwork, the shaping and handling of the material, can itself transform the experience for the artist, for it to be experienced as art by the spectator two things seem to be necessary: effective use of metaphor to give the work wider resonance in the world, and powerful presence on the part of the performer.

In Leeny Sack's *The Survivor and the Translator*, spectators witness her coming to terms with the horror of her family's experience under the Nazis. In a remarkable monologue in which she functions as her grandmother/survivor and herself/translator, she recites a recipe for *gefilte* fish, first in a terrified, passionate Polish, then in a flat, non-inflected English. The effect of this juxtaposition is that the grinding of the fish bones becomes a horrifying metaphor for the extermination of her people.

Sack's performance transcended self-referentiality to become a tribute to endurance. The intense physicality of the Grotowski-influenced performance style she used challenged her own physical endurance and heightened the spectator's sense of the immediacy and urgency of the event being witnessed. Vitality was transmitted

and moved the audience physically, viscerally, as well as emotionally. The spectator witnessed traces of the emotional ordeal or
conflict at the base of the work and the full physical effort involved
in performing it.

The crucial difference between witnessing this direct expression
and attending the theatre is that there the experience has been
distanced by the creation of characters and actors representing
something. In autobiographically based performance art, the only
mediator between the experience and the spectator is the presence
of the author/performer him- or herself.

Similarly, the Wooster Group's juxtaposition of autobiographical
material from Spalding Gray's life (his mother's madness and suicide) with abstract images created by LeCompte and the performers
in *Rumstick Road* resulted in a performance far more powerful than
most conventional plays. When Gray's grandmother, her actual
words documented on tape, talks about readiness for death, the
effect is more compelling than, say, Jessie in Marsha Norman's
'night Mother (1983). When we hear a recorded conversation, we
know this really happened, it actually took place. When documentary material is handled abstractly, framed and shaped to create a
performance text with resonances and associations the spectator
can read in a non-literal way, it is often more surprising and exciting than imagined situations manipulated in a 'realistic' style.

What of the argument that, since theatre is artifice, identifying art and life, as some performance does, is not honest. On a
reality/artifice continuum, it's all a matter of degree. There cannot
be theatre that is 'more' authentic, more truly life, because artifice
in theatre is real, too. It is really pretending.

Part of the reason autobiographical performance art flourished in
the 1970s is that it offered the spectator the experience of catharsis.
One can argue that catharsis was no longer available in conventional theatre, where the mental and emotional structures and
forms are inherited formulas that don't correspond to the contemporary experience of reality as a series of shocks and fragments. After Vietnam, after the shocks of the 1960s, audiences
were interested in art that could be healing. In the best of this
work, witnessing a performer coming to terms with fragments of
actual ordeal or conflict in an immediate, direct way felt exciting
and empowering.[6]

The use of autobiography as material is still typical of the art
form, but now there is irony about the self as a valuable source for

work. In *Tennytown* (1988), Jessica Hagedorn's satire of a stand-up monologue, she sarcastically observes, 'Even your major disappointments are turned into artistic material. Every little second of anguish has value. You're expressing yourself'.

Today performance is not evaluated in terms of degrees of anguish, self-expression or conflict. The original anti-commodity impulse of performance is a thing of the past as audiences and producers expect a slicker, more sophisticated package, and performers expand their range of concerns.

Early performance artists were entrepreneurs, operating on the margins of the system. Performance art in its solo form can be economical. In *Some Kind of Dance* (1982), Stephanie Skura packed all her props into her back-pack and performed the solo performance artist walking home, alone. Now Skura has a dance company, and travels with trucks and technicians. For many artists, solo performance offered a way to work without entailing the expenses of theatre or dance companies. Even in a poor theatre, actors have to pay rent.

Many performance artists today are rediscovering theatre, as solo performers, dancers and visual artists use text extensively and work to larger scale, but this work rarely resembles a traditional play. When it does – for example, Karen Finley's latest foray into the American family drama, *Theory of Total Blame* (1988) – it is more parody than imitation, more outrageous challenge than homage. Like an Alfred Jarry (or Ubu Roi) for the 1980s, Finley farts on convention and blows the audience away, alternately offending them and reducing them to laughter as she brings to light what the culture represses.

Where is the provocative work now? As performance gets more theatrical and seeks a wider audience, spaces with technical possibilities are preferred to more rudimentary gallery settings. Alternative dance spaces, such as Performance Space 122 or Dance Theatre Workshop, with their adventurous audiences, have been particularly open to performance. As the decade progresses, work veers from elegant irony to something wild and manic.

III

You should be on Johnny Carson.
– Martha Wilson

Where sincerity and authenticity, and a somewhat raw emotional intensity, were hallmarks of performance in the 1970s, the stylish performance attitude in the 1980s is one of studied irony. Audiences are changing with the generation. Whereas 1970s audiences wanted to 'share' the experience with the performer, or be challenged by complicated structures, jaded 1980s audiences just want to stay awake. They want to be entertained and stimulated; ideas have to be slipped in between fast-paced image shifts. This desire on the part of the audience has always been problematic for experimental work, but is being met today by work that is both provocative and entertaining.

The change of venue from galleries and art spaces to clubs and theatres has generated a different performance style and subject matter. Whereas 1970s performance art tended toward conceptual or autobiographical work, 1980s performance is more self-consciously entertaining and often comments on mass culture and borrows from it. Performers from the visual arts world still tend to approach the form more conceptually and from a theoretical base. But young people with a theatre or dance background are fascinated with the everyday materials at hand: headlines from the *National Enquirer*, reruns from the *Lucy* show. Anything from television or the mass media is considered fair game. Mass audience material is used as subject matter/content, as form, and/or as both.

For instance, in Spalding Gray's monologue, *Nobody Ever Wanted to Sit Behind a Desk* (1981), Gray read a clipping from a tabloid about a woman who saw the face of Christ in a tortilla. He didn't comment on it, just read it before he started telling his stories. It functioned as a frame, setting his subsequent ruminations on contemporary life in a weird context of irony and wonder.

In the mid-1980s, Elizabeth Prince and Michael Stiller did a duet called *The Giveaway Sale*, which was like a live cartoon. *The Giveaway Sale* changed every time it was performed. In one incarnation, Liz, wearing an evening gown created from plastic Bounty brand paperbags, played 'Onward Christian Soldiers' on her saxophone as Michael, wearing a Chiquita banana jacket, sang 'I Did it My Way' after giving away a million dollars to Nino Rota music. It was very fast, but contained a cogent and intelligent critique of American capitalism in the distortions, juxtapositions and sheer number of mass culture images layered into the piece.[7]

A lot of performance art in East Village clubs is of this style: cartoon-like in gesture and timing, full of accumulated objects, and intentionally messy in execution. There are several reasons for this. One is the short attention span of today's audiences, partly as a result of television, partly, in the case of club performance, because the audience may have consumed alcohol and drugs; to keep their interest the performance energy has to be manic. In addition, today's younger audiences are more image literate and sophisticated, and enjoy the great leaps in analogies that can be made by quick image juxtapositions. Today's artists often integrate the jump cut as a performance mode.

DanceNoise, a duo composed of Lucy Sexton and Annie Iobst, hosts a performance series at the WahWah Hut in the East Village. They sometimes perform with Jo Andres (a choreographer who makes films and exotic visual projections), Mimi Goese, and Tom Murrin/Alien Comic at P.S. 122 in something called the 'Full Moon Show'. All of these performers, like Karen Finley, whose raw, aggressive quality they share, made their name in clubs, where audience expectations and performance conditions call for high shock value. Some of DanceNoise's comes from their costuming – they strip down to teddies and combat boots to cartwheel across the stage in tandem. These two physically powerful women play with sexually charged images (the *noir*-ish image of the woman in a white slip, hand on hip, chain smoking cigarettes) in a way that de-feminises, de-objectifies them. They walk around in their nearly nude bodies like guys in the locker room, they waltz together, they get into fights and throw things. In *Half a Brain* (1988), they remove fish from their underwear and drink water from fish bowls with fish swimming in them.

DanceNoise also make simplistic, ironic social critiques. For instance, while a tape of romantic music plays, a placard announces the situation: 'a romantic evening'. Then a series of large word cards spell out the components: roses, champagne, candlelight – contraceptives, money. Later, they emerge from a trunk wearing military helmets with penis-like topknots; they strip off their uniforms and pour fake blood on themselves.

Mimi Goese, who sings in the band Hugo Largo and sometimes dances with Andres, likewise makes an aggressive spectacle of herself. She throws lighted cigarettes at the audience or, asking for a volunteer who has hassled women on the street, ties him up and yells 'asshole' in his face. Clearly, part of the appeal of DanceNoise and Goese is to see how far they will go; what irreverent insult they'll come up with next.[8] There's a kind of adolescent rebelliousness, a bad girl quality to their work that provokes a vicarious pleasure in boundary breaking.

With club performance and 'new vaudeville', performance art becomes a meeting ground of high art and popular entertainment.[9] Increasingly, references are to mass market images of things, rather than to the original source of the image, that is, the experience or thing itself. With references to references, we may be in the mannerist phase of performance art.

IV

Post Script: In The Art World

Where is performance in the art world? Where it began? In the wake of an infusion of deconstruction and feminist and psychoanalytic theory, the art world is rife with challenges to authority in the early 1990s – words, ideas, commentary are more important than, or as important as, the image (think of woe by Jenny Holzer and Barbara Kruger, Hans Haacke and Marcel Broodthaers). Art world performance borrows from the persona impulse of performance, runs it through a theory grinder, and comes up with irreverent plays on fashionable concepts. Knowing girls in power suits with lots of attitude tease and provoke the audience to side with them in favour of difference.

Mastery of current theoretical discourse informing the art world and its ironic deconstruction is the strategy used by the V-Girls, a five member reading and performance group, and in the solo performances of Andrea Fraser (one of the V-Girls). The V-Girls (Martha Baer, Erin Cramer, Jessica Chalmers, Fraser, and Marianne Weems) stage mock-serious panel discussions and paper presentations that display their knowledge of psychoanalytic and literary theory while lampooning the jargon and punching holes in the systems' claims to explain everything. In their panel on Manet's Olympia (based on the painting by that title), Weems talks about 'Dogged Desire' and 'The Gaze' as a slide of a cocker spaniel is projected; Fraser reads a paper on 'Mayonnaise Olympia', which consists of a recipe but which, in this context, seems like a weird description of Manet's process and materials. In a send-up of the very notion of a panel of authorities, one panelist righteously questions the absence of critical commentary on the presence of the black woman in the painting (paralleling the marginalisation of Third World people and women in the West), until another notes the absence of a black woman on the panel.

Fraser's solo performances are in the guise of a museum docent or tour guide. Her site-specific works are a *mélange* of historical facts about the actual museum (the physical plant, the social and cultural role of the institution in the particular city), deconstructions of psychoanalytic theory, and commentary on both the art work itself and its setting.[10] In a recent Philadelphia Museum tour, she took the audience through the various rooms – the rest rooms, the cloakrooms, the dining rooms, the museum shop – while she kept up a non-stop, zany commentary that emphasised the ideology underlying the museum and its selection process. Squarely in performance art's tradition of dissent and provocation, her witty, intelligent work, like that of the V-Girls, is an entertaining, ironic play with authority.[11]

NOTES

1. Body art, such as Vito Acconci's masturbation piece, situated the artwork in or on the artist's body. Sometimes this took the form of physical mutilation, as when Chris Burden had himself shot in performance. Other artists, such as Linda Montano, who applied acupuncture needles to her face while speaking of her former husband's death, found metaphors for trauma.
2. In one performance, Laurie Anderson played her violin while wearing ice skates set into blocks of ice. The performance was over when the ice melted.
3. In true performance art persona work, the self of the performer shows through the character. Martha Wilson isn't really convincing as Nancy Reagan; she's commenting on her. Persona explorations are different from the impersonations that performers such as Eric Bogosian, Ann Magnuson or Whoopie Goldberg do. This style of performing is closer to acting and being an entertainer in a stand-up comedy tradition. The performer/comic Reno, for instance, has brought her downtown persona and material to a wider audience in a larger sphere. Performers who specialise in playing characters, rather than taking on personas, often move into the financially lucrative area that has been opened up by the success of satirists such as Lily Tomlin.
4. Theodore Shank, 'Mitchell's Death', *The Drama Review*, vol. 23 (1979) no. 1, pp. 13–14.
5. It was a big shock for women whose work was criticised as 'confessional' when the same form was praised when adopted by

male colleagues in revealing monologues. Along with David Cale, the best-known male performers using the monologue form are Spalding Gray, Eric Bogosian, and San Francisco's John O'Keefe, whose solo work, *Shimmer* (1988), is based on his boyhood experiences in a midwestern reform school. All of these performers use autobiographical material and imagery to some extent, although Bogosian, as previously mentioned, tends to model his characters on types he sees in the culture. Gray has expanded his material from reflections on his boyhood to his adventures in India and after. In *Terrors of Pleasure* (1986) he addresses the crises of buying a home; in *Swimming to Cambodia* (1984), written while he was filming *The Killing Fields* and made into a film by director Jonathan Demme with music by Laurie Anderson, he reflects on that country's difficult relationship with the US and with his personal (mis)fortunes. All of these performers work as actors and have had their monologues published in book form. Gray is currently working on a lengthy novel.

6.   Another way of looking at performance as a means of satisfying desire for catharsis or of providing the occasion for communal witnessing of a private ritual is to think of the religious origins of theatre, and the functions theatre may attempt to fulfil in a secular society.

7.   I think this work is more sophisticated conceptually than the satirical character sketches of performers who impersonate a range of contemporary types without implying a larger critical framework that includes the audience. In terms of scale of intent, it's the difference between making fun of someone 'other' by indicating 'what a fool this guy is, thank God we're different' and critiquing something we're all part of (that is to say *Giveaway Sale* = American Dream).

8.   The acknowledged master of this is Karen Finley, who breaks taboos and makes a special target of sacred cows. Her vivid and violent imagery is delivered in a shrill and enraged tone. She relieves her intense and exhausting verbal rants with visual foolishness, such as getting naked and shaking up raw eggs and stuffed animals in a plastic bag, painting herself with the wet bunnies, then applying glitter. This viscous image is the physical equivalent of some of her gutsy word pictures. Finley and other other messy, boundary blasting performers owe something to the Kipper Kids, who pioneered this style in the 1970s.

9.   Some noted proponents of the 'new vaudeville' are the virtuoso clown/performer Bill Irwin, the juggler Michael Moschen, and Paul Zaloom, who manipulates object in his fast-paced lecture demonstrations to score points in arguments for environmental and political change. Tom Murrin, aka Alien Comic, is a wizard with objects, garbage and stuff of all kinds. His rapid-fire delivery of puns and cultural commentary is matched by witty, non-stop play with strange and ordinary materials, transformed into original, surprising costumes and props. Stuart Sherman, known for his

quirky ideas and silent manipulations of objects on a portable folding table, has expanded his formal explorations into film and now speaks, and even sings, in performance.

10.   Another important site-specific artist is Scottish-born Fiona Templeton, whose *You, the City*, a large scale performance for an audience of one, premiered in 1988. In this work, re-created for London in 1989, each 'client' was individually guided through a series of encounters with the city as set by a series of performers stationed at various locales, all of whom address 'you' (the spectator/participant). A former member of the performance collective Theatre of Mistakes, Templeton makes work that is theoretical and conceptual at base; she uses language for its abstract and poetic rather than narrative possibilities. This piece raised intriguing questions about the aestheticisation of everyday life, the significance of chance encounters and the appropriation of the city as spectacle.

11.   Other significant art world performers are Laurie Anderson, who, by virtue of her success in the music business, is probably the most well-known performance artist, and Constance deJong, who was in the latest Whitney Biennial. Both performers offer ironic observations on how human communication is affected by technical interference, and critique society's misguided efforts to control conditions with technological 'mastery'.

10

Performance Artist/ Art Performer: Laurie Anderson

MEL GORDON

I always felt it was a mistake being labelled as an autobiographical artist . . . Most of the work that I do is two-part or stereo, not monolithic at all – so there's always the yes/no, he/she, or whatever pairs I'm working with.

Laurie Anderson, 1979

Since her first performance work in 1974, Laurie Anderson has found herself concerned with a basic aesthetic dilemma that has troubled a number of other performance artists: how to create an intensely personal art that is not just simple autobiography. That is, how can the performer-author bring raw, unmediated materials from their life and structure them to strike a balance between their own needs and those of the audience? For Anderson, the resolution is not only intellectual but technical. It is one that leads to a new performance style.

What Anderson calls a 'system of pairings', of placing polar opposites side-by-side or before one another, of incorporating (or transposing) a spiraling dialectic of styles and frames of reference pattern her productions like an electrical grid. Her performance methodologies revolve around a network of dualities: artist as person/character, language/sound, private/public activity, memory/fantasy, audio/ visual space, male/ female, nineteenth-/twentieth-century musical instrumentation, history/prophecy, filmic/live presentation.

Even Anderson's reception as a performance artist has a dual aspect to it. Despite the dense theatricality of her work, her early support and renown came almost exclusively from the art world, where she had an enthusiastic following. Although a *Life* magazine photo-essay (January, 1980) described her as 'a former teacher and critic, who may be the most popular performance artist', relatively few individuals in experimental theatre at that time were aware of her work. Possibly, the difficulty in actually seeing Anderson's presentations – she normally performs only once or twice a year in New York, where she lives – and her first tendency to mount her productions in art galleries and museums may also explain why she has been generally overlooked in theatre circles.

Born in 1947 and raised in northern Illinois, Laurie Anderson feels her early childhood may have had an especially lasting influence on her artistic thinking. One of eight children, she remembers a family ritual where everyone sat around the telling stories about what had happened to them that day. Amidst this mob scene, young Laurie quickly learned that the simple narration of interesting experiences did not always lead to interesting stories. Reports had to be tailored in places, expanded in others, points of view sometimes had to be altered, occasionally missing details or supplying more dramatic conclusions. Besides stories, family members played musical instruments, composed private songs, did voice imitations. Anderson also discovered at this time, like many tellers of yarns, that one often forgets what reportage is factual and what is invented. This sometimes leads to a certain artistic confusion or complexity (during a piece she presented at the Whitney Museum in 1976, for example, where she related a personal story, her father was heard relating another version of it in the audience).

During the 1960s, Anderson studied at Barnard College, graduating with honours in art history. Later she took a master's degree in sculpture at Columbia and began teaching 'Principles of Art History', which she subtitled 'Skrooples', at City College in New York. Both in and out of the classroom, Anderson found herself fascinated with the perceptual contrasts of words – whether handwritten, printed or spoken – and visual imagery. The notion of students filling notebooks in the coloured light of projected slide transparencies while she lectured struck Anderson as a bizarre aesthetic relationship.

Around 1972, Anderson's interest in paper sculpture and in art generally began to fade. Instead, she turned to writing, a kind of conceptual style that consisted of one-sentence books, diary entries, even a dream series that resulted from the mixing of daydreams, memories, real dreams and paintings that were projected on the screen during an art history class. During the summer of 1972, Anderson and a friend organised a performance event in a small Vermont town. Every Sunday evening, residents of Rochester would drive up to their park in automobiles, trucks and motorcycles to hear music played by a local band. Without ever leaving their car seats, the spectators would sit and honk their horns to show approval at the end of each section. Enthralled by the *naïveté* and unintentional sophistication of the situation, Anderson managed to reverse the audience/entertainer relationship by forming an orchestra of the small vehicles. This time the people in the driver's seats made the music with their horns and spectators sat in the park's gazebo.

Laurie Anderson's first major performance piece, 'As: If', was mounted at the Artists Space in SoHo in 1974. Encouraged by the performance artist Vito Acconci, she attempted to structurally blend different personal stories with oversized projections of words. On one side of the screen was a word concerned with language, and on the other, separated by a colon, was a word related to water (for example, 'SOUND: DROWN'). The slides were used as a subtext to both highlight and diagram the narration.

In the summers of 1974 and 1975, Anderson performed 'Duets on Ice' in various outdoor locations in New York City. Standing in ice skates, whose blades were embedded in blocks of ice, she played a violin that contained a built-in speaker. Wired to a hidden tape recorder, the violin could produce pre-recorded sound as well as live music. In this way, Anderson was able to perform a duet with herself. More than a simple Dada-type escapade, 'Duets on Ice' revealed a number of central features in Anderson's ethos – notably a deep concern with performance time and objects. Possibly influenced by her storytelling and teaching experiences, Anderson tries to keep the length of her performances within set limits, usually less than sixty or seventy-five minutes. In 'Duets on Ice' the melting of the ice regulated the performance time in an obvious, graphic fashion.

For Anderson, certain personal objects play a significant part in the production. Unlike standard stage props, these special items, or what Anderson calls 'dense objects', signify a whole range of private memories or emotions, while remaining entirely functional to the piece. The ice and the skates take on personal and metaphysical expressions of time passing, of internal and outer balance, of musical and anatomical rhythms. Of all the 'dense objects' in Anderson's repertoire, none is so readily associated with her as the violin. Used as an instrument, a partner, a piece of machinery, a screen, a weapon, the violin and bow (or, symbolically, wood and horsehair) have undergone dozens of technical incarnations in Anderson's work. Sometimes electrified, at other times played naturally, Anderson's most innovative violin-creation has consisted of an instrument whose strings have been replaced with an audio head from a tape recorder and whose horsehair on the bow has been replaced with recording tape. This 'tape-bow violin' can create a sound-speech that has never existed before. As the bow is passed across the audio bridge, a totally reversible music-language is heard: 'no' on the up-bow becomes 'one' on the down-bow, 'yes' becomes 'say'. All a demonstration of the liquid nature of language.

After 'Duets on Ice', Anderson's work began to exhibit a more sophisticated blending of personal narrative and complex technology. For one thing, her sculptural sense of space became more pronounced. In an early version of 'For Instants', presented at the Whitney Museum in February 1976, a film shot from Anderson's loft window was projected against a white wall. After a few moments, she appeared in a white dress with an electric violin. Flush against the film image, looking like a kind of bulge in the two-dimensional plane of a window, she started to play her instrument, occasionally glancing back at the projection. The concert and film ended simultaneously. Anderson then lay down on the floor with a candle and read a text, which described the difficulties she had in filming, in understanding film time, in writing songs (It's like walking up the stairs in the dark and you think there is one more step than there actually is, and your foot comes pounding down on the top step . . . '). While she spoke, her breath caused the candle flame to move in and out of the path of a photo cell's beam, which in turn guided the electrical circuit of the spotlight in a joining and broken pattern. Therefore, the readings' illumination was solely based on the 'breathiness' of its words.

Later in 1976, Anderson prepared a new piece for the Berlin Festival, called 'Engli-SH'. Knowing little German, she attempted a performance that explored the areas between the languages, emphasising 's' (actually 'z' in German) and 'sh' sounds. At first, she appeared before her audience with simultaneous slide projections of German translation as she spoke. But, after a while the subtitles went out of sync, and the performance took on a new rhythm. Almost every word had a 'zzz' sound in it, which became the buzzing of a fly, the noise of snoring, the resonance of bad violin playing. (Curiously enough, small sections of the audience responded by locking arms and replying with the own 'zzz' sounds.) Anderson also played a violin as she ran back and forth between two microphones, merging the images of crossing language carriers and violin playing. The staccato sounds of the violin rapidly going in and out of the microphones' range increased until they resembled the frenzied report of a machine-gun. Anderson then stopped to tell a story about carrying a violin case in Chicago. She performed her violin duet, and on an up-stroke she released the bow, which sailed to the wall, hitting a projected image of an apple, which transformed into the character of William Tell, as other images began to multiply.

Laurie Anderson's first long piece, *Americans On the Move: Parts One and Two* was presented at the Carnegie Recital Hall and at The Kitchen (literally, uptown and downtown in New York City) in the spring of 1979. Here Anderson presented herself as a vivacious, if self-conscious, one-woman performer. Using cartoonish moving projections and overlays of maps and lines, Anderson charmed her audiences with anecdotes about traveling across America (staying in a nunnery, being picked up by a sex crazed truck driver, flying in an out of control airplane, and so forth). During each story, a gesture, a phrase or sound was repeated from the one before. This stimulated Anderson into a new musical phase: whether dancing/gesticulating hysterically, belting our a punk rock song (with her band), making strange electronic noises or doing increasingly abstract imitations of her story characters. Each final moment led associatively to another story: the waving goodbye of a violin bow became a windshield wiper; the word 'currents' gave rise to an anecdote about Thomas Edison and his arch-rival, the otherworldly Nikolai Telsa. As *Americans on the Move* unfolded, the audience began to notice the constant repetition of objects, gestures, words, shapes and sounds, which accelerated into an outer space finale.

Anderson's next production, *United States Part II* received a considerable amount of coverage in the New York press in the last week of October 1980 with extensive reviews in *The New York Times* and *The Village Voice*. One downtown weekly, *The Soho News*, devoted an entire cover story to her. The three performances that were announced for the Orpheum Theatre on Second Avenue were extended for several more presentations. Although their composition varied each night, the spectators seemed to consist of an unusual fusion of SoHo intellectuals and East Village punk rockers. All of this confirmed reports that Laurie Anderson had broken through the art and art performance barriers to find new audiences in the music and theatre worlds.

United States Part II was now announced as the second piece of a four-part project that would later be mounted at the prestigious Brooklyn Academy of Music's New Wave Festival. Once again, Anderson blended spectacular visual and aural effects within a complicated and seemingly disconnected narrative and musical structure. The performance itself was divided into thirteen sections and lasted seventy-five minutes. Anderson was accompanied by a band of seven vocalists and musicians. There was also a technical crew of four, who ran two film and two slide projectors.

The following description of the 1980 production of *United States Part II* serves as an introduction to Anderson's basic techniques and unique structuring devices:

1 **Superman Theme** The band plays hard rock-like music. Anderson tells an anecdote about how speaking French without really knowing it resembles the action of reading the list of unhealthy ingredients on a cereal box as you eat the chemically treated grains. She then relates that in France baby carriages are pushed out into the street between parked cars as a kind of traffic-tester. Anderson begins to beat a plastic toy gavel that gives off a beeping sound. An image of a clock at midnight appears on the back screen. It disappears, and Anderson turns on a wristwatch with a lighted dial. She hits it with the gavel.

2 **Superman! (for Massanet)** The sound of the gavel is picked up on a harmoniser that creates a pulsating beat. At the edge of a wide spotlight, Anderson makes hand gestures, such as the shooting of a gun, that leave large shadows on the screen. Occasionally her gestures are coordinated with the lyrics of a song she is singing. The song refers to Superman, her mother and father, and the leaving of messages on a

telephone answering machine. It concludes with a statement that after love is gone there is always justice; after that, there's force; and after force, there's Mom.

3 **Talkshow (for Electric Dogs)** Anderson explains that during a television strike, print journalists had to substitute for TV reporters and that management felt everything they did was wrong: they squinted into the camera, they used big words, and so on. Instead, they were instructed to use two-syllable words, 'buzz-words'. On the screen, these buzz-words – like 'update', 'hotline' – appear. The word 'gridlock' is followed by a large grid projection. Suddenly, there is a film of hand gestures projected over that. Anderson plays an electric violin in the manner of a ukelele. A variety of images are projected, each one turning into – actually 'becoming' – the next: a clock; a plate; a round map of Iraq and Iran; a plate of helicopter drawings; dancing hands silhouetted like animals. The sound of dogs barking is heard.

4 **Three Dreams: For Tape, Voice and Film** An image of wrinkled sheets is seen. The stage is now bare. An audio recording of a boy talking about a surreal dream is heard over music from TV sitcoms. Anderson appears and comically describes a dream she had about being one of Jimmy Carter's many wives, none of whom has seen him. Paper silhouettes of a person are flashed to show movement. Slides of sheets levitating and dissolving are seen as an audio of Anderson is heard mysteriously repeating dream longings. She also explains how walking is just falling sideways. Finally a story is projected in red letters about how Anderson and her sister played a game called Red Hot, where they pretended that the ceiling was red hot and gravity had lost its pull as they struggled not to float upwards.

5 **Private Property** Using a device that slows down her speech and lowers her pitch, Anderson relates a story about how William Buckley, the conservative author, was ejected from an Illinois mall for hawking his book because the mall owners told him he was on private property. Another anecdote told in that voice concerns the smoke rising from the barbecue pits of apartments that replaced broken-down factories. A film of trains entering and departing from a

subway station is seen as electric sounds suggestive of railroads are heard. Anderson entones, 'Do you want to go home? You are home.'

6   **Neon Duet for Tape and Violin**   Anderson plays a violin with a large neon-lighted bow. She continues the keening sound heard in the previous section.

7   **Let X=X**   Vocalists and band accompany Anderson in her song 'Let X=X'. As they sing, a map showing the time zones in North America appears with moving images of video-game rockets and flying saucers. Later a block drawing of a growing boy and girl replaces the map. At the end of the song, Anderson breathes into the microphone, 'It's a day's work just looking into your eyes'.

8   **The Mailman's Nightmare**   The face of a mailman is seen on the screen with the image of a sheet. A recorded voice is heard. The mailman tells of a dream where everyone but him is a huge baby.

9   **Language Is A Virus . . . (for William Burroughs)**   Anderson says, comically, 'Welcome to the difficult listening hour'. In an octave lower and with an echoing effect, she tells a story of a man coming home, finding all his wallpaper samples destroyed, and asks a stranger what he is doing in his house. The stranger replies that he is a soul doctor and that 'Language is a virus from outer space'. This begins the song for the entire band. As they repeat the refrain, 'letter words', such as 'A Frame', 'B Flick', 'C Note' are projected alphabetically ending with 'V Sign', 'WWII', 'X Ray', 'Y Me', 'Zzzzzzzz'. Speaking in the song, Anderson explains that Japanese is not a language, just sounds and characters, as Space Invader figures crowd the screen. The words 'Game Over' flash.

10 **Solo for Resonant Head, Violin and Pillow Speaker**   Anderson places microphone-goggles over her face and pounds her temples to create amplified knocking sounds. She picks up an electrically amplified violin and plays it. She puts a small flat speaker into her mouth and by inhaling and exhaling makes harmonica-like whining and roaring sounds.

11 **If You Can't Talk About It – Point to It: 2 (for Ludwig Wittgenstein)**   Anderson waves a baton maniacally, forming the sign of the cross. Paper figures are flashed on the

screen. She points to a spectator. Insignias of a moving hammer, a rabbit, and airplane appear. Anderson repeats a nursery rhyme, 'I see London, I see France, I seen those peppy Germans dance . . . ' She strikes her watch with the toy gavel.

12 **Don't Look Down** Zooming and rapidly intercut negative images of Manhattan building are seen. Speaking in a little-girl voice, Anderson tells stories about how she broke into a staff meeting of a military headquarters, about a crippled dog, and about a man standing on the ledge of a building, with the crowd below shouting, 'Jump'.

13 **Finnish Farmers** Anderson relates another anecdote about how Russian paratroopers often died during the Second World War because their parachutes didn't work. During the invasion of Finland, Russian paratroopers sometimes fell through the snow fifteen feet into the earth. The Finnish farmers would then find the holes and shoot directly into them. Another anecdote: during the 1979 drought in the US, American farmers sold property to the government for the contruction of missile silos. An image appears on the screen of an American flag tumbling around and around in a washing machine. Anderson begins to play the keening sound on her violin. The Statue of Liberty is projected in negative. Words are projected over it: 'Melting Pot', 'Melt Down', and finally 'Shut Down'.

Following the Orpheum concert-performance, Anderson's career began to change rapidly as her fame as a performer, musician-composer and artist grew. One song in *United States Part II*, 'O Superman', was recorded on a 45 rpm disk in 1981 and reached number two in the British pop charts. Warner Brothers Records quickly signed her as a recording artist and two long-playing albums, 'Big Science' and 'Mister Heartbreak', were issued in 1982 and 1984 respectively. Galleries and museums in Europe and America vied for her conceptual sculptures, 'paper objects' and various musical inventions, such as the 'Acoustic Lens'. Major exhibitions and installations of her works were mounted at the Institute of Contemporary Art in London, the University of Pennsylvania and Queens Museum in New York City. In 1982 alone, articles and interviews with Anderson appeared in such mainstream publications as *Rolling Stone*, *Gentlemen's Quarterly*,

Esquire, the French monthly *Actuel* and the airline magazine *TWA Ambassador*. Two years later, Anderson's image was so well known that her face, without caption, highlighted the American Express print campaign.

On 3 and 4 February 1983, Laurie Anderson presented her long-awaited and grandiose *United States: Parts I–IV* at the Brooklyn Academy of Music. This time her audiences were much more upscale, many coming from corporate and philanthropic backgrounds. Supported by twelve musicians and vocalists as well as a team of technicians, *United States* was divided into seventy-eight parts, given over two evenings. Both newspaper and magazine previews enthused over a new-found, if somewhat shy, performance artist personality. In 1984, Warner Brothers issued an extraordinary five-record album of Anderson's project *United States* live. Still two years later, in 1986, Anderson rephrased much of *United States* performance in a feature-length film, *Home of the Brave*.

Since the BAM success, Anderson has explored new video and dance venues. Critics, almost all sympathetic, have articulated a feeling that Anderson should pursue smaller and more personal presentational work. The Wagnerian proportions of *United States* and *Home of the Brave* have begun to dwarf Anderson's considerable storytelling, comic and musical talents. In fact, she had already moved into that direction. At the end of the 1908s, Laurie Anderson, whom Jack Kroll of *Newsweek* labelled an 'Electric Cassandra', once again returned to small-scale performance art.

11

Contemporary American Dance Theatre: Clarke, Goode and Mann

THEODORE SHANK

After two decades of American post-modern dances in which structure, abstract movement and kinetic energy were the principal content, we have entered a new era of expressiveness. The works of Martha Clarke are important examples of this new expressionism. However, she is not alone in making dances comprised of emotionally expressive images rather than formal ideas. Images imbued with emotional content are also important in the works of Pina Bausch and Susanne Linke in Germany, Anne Teresa de Keersmaeker and the Need Company of Belgium, Maguy Marin of France, Parco Butterfly of Italy, Second Stride in London and even the butoh dance companies of Japan. In the United States companies that share Clarke's emotive interests include two in San Francisco – Contraband, directed by Sara Shelton Mann, and the Joe Goode Performance Group. All of these dance companies use narrative (although fragmentary), character, expressive costumes, décor, lighting, music and language; in fact, they use whatever materials serve to express the feeling of living in their culture. Is it any wonder that much of their work expresses violence in one form or another?

Culture evolves organically and the arts tend to catch up with it by jerks as the discrepancies between the culture and the art expressing it become apparent to artists. One such jerk occurred in 1962 when the students of Robert Dunn presented their first concert at Judson Church in New York. They became the vanguard of post-modern dance choreographers. Much as the modern dance choreographers a generation earlier had rejected the restrictions of the ballet vocabulary, these young choreographers of the 1960s ane 1970s, who came to be called 'post-modernists', set out to release dance from the restrictions, inhibitions and vocabulary that had developed out of the sensibilities of the modern dance choreographers. The post-modern dancers set out to explore anew the possibilities of dance beginning with the human body. Their mentor, and at the same time someone to push off against, was Merce Cunningham who in the 1940s had set a course away from the mainstream of modern dance. To him any movement of any part of the body could be dance, it could be presented any place, and its principal content was not about something outside the dance, it was about the movements of the human body. And to assure that a dance was not influenced by the music, those two elements were sometimes brought together for the first time in performance. To Cunningham movement, music and setting were of equal importance but independent of each other though they could share the same time and space. The result had the chance correlations and divergences of real life and was not intended to give the spectator a predetermined meaning.

During the 1970s and early 1980s those choreographers whom Sally Banes calls 'analytical post-modernists' focused principally on movement to the exclusion of other elements (Banes, 1987, p. xx). Movement, the body and abstract form was the exclusive content of their work. Ordinary movements and tasks were transformed into art by being placed in an aesthetic frame.

These innovative choreographers tended to strip away all potentially expressive elements except movement. Instead of narrative they devised structures based on mathematics, sports, games or other abstract compositional ideas (Trisha Brown, Laura Dean, Lucinda Childs). Instead of characters in costume, they presented performers in motion wearing uniformly neutral clothing (Lucinda Childs and Molissa Fenley) or they wore street clothes (Thrisha Brown) or were nude (Carolee Schneemann). Often the performers were so undefined that they projected an androgenous presence, and the movement was sexual. Instead of psychological interaction of characters, there was abstract interaction such as the contact improvisation of Steve Paxton. Instead of character emotions, there was raw performer energy. Instead of stylised imagistic movement presented in an idealised dream time, everyday movements and tasks were presented in real time and revealed whatever difficulty was actually involved. Instead of working with trained performers, some of these choreographers used non-dancers (Anna Halprin, Deborah Hay). Instead of scenery and theatrical lighting, their dances were presented in bare performance spaces under ordinary lights. Instead of especially composed music, performers sometimes produced their own sound either vocally or through body percussion. As in the work of Merce Cunningham, the music and the movement were sometimes unrelated to each other except for the fact that they shared the same time and space. Instead of insisting on precisely determined moments, the element of chance was acceptable and sometimes intentional. The creative group process was often more democratic than the hierarchical structures which preceded and followed the 1970s.

These choreographers were formalists, not expressionists. Their work was abstract rather than representational. They avoided personal expression, emotive content and themes. The dances were for the sake of movement for structure, they were not metaphors for something in the culture. In this respect certain works of choreographers Yvonne Rainer, Lucinda Childs, Steve Paxton and Molissa Fenley parallel those of minimalist composers such as Philip Glass, Terry Riley and Steve Reich. These choreographers also parallel the work of theatrical formalists such as Robert Wilson, Michael Kirby and Alan Finneran.

The spirit of the 1980s retreated from the austerity of minimalism and by mid decade there was a resurgence of expressionism in painting, theatre and music as well as dance. This new expressionism has two somewhat different tendencies, and both seem related to the pressures and tensions and the perceived violence of the time. One tendency focuses outward to the experience of people in the culture and results in work intended to have an impact on society. The other tendency involves the choreographers looking inward, seeing themselves as microcosms of the culture, and expressing in their work the experience of living in a brutalising society. Although these two tendencies are different, they can exist in the same work.

Sara Shelton Mann and her San Francisco company, Contraband, exemplify the broader view of violence in the culture. Since forming her own company in 1979 an important focus of her work has been to integrate aspects of herself and her environment. It is a struggle against the potential violence which she believes lies within all individuals. Her productions reflect this concern and present both the violence, individual and communal, as well as the hope for healing it. For example, *The (Invisible) War* (1987), created for presentation in indoor performance spaces, was an investigation of personal conflict. Although there are four performers in the work, it was created principally by Mann and Jess Curtis and explores the relationship of 'the couple' – the passion, the tenderness, the viciousness, and the comic.

A recent site-specific work is more elaborate and is concerned with more complex social issues of violence. *Religare* was originally created in 1986 for presentation in a giant hole in the earth left when arson destroyed a low-income residential hotel and killed twenty-five people. The performance involved the nucleus of dancers from Contraband as well as visual designer Lauren Elder, composer Rinde Eckert, several painters and scored of people from the area who participated in the celebratory event. The production, described in the programme as 'a ritual of raucous dancing which seeks meaning in the ruins of modern life', was presented at night and lighted by paper lanterns and bonfires. The theme of the work is suggested by its various subtitles: *Binding Back to Source, Hope of the Impossible, Wounds That Heal*. As Mann studied the site she began to think about the meaning of home, the meaning of source.

> There was a wound in the center of the Mission District. We wanted to go in and meditate, we wanted to reclaim energy from below that wound and pull it up through the earth and create some kind of a ritual there. Then these other issues came up. We had to deal with discarded dirty diapers and used hypodermic needles, and we had to deal with the gentrification was that was going on in the area. As the process went on we began to feel we were survivors of a war and we could only remember fragments of who we were. We performed these broken memories of our past lives trying to put them back together so they would mean something. So the piece is simultaneously in the past, in the future, and in the present.
>
> (Mann, 1989)

In 1989, with the help of some eighty community participants, *Religare* was reincarnated in the midst of an urban ghost town in a desolate ghetto area of San Francisco. The high-rise apartment buildings surrounding the performance site have been abandoned, the doors and windows have been removed to make them uninhabitable. Contraband and their community volunteers attempted to reclaim the derelict buildings aesthetically. In addition to the performance they made paintings, graffiti, sculptures and music. Pieces of furniture were hung on the sides of the buildings. In front of the main building a large area of sand was carefully raked into a pattern. It is here that most of the dance performance took place.

The performance begins at dusk when the spectators arrive and observe the site from the raised parking lot area. They have a view of the derelict buildings, the sculptures and the performers who have arranged themselves in a circle and are singing non-verbal songs. Then the spectators are admitted into the space to walk among the sculptures and watch several mini-performances, which are taking place simultaneously. A woman with a painted red face, who calls herself the 'cleaning lady of the world', stands beside a house she has made from discarded aluminium cans. She nails more cans to the building as she says, over and over, 'Six and a half pounds buys a bottle of Ripple [wine]'. A nearly naked man stands shivering and suggests, 'We better all huddle together; this place is scary'. A woman in white does acrobatics at the top of a fire escape ladder on the roof of one of the buildings. A group of three sculpted figures, lighted from within, looks out of a second story window. As night approaches groups of performers begin to dance and sing, making non-verbal vocal sounds. As it becomes darker, spotlights on top of the buildings light the performers in the sand area and the performance has a single focus.

The performers (approximately twenty-five) are now costumed in off-white muslin and gauze. Each is unique, however. One woman wears a dress with corset over it and a bulge in her crotch. The programme says 's/he doesn't know who s/he is'. Others sometimes put on black shirt-dresses over their basic costumes.

The narrative, actually more of a theme, has to do with combat, violence, death and rebirth. It is as if they are a group of aborigines from a pre-language time in the past. Mann, identified in the programme as 'a witch from the south', dances with a blown-out black umbrella. There are battles between two women and then two men. One of the men is killed and the performers create a funeral dirge and carry the body to another area where a ritual is performed. At the end of the performance the performers and spectators form a large circle around a conical wire sculpture which is set on fire. They hold hands and sing together.

Instruments used in the performance include wailing cow horns and seaweed horns, metal barrels with cello-like necks and strings which are hit with sticks, and other home-made instruments. Often the percussion consists of hitting sticks against the concrete walls or metal pipes. There are a few conventional instruments, including a tuba, which are used unconventionally to make sounds suggestive of those that might have been made by an ancient tribe. The company has blurred the distinction between singing and dancing – at least in their own minds. Jess Curtis says the vibration of vocal cords is just the movement of a part of the body. 'The understanding of resonance and vibration is one of the things we're working on. It is less and less clear what is singing and what is dancing' (Mann, 1989).

Mann has developed her own unique concepts for employing language, song and expressive movement to create performances which are metaphors for our violent culture. But her work also expresses her hope for a spiritual healing. Mann performs in all of her productions and directs the collaboration of Contraband dancer/actors, designers, composers and volunteers from the community.

Like Contraband, the Joe Goode Performance Group creates large site-specific works as well as more intimate indoor performances. Goode's intimate productions, like those of Mann, tend to be focused on personal relationships. Joe Goode studied with Merce Cunningham, Viola Farber and Finis Jhung and performed off Broadway before moving to San Francisco and becoming a member of the Margaret Jenkins Dance Company in 1979. With Jenkins, he says, he 'learned to explore what happens when the interior is made exterior, and big feelings and emotions are turned into gestural reality onstage' (Goode, 1989, p. 48). In 1980 he began making pieces on his own. Goode says that he thinks of himself as a fairly angry person and that much of his work 'is generated from having that anger and having to process it' (Goode, p. 50).

The Disaster Series (1989) consists of several short pieces related by the theme of unexpected but imminent natural disaster or personal catastrophe. The unforeseen events often express anguish, sometimes humour, and frequently reveal an ironic perspective. The thematically coherent short segments of ten to fifteen minutes are linked together by Joe Goode's solo bits in which he is knocked around by an imaginary force, perhaps a hurricane or an earthquake. The performance style is raw energy and often involves violent movement. The performers throw themselves against the walls and the floor and their bruises are evident. Life is hard, punishing; the anguish of it is nearly impossible to endure, but life goes on.

In 'Disaster Number One' Joe Goode performs solo. Wearing a hat, white turtleneck shirt and pants he stands behind a table which holds a ceramic sculpture of a tiny house on a hillside. 'Anything can happen', he says, and this refrain is repeated often as he narrates events in which unexpected disasters occur. Many of these events refer to his own family. 'Like my mother who saved all her life for a sewing machine so she could take on jobs.' Goode takes a watering can from under the table and pours water on the house and hillside as he tells us that a flood came and washed everything away including the Singer sewing machine. 'Too big. Too many feelings. Inappropriate.' This is another repeated refrain. 'Like my mother', he says, 'you can have a singing career with one lung and run backstage between numbers to suck on the oxygen machine'.

In another segment a woman stands on a stool in a solitary spotlight attempting to find sufficient will to jump. She tried to talk herself into it as the most desirable alternative. 'It's an option', she says. Four other performers in the background, wearing black, dance blindfolded.

Near the end of the performance Goode makes an entrance through the audience, bellowing in anguish. Once on stage he says, 'You can be a real princess with hair like Alice in Wonderland'. 'The boundaries between what's you and what isn't can begin to blur.' He takes a tiny house from his pocket and holds it in his hand as he pours water from a watering can on it and says, 'You can watch the big wave coming'.

Throughout the performance potential sentiment is undercut with irony and the physical punishment of the movement. If grace or beauty is suggested, it is mocked. But the performance is more than a metaphor for a brutal world, the actual performance itself has a brutal impact on the performers. Here is genuine commitment to an art; it requires the performers not only to give their skills and mental concentration, but to risk their bodies as well.

Martha Clarke, like Goode and Mann, aims to create forms that express her experience in the world. Clarke has the ironic perspective of Goode; she is able to look inward and outward at the same time, or at least alternatingly, and she is often amused by what she sees. However, unlike Goode, her amusement is not so tinged with bitterness.

In contrast with the post-modern formalists such as Lucinda Childs, Clarke uses all appropriate means to imbue her works with emotive content and create performances that are metaphors for our culture. Music is specially composed for each of her productions, and she uses scenery, lighting, costumes, character, narrative and even language. Although movement is important in all of her work, Clarke likes to explore new areas. She says that she has always been drawn to theatre and film and thinks of Ingmar Bergman and Fellini as choreographers. Her work, she says, 'comes out of emotions, motions from emotions' (Clarke, 1987c, 1988c; unless otherwise noted all quotations and paraphrases of Martha Clarke are from the author's interview and conversation cited under these two sources). It 'comes out of my own life and out of my own gut'. In addition to working with well-trained dancers, composers and visual designers, she has worked with artists not normally associated with dance – actors, opera singers and writers.

In the early 1960s, at the age of fifteen, when she was at the American Dance Festival, Clarke saw the work of modern dancer Anna Sokolow for the first time. Works such as *Rooms* and *Dreams* had such an impact on Clarke that she believes their 'emotional expressionism' has been the impetus for everything she has done since then. She studied dance at Juilliard and when she graduated in 1965 she joined Sokolow's company. Two years later she quit dancing, went to Italy, had a baby and moved to Connecticut where she still has a farm. In 1971 she joined Pilobolus Dance Theatre in New Hampshire. After seven years with Pilobolus (1972–8) she formed Crowsnest with French dancer Felix Blaska, who still dances in some of Clarke's productions. Her interest in theatre and acting was heightened when she directed three pieces with actor Linda Hunt between 1977 and 1982. One of these, *Elizabeth Dead* (1980), was Clarke's first experience directing a production with text. Another, *A Metamorphosis in Miniature* (1982), based on the Kafka story, won Clarke her first Obie. It was produced by the Music-Theatre Group where the producing director, Lyn Austin, has nurtured the work of many experimental artists. Austin became one of the producers of the next three works by Clarke.

The Garden of Earthly Delights (1984) was the first of the four major works for which Martha Clarke is best known. While she does not consider the work exactly dance, like the work of her mentor Anna Sokolow it could only be done by dancers. The first half of the new piece was a final gesture to the athletically demanding gymnastic work of Pilobolus.

Beginning with *The Garden of Earthly Delights*, the subject matter of Clarke's productions has been Heaven to Hell, a reflection, she says, of extremes in her own life:

> Each piece is really about the same thing – it's about innocence to decadence, rises and falls, humanity and cruelty, love and hate, laughter and tears. They're all the same piece, just in different clothes.

The inceptive ideas for her works are nearly always visual and she always has a painter in mind. *The Garden of Earthly Delights* used the fifteenth-century triptych of the same name by Hieronymous Bosch as more than an inspiration; it became a source of many images and provided the broad overall structure of four sections: Eden, The Garden, The Seven Sins and Hell.

Clarke brought together six dancers, most of whom she knew from Crowsnest or Pilobolus, and three musicians. For the next two months they improvised images and movement. While some images may have started out as literal borrowings from the painting, the final result was from their own intuitions as stimulated by the painting. During the rehearsals notes and drawings were made so as to remember the raw material being developed. Clarke danced in the original version of the piece, so during these rehearsals she had a dual function. Richard Peaslee was brought in as composer. He would watch the dancers and listen to the musicians improvise and them respond with what eventually accumulated into a score. Finally, the material that had been invented was screened for its usefulness in the work and a structure was created.

The left panel of the painting presents a surreal Garden of Eden. Adam and Eve sit and kneel, naked, on either side of Christ. In the foreground are birds and small animals which at first seem peaceful, but a closer look reveals that they are eating one another. In a small pool a winged fish is about to fly. The apple tree is nearby. In the background larger animals feed and drink from a small lake. This panel served as primary inspiration for 'Eden' which is the first section of Clarke's *The Garden of Earthly Delights*.

From the beginning of the 55-minute performance there is fog in the air so the beams from the spotlights are visible. It is the time of creation as described in *The Book of Genesis* and transformed through the imaginations of Bosch and Clarke. The performers wear skin-tight flesh-coloured body stockings and at times add costume pieces. They appear to be in a void which is created by a black surround. The musicians, playing cello, woodwinds and percussion, are visible upstage and sometimes participate in the action. The first sound is a musical bellow suggesting some giant creature – perhaps the elephant from the Bosch painting. A man enters with a tree in each hand, bare of leaves. Six performers enter, walking on hands and feet like graceful gazelles. Two of the animals copulate lovingly. Eve, who has extraordinarily long hair like the Eve in the painting, dances sensually with Adam as they explore each other. Two cherubs fly in, briefly look down on the loving pair, and fly off. A two-person serpent produces an apple from its crotch which suggests both a vagina and the mouth of a serpent. The human couple taste the apple and then make love as the tree turns away in embarrassment. Adam and Eve exit, expelled from Eden, hunched over from the weight of their sin.

The next two sections of the dance – 'The Garden' and 'The Seven Sins' – were inspired by the central panel of the triptych, which depicts some of the earthly delights. The world is now populated with many naked human beings; the animals have multiplied and many are being ridden by the humans. In the performance a woman reclines on the lap of a man as he plays a glockenspiel which rests on her bosom, an image suggesting he is playing with her breasts. Another man and woman lie entwined as he plays a reclining cello. There are images of the water world. Three men roll on the floor as if they were logs in a lake while women balance on them with the help of sticks. A man transforms into a boat with a woman punter. Two women row an imaginary boat. A woman flies above, fluttering her feet like the tail of a fish. Men lying on their bellies swim/fly carrying women

on their backs, then they gradually transform into upright earth
creatures. Women beat the floor with tree branches and then use
them to send semaphore signals. A man wearing wooden clogs
enters ringing a bell. He is controlled by two others holding a long
stick attached to his neck. Six figures put on tunics and hoods like
Brueghel peasants. One of these men urinates in a metal pan. A
pile of potatoes is dumped on the floor. A glutton, with this head
in a bucket, sleeps and snores; he awakens and vomits into the
bucket; then he 'eats' one potato after another as his tunic bulges.
He farts loudly with the aid of a musical instrument. Potatoes fall
from under a peasant woman's skirt like turds. A man makes love
to a woman; another woman, in a fit of jealousy, cuts the throat of
the first. In sharp contrast to these crude activities, the performers
dance a minuet.

'Hell', the final section of Clarke's piece, relates to the right
panel of the painting which shows the torments of the damned
as fantasised by Bosch. Among other torments several figures
have been skewered with swords or arrows and two figures
are being tortured on a giant musical instrument. This section
of the performance begins with a woman being hoisted above
the stage with a pulley and rope; soon she is lowered upside
down. A man, suspended from a rope, twirls and twirls, upside
down and right side up. A bass drum is placed on top of a
reclining man and is thumped as if the man were being beaten.
Two figures fly out over the audience and others are suspended
over the stage. Two women ride on the backs of men. A man
playing a glockenspiel is set upon by two others who beat the
instrument with hammers until it is destroyed. Chaos is taking
over as musicians beat instruments. As a cellist plays, a woman
tries to get his attention. She finally takes the bow from him.
Silence. She lies on her back, legs spread to him. He places the
spike of the cello on her chest and skewers her. By now the stage
is littered with potatoes, musical instruments and other props. A
man enters using two sticks as canes and all exit. The final image
is of the long-haired woman, alone, flying above.

The performance uses no words, but there is a narrative which
is basically that of the Bosch painting. It is the mythological story
of humankind beginning with creation and continuing through
the expulsion from Eden, the sinful enjoyment of earthly delights,
and ending in the punishment of hell. The feeling is elaborately
sensual and joyous; the tortures of the damned are never quite

serious. The movement at times is gymnastic, but mostly one is held by the images, which often involve flying or the interaction of human figures engaged in sex, brutality or subjugation. The sins depicted are more in a spirit of innocence than sinfulness; and the experience is often sensually satisfying or grotesquely funny. The flying performers and the playful score of Richard Peaslee add greatly to the sense of fantasy and the buoyant spirit of the work.

Clarke's next work, *Vienna: Lusthaus* (1986), again made use of paintings, but not so exclusively as *The Garden of Earthly Delights*. The new work was greatly influenced by the social atmosphere of Vienna at the turn of the century. While the earlier work, like *Vienna: Lusthaus*, incorporated psychological interactions between characters, the social ambience projected was based on Christian mythology rather than social history. 'The Seven Sins' section did have the performers dressed in medieval costumes, but the attempt was not really to deal with medieval society. The costumes for *Vienna: Lusthaus* more precisely suggested the period in which the production was set. Often these costumes were white under-garments and at times the performers were nude. Both the set and costumes were designed by Robert Israel whom Clarke has some to consider her closest collaborator.

The Garden of Earthly Delights made use of some strenuous gym-nastic movement of the sort that was the staple of Pilobolus. In *Vienna: Lusthaus*, although most of the performers were technically proficient dancers, such athleticism was not required. As a result Clarke was able to blend dancers, actors and musicians so that the spectator cannot identify their particular skills ('Symposium', 1988).

Another major difference between these two works is that *The Garden of Earthly Delights* used no language while *Vienna: Lusthaus* had a text that accompanied the movement images throughout but did not have a realistic connection with them. The text, written and compiled by Charles L Mee, Jr, consists primarily of monologues describing dreams which, for the most part, were invented by the writer; but the text also includes borrowings from Freud's *The Interpretation of Dreams*.

The beginning idea for the piece was a touring exhibition of Viennese art from the turn of the century called *Dream and Reality* which Clarke had seen a couple of years earlier. Originally she planned to do a historical Vienna, a Vienna with waltzes and the assassination of Archduke Ferdinand, but 'the piece rejected waltzes, it rejected reality, it rejected historical details, and it became about dreams and the subconscious' (Bartow, 1988, p. 56). What was left of the waltz idea was a section in which the performers mimed skating to a silent Strauss waltz. Nonetheless Peaslee's music at times echoed the music of Strauss with six musicians playing harp, violin, cello, woodwinds and French horn.

Most of the physical images in *Vienna: Lusthaus* are intentionally ambiguous but sexually evocative in their suggestion of dreams, the boudoir, death, horses, soldiers. Although the predominant subjects reflected in the text and in the movement images are sexuality and death, these are seen through the mist of grace and gentility. The distancing of raw flesh and the harshness of death is accomplished not only be the physical grace of the performers, the past-tense dream narrative of the text, and the music borrowed in part from Johann Sebastian Bach and Johann Strauss, but also by Robert Israel's set. Although the bare walls are clinical white, they tilt expressionistically and the entire performance is seen through a white scrim which creates a kind of impressionistic fog. Despite the distancing, Clarke insisted on strong contrasts and mentions her agreement with certain aesthetic principles of the novelist Milan Kundera: harsh juxtaposition instead of transitions, repetition instead of variation, and heading straight for the heart of things.

For *Vienna: Lusthaus* Clarke assembled a larger company than was used for the previous production. Eleven dancer/actors were involved and six musicians. Clarke did not perform. Working in much the same way as before, the group improvised approximately 100 movement–image fragments, which were then winnowed down to 44.

At the beginning of the 65-minute performance a waltz is heard, but the performers are not dancing; they are walking and talking indistinctly. A man sits on stage playing a French horn as a woman circles around him moving in imitation of a horse and making clopping sounds. Two fully clothed women (one dressed as a man) dance to harp music and then undress down to chemises and corsets.

The text is spoken by the characters on stage as if they were dreaming aloud. A young man in a cafe tells of attending a performance of *Fidelio* with Leonard when 'all of a sudden, without any warning at all, Leonard flew through the air across the seats, put his hand in my mouth, and pulled out two of my teeth' (Mee and Smith, 1987, p. 45).

Six women are alone in the boudoir wearing chemises. One of the women describes a dream or an imagined experience she had in India. She was fondling a horse, she says. There was a blond boy on the horse and soon she was fondling him:

> And then he came down from the horse and kissed my quim.
> And I was very glad.
> And so we danced.
> And I saw that he was very strong, and hard as a rock.
> His penis was small, but very firm and round and powerful, and I loved it.
> And I was ready to have him come inside me.
> But he didn't.
> I thought: perhaps this is the way it is in India.
> Penetration is not important.
> And I felt like a barbarian, expecting entry when he had something more civilized in mind.
>
> (Mee and Smith, p. 47)

At the end of the story the speaker kisses another woman long on the mouth. The projection of faint clouds are seen on the back wall.

A man and woman entwined in a love-making position roll across the stage in slow motion. Two nude women sit with their backs to the audience and move sensually. An old woman quietly sings a song in German while holding a large butcher knife.

A young woman tells the same dream heard earlier about how Leonard flew across the opera house seats and pulled out two teeth. As she speaks a young man repeats the phrases out of sync. The woman continues, telling of meeting a little girl on the stairs and 'copulating with her. . . . Well, not copulating really; in fact, I was only rubbing my genitals against her genitals' (Mee and Smith, p. 52). By this point the young man is ahead of the woman in relating the story. He sees her and runs off.

A man puts shoes on his hands and through various Pilobolus-like contortions creates the suggestion that he is two people making love to each other.

As snow falls the performers mime skating to a waltz and four young men in military uniforms throw their large shadows on the back wall. One slaps another. In abstract movements they convey the idea of a challenge. Two of the soldiers march about, then fall to the ground, their feet still marching in the air.

A middle-aged man tells of returning home to find a giant rat which looked him straight in the eye and refused to be frightened away. The man tried to choke it, but it wouldn't die. A young woman hugs and kisses a dead soldier, shakes him and hits his head against the floor perhaps in an attempt to bring him back to life.

The performance ends with the dead soldier asking the middle-aged man what colours the body passed through after death. The man answers, 'Light pink, red, light blue, dark blue, purple-red' (Mee and Smith, p. 58).

As in *The Garden of Earthly Delights*, *Vienna: Lusthaus* moves from harmony to discord. While the work reflects Clarke's subconscious unhappiness, she also believes it is very much a product of the people's lives who work with her. 'The individual parts', she says, 'were in a way tailored out of their personalities' (Bartow, p. 17).

Although she found Charles Mee's text to be beautiful, it took her a long time to discover how to use it. She had worked with text before on shorter pieces, but for *Vienna: Lusthaus* it was almost like starting from the beginning as she explored ways to use text together with her movement and images. The short narratives were all monologues even though in a couple of instances she had two performers speaking them together out of sync. Usually these monologues accompanied the movement images with evocative, rather than direct, relationships between the text and what the performers were doing. The success of *Vienna*, which is her favourite piece as a whole, apparently gave her the confidence to use text even more extensively in her next work. The material for *The Hunger Artist* (1987) is from several writings of Franz Kafka – 'The Country Doctor', 'Letters to My Father', 'The Metamorphosis', 'A Hunger Artist' – as well as diary entries and letters to, from and about the author. These writings were adapted for the production by Richard Greenberg. Given Clarke's expressionist interests, Kafka was a natural source for her. As she had done previously, she also looked at paintings – in this instance the paintings of Chagall and Goya – and she studied photographs of the period. She also studied the work of her favourite film-maker, Fellini, giving special attention to his film *8 1/2*.

The theme of *The Hunger Artist* concerns emotional and physical starvation. In the story that gave its title to Clarke's piece, a man starves himself to death; and in 'Metamorphosis' Gregor, the young man who turns into an insect, is not fed by his family. Clarke says that Kafka, in his personal life, was emotionally starved – especially in his relationship with his father, but also because he denied his appetite for marriage and a well-balanced life (Gussow, 1987).

The first step in developing *The Hunger Artist* was the set design. Robert Israel conceived a set with two parts. The rear part had been suggested by a 1910 postcard photograph that Clarke had sent to Israel. It shows four girls playing handball against two walls. This became the corner of a room with expressionistic out-of-kilter walls, a ceiling, one small window, a rocking horse and a piano stool. The part nearest the audience was like a room-sized sand-box filled with earth. In this part, standing upright in the earth, was a smaller-than-usual functioning door and frame; there were also furniture pieces and in the middle was a pit resembling a grave.

The relationship of text to characters and movement was more literal than in *Vienna*. The text was used somewhat in the typical mode of story theatre. Performers spoke the first-person segments as the characters they were playing at the moment, while the third-person narration was spoken by actor Brenda Currin. The dancer Paola Styron did not speak, but played many of the women in the stories and in Kafka's life. The actor Anthony Holland, the dancer Robert Besserer, and the child David Jon played some of the fictional characters as well as aspects of Kafka. The two musicians, Jill Jaffe and Bill Ruyle, also entered the action.

At the beginning a folk song in Czech is heard; as the lights come up a young man, wearing a checkered three-piece suit, and a young woman are sitting on the ground with their feet in the grave-like pit as white fog rises from it. She narrates the story of 'A Country Doctor' who is played by the man. The Doctor is on his way to the bedside of a dying boy. As the story continues another man and woman enact a scene back at the doctor's house. The doctor's maid is bent over a chair and raped. In the 'Metamorphosis' section Gregor's sister narrates the story; then it is acted out by the men. The last section, 'The Hunger Artist', is in the spirit of a dark carnival with illusionist tricks, performed by Besserer who creates fire in the air and turns eggs into live white mice. In the final moments the performers go to the pit where the artist lies dead. The five huddle together as one of them tells with pleasure of the food he was served in the sanitarium.

In retrospect Clarke thinks *The Hunger Artist* 'had some of the most successful and least successful' moments of all her works. 'The first ten minutes . . . really married song, movement, and text', but the 'Metamorphosis' section 'just didn't work'. She has some to believe that she was to literally tied to the Kafka stories. When there is so much text one is inclined to let it become background sound so as to focus more keenly on the flow of imagery.

In her next production, *Miracolo d'Amore* (1988), Clarke did not use language. At the outset she had expected to work with a writer, but she kept delaying decision because she wanted 'to work on the imagery and the style of movement first'. But then, at one of the rehearsals she asked a performer to scream for her. 'It was so horrifying', she says, 'and so much larger than words in resonance' that words would 'intellectualise and diminish this very strong emotion'. So Clarke decided not to use language and substituted gibberish and non-verbal vocal sounds created by the performers – 'visceral–emotional' material such as laughing, crying, snoring, snorting like pigs and honking like geese. In deciding to put vocal and physical imagery first she was attempting to reinforce the direct expression of feeling without the more conceptual process which is inevitable with words.

Initial sources for *Miracolo d'Amore* were fairy-tales – first those of the Grimm brothers and then the Italian tales of Italo Calvino – but in rehearsal Clarke kept resisting the written stories and the group started inventing their own. 'The narrative of motion', she says, 'is much more abstract than having to follow the literal story telling'.

The most important sources were the eighteenth-century hunchback Punchinello drawings of the Venetian, Domenico Tiepolo, and *The Court of Flora* drawings of the nineteenth-century French illustrator J J Grandville. These sources served as inspiration for improvisations and costumes. The men in *Miracolo* were modelled after the Punchinellos with the humpbacks, tall tapered white hats, scalloped collars and loose-fitting white tunics and trousers. The women were sometimes nude and at other times wore costumes suggested by the Grandville drawings of women dressed as various flowers. The works of both artists also had an impact on the spirit of Clarke's production.

The music was composed by Richard Peaslee, but this time, much of it was vocal. The composer began by looking at the madrigals of the Italian Renaissance composer Claudio Monteverdi who had used some of Petrarch's lyrics including 'Miracolo d'Amore'. These songs are concerned predominantly with love and rejection, which was the theme taking shape in Clarke's rehearsals. Peaslee began work on the music six or seven months before opening. A couple of times a week he would come in with choral pieces and the performers would sing them. The work was developing on two tracks – the movement and the vocal music; later the two were put together in a process that Clarke calls 'mixing and matching'. At that point Peaslee would see what else was needed and would write new material, often responding directly to what the performers were doing. For example, in one section of the work a suggestion of Egypt is created with a palm tree and a woman riding on the back of a camel (a man on all fours). When Peaslee saw this, he wrote mock-opera music with an exotic Eastern flavour to accompany the image (Peaslee, 1988).

Miracolo d'Amore uses fifteen performers, most of them combining at least two of the required skills of dancing, singing, acting and playing musical intruments. The coloratura plays cello, the mezzo is also a violinist as is one of the counter-tenors, and another counter-tenor sings baritone and tenor as well as playing flute, recorder and percussion. As in *Vienna: Lusthaus* all of the performers are integrated in such a way that the special skill of each is largely indistinguishable. Everyone in *Miracolo* is costumed and everyone sings and moves.

Images discovered in rehearsal were linked together as the premiere approached and were staged in Robert Israel's set which resembled an Italian Renaissance courtyard with canted brick-red walls, alcoves and open doorways. The piece has no overall narrative, but is a series of narrative moments unified by the theme of love. The images often involve violent, forced love-making and strong contrasts of mood. Punchinellos forciby kiss and rape the women and even each other. A nude woman and skeleton are seen in a raised window. The woman manipulates the skeleton so it seems to be making love to her. A hand of the skeleton caresses the woman's hair and breasts, and the woman kisses the skeleton on the mouth. At another time a woman in the window seems to have four arms (another woman is standing behind her). One pair of arms echoes the other as the woman gestures and blows her nose. A woman on the floor laughs hysterically as she is sodomised by a skeleton (manipulated by the woman); and then the other performers stand in a doorway and sing 'Miracolo d'Amore'. Two women compete for the attention of a Punchinello. One bares her breasts, the other does likewise. The second woman starts giggling manically and the first stops her by pinching her nipples. A woman carries on a skeleton and lies down with it. Four Punchinellos enter and rape her against the wall. She falls on the floor sobbing. One of the Punchinellos comforts her and carries her off. The four-armed woman brushes her hair with two hands and holds a mirror with another. One Punchinello violently tickles another. A Punchinello sobs as he is raped by a skeleton.

The work has a broad emotional range with layers of sharply contrasted feelings and images. Music and sound often contrast harshly with visual images, sometimes as ironic counterpoint and sometimes creating sudden shifts of mood. Following the rape of a woman by a skeleton, the sweet song 'Miracolo d'Amore' is sung; and then a man, nearly nude, is seen in an image of Christ on the cross, but the scene turns funny when he is fed a bowl of spaghetti. Two Punchinellos enter with rifles and aim at geese flying overhead while making the sound of the geese themselves. At the very end of the performance a woman in the raised window with the skeleton waves her companion's bony hand toward the audience and in a sweet voice says, 'Ciao'.

Since *Vienna: Lusthaus* Clarke's process for developing a piece has been much the same. Before beginning work with the performers on *Miracolo* her research involved reading and looking at paintings. In April 1987 she visited Venice, and when she met with Robert Israel in May she had a book full of notes and drawings. Clarke and Israel made a list of materials and sources that they thought might be useful: 'Marionettes, painting, ladder to the sky, geometric shapes, white ducks, wicker baskets, prosthetic noses, Grandville, flower detail, removable vases, 1840s ballet skirt, bed sheets, tree, table, fruit, roof, Seurat clowns, dead fish, women to be naked'.

Rehearsals for *Miracolo d'Amore* began in October, with a nucleus of seven performers, and opened late the following May. From nearly the first rehearsal the men were dressed as Punchinellos with their humps as it was important for Clarke to see them in costume:

The process is really improvisational. Sometimes it's structured, sometimes it's an image from a painting. I was looking at Goya's 'Destructions of War' and there was a little girl with her mouth open and arms outstretched. One of the women is doing a solo based on that. . . . So I have them improvise for me and then when I catch something, I begin to mold it.

Clarke also discovers images and movements when performers are caught off guard:

I'll see someone combing their hair and I'll say, 'That's a great angle'. Just yesterday John Kelly was stretching and he looked exactly like a crucifix, so Rob [Besserer] took most of his clothes off and went behind the cross and hung from the back like a Jesus figure and it became a very strange insidious thing.

She puts down in words and drawings everything that might be useful. On a good day this might amount to four pages. After developing raw material, she begins to make clusters. For example, she says, 'I'll put the religious imagery together, but I may recap it. I'll either introduce it early and then do a section of it later or I'll do a big section and then recap it later'. The final stage is shaping it for performance, combining it with the music and set:

I go into a kind of trance the last two or three weeks when putting it together. . . . I intuit my way through the quilting of the piece. . . . It's through association. . . . One image will make you think of another. I never know exactly what they mean.

In the final stages all of the collaborating artists are there – Robert Israel, Richard Peaslee and lighting designer Paul Gallo. Visually the process is very collaborative, but Clarke has the final decision on everything. Much of the work done during the development phase is thrown out. This is true of her own choreographic images as well as the work of her designers. It is not uncommon for more than half of the movement–image fragments developed in rehearsal to be discarded. For *The Garden of Earthly Delights* an entire set designed by Jun Maeda was built and then eliminated when Clarke found she didn't know how to use it (Bartow, p. 55).

Clarke says her recent works are like dreams. *Miracolo* is a 'fractured nightmare'. Some of it is 'legible' and some of it is left to the viewer. However, her aesthetic is not that of Merce Cunningham, for example, who considers any meaning correct.

The work of Clarke, Goode and Mann has more in common with contemporary European expressionism than with the predominant direction American avant-garde dance has taken in the last two decades. The work of these American choreographers, in their use of narrative, character, imagistic movement (which often express psychological states), and the implicit conflict and violence, suggests the work of the Germans Pina Bausch, Reinhild Hoffmann and Susanne Linke as well as that of certain French and Belgian choreographers. While the American tendency set off by Cunningham, and reinforced in some respects by the Judson group, focused on movement for its own sake, these Europeans are interested in emotion. Pina Bausch says she is 'not so much interested in how people move as what moves them'. Her pieces grow from the inside outwards (Bausch, 1984). Similarly, Clarke says her work comes out of her own emotional life.

While the realism in Bausch's work may relate more directly to the work of Joe Goode than to Martha Clarke or Sara Shelton Mann, all three of these choreographers are concerned with emotion and the expression of it in their dances. They deal with love and rejection, with fear, loneliness and sometimes joy. They express anger, brutality, conflict (especially between the sexes) and gentleness. These three choreographers and a few others are the vanguard of new American expressionism which seems on its way to becoming the dominant style of dance in the 1990s.

BIBLIOGRAPHY

Banes, S. (1987) *Terpsichore in Sneakers: Post-Modern Dance* (Middletown, Conn.: Wesleyan University Press). An excellent discussion of the development of postmodern dance.

Bartow, A. (1988) 'An Interview with Martha Clarke', *American Theatre* June, pp. 13–17, 55–7. The interview has also been published in Bartow, *The Director's Voice: Twenty-One Interviews* (New York: Theatre Communications, 1988).

Bausch, P. (1984) *Pina Bausch–Wuppertal Dance Theater; or The Art of Training a Goldfish*, Patricia Stadié (trans.) (Köln: Ballett-Bühnen-Verlag).

Chopra, J. (1981) *Martha Clarke Light and Dark*, a film in collaboration with Martha Clarke, broadcast by PBS (Martha Clarke is shown developing dances in her studio for her company Crowsnest).

Clarke, M. (1986) *Vienna: Lusthaus*, performances seen in the Newman Theatre, The Public Theatre, New York, 21 June (also at the Kennedy Center Eisenhower Theare, Washington, DC, 16 Sep.).

———. (1987a) *The Hunger Artist*, performance seen at St Clements Episcopal Church, New York, 19 March.

———. (1987b) *The Garden of Earthly Delights*, video tape of a performance, 11 Dec.

———. (1987c) A taped interview with Theodore Shank, 19 Dec.

———. (1988a) *The Garden of Earthly Delights*, performances seen at Seattle Repertory Theatre, 15, 16 Jan.

———. (1988b) *Miracolo d'Amore*, performances seen in the Newman Theatre, The Public Theatre, New York, 23, 26 June.

———. (1988c) A telephone conversation with Theodore Shank, 28 June.

Contraband (1989a) *The (Invisible) War*, performance seen at Theatre Artaud, San Francisco, 19 Feb.

———. (1989b) *Religare*, a site-specific performance seen at a site in a desolate area of San Francisco, 5 May.

Curtis, J. (1989) A conversation with Theodore Shank, 5 May.

Goode, J. (1989) *Disaster Series*, performance seen at Sushi Performance Gallery, San Diego, 20 May.

———. (n.d.) *Speak for Me*, a video tape of the performance.

Gussow, M. (1987) 'Clarke Work', *The New York Times* magazine, 18 Jan.

Israel, R. (1988) Conversations with Theodore Shank, 20 June, 10 July.

Kreemer, C. (1987) *Further Steps: Fifteen Choreographers on Modern Dance* (New York: Harper & Row).

Mann, S. S., and Curtis, J. (1989) A taped interview with Theodore Shank, 16 March.

Mee, C. L., Jr and Smith, A. (1987) 'Martha Clarke's *Vienna: Lusthaus*; Play Text and Photo Essay', *The Drama Review* (T115) 31.3, fall, pp. 42–58.

Peaslee, R. (1988) A telephone interview with Theodore Shank, 28 June.

Ross, J. (1989) 'San Francisco's Joe Goode: Working Hard to Be the Bad Boy of Modern Dance', *Dance Magazine*, Jan., pp. 47–50.

Shank, T. (1982/1988) *American Alternative Theatre* (London: Macmillan Press/New York: St Martin's Press).

———. (1989) *California Performance: Volume One/San Francisco Bay Area* (Claremont, Cal.: Mime Journal).

'Today' session of 'German and American Modern Dance: Yesterday and Today' (1986) A symposium presented at Goethe House, Nov. 1985, *The Drama Review* (T-110) 30.2, summer, pp. 46–56.

12

From C-R to PR: Feminist Theatre in America

ALISA SOLOMON

Early in Wendy Wasserstein's Pulitzer Prize-winning play, *The Heidi Chronicles* (1988), the hero visits a consciousness-raising group in Ann Arbor, Michigan. It's 1970, five years into the chronicle that will follow Heidi to 1988. The scene in an Ann Arbor church basement serves as one of many occasions for Wasserstein to score some comic points off the American women's movement. Wasserstein paints the C-R group as a touchy-feely hugfest where women embrace each other evey couple of seconds, and declare their love. Heidi, who is just visiting, remains critical, outside and unmoved, until she lets loose about an inattentive arrogant boyfriend. 'I hope our daughters never feel like us,' she concludes. 'I hope our daughters feel so fucking worthwhile. Do you promise we can accomplish that much?'

Because of lines like these, and because Heidi is an art historian uncovering forgotten women artists, mainstream critics have called the play feminist. In fact, it is the opposite. For as the years roll by, and Heidi remains tied to the same obnoxious boyfriend (though he has married someone else), she becomes increasingly disappointed in the women's movement for not keeping what she took to be its promises: unhappy and alone, Heidi blames the women's movement – not our tenaciously patriarchal culture – for her failures. And the play suggests that it's the fault of feminism – not men's unwillingness to contribute to childcare, for example – that having both a career and a family remains so difficult.

In addition to the Pulitzer, *The Heidi Chronicles*, which moved to Broadway after a brief run at off Broadway's Playwrights Horizons Theater in December of 1988, also won a Tony Award – among other prizes. For some, this success is a measure not only of the extent to which the play is tuned into these 'post-feminist' times, but also proof of how much has changed in the theatre over the last two decades that a woman could be so valorised. You might say she has benefited from the very movement her play mocks. *The Heidi Chronicles*, at once the culmination of one aspect of the feminist theatre movement and the nemesis of another, provides an instructive lens through which to view the development of feminist theatre in the United States.

As in the women's movement in general, the feminist theatre movement has covered a broad range of interests and approaches, represented by various groups that have often come into conflict over strategies and purpose. Two groups might share absolutely nothing in common other than that they call themselves feminist – and they will even differ on how they define that term. Some might mean that they argue for a complete restructuring of a patriarchal culture, others simply that they value female experience and want to put it at the forefront; some might want to provide a place where a female artist can create freely, unencumbered by the intimidations and conventions of a male-dominated theatre; others want to nurture women and send them out newly forged as able competitors in that male-dominated theatre. And sometimes, groups that take on these same tasks will adamantly oppose being described with the now discredited 'f' word.

As in any sweeping social movement, organisations in the feminist theatre movement formed without following any prescribed pattern, sprang up successfully in their localities without achieving wider recognition, or dissolved without leaving much of a trace. As a result, it is impossible to account for all the work of the feminist theatre movement in the US, and nearly as difficult to generalise about the work that has been recounted. Still, the outlines of an unprecedented theatre movement can be sketched out, even if it can make no claims to being complete.

Broadly speaking, the feminist theatre movement has paralleled the women's movement, fostering groups devoted to creating a tributary through which women could flow into the male-dominated theatrical mainstream (much as one branch of the women's movement concentrated on getting women into executive positions in corporations) and giving rise to others who considered theatre a powerful tool for advancing radical, feminist causes. In other words, some women sought to change the world of theatre while others used theatre to change the world at large – and, of course, there have been numerous groups that have taken aim between these two goals, and even some that have tried to achieve both.

Coming at a time when advertising campaigns herald 'the neo-traditional woman' and recent college graduates plan a conference entitled 'I'm not a feminist, but . . . ', *The Heidi Chronicles* marks what has become acceptable, even marketable, of the women's movement: it refers to feminist ideas without engaging them, and above all, it poses no threat to the established order. (Indeed, the play ends with Heidi finding fulfilment by adopting a baby.) While a few women critics have pointed out how the play participates in the late 1980s backlash against feminism (see, for instance, Laurie Stone's 'The Women's Movement Carried Off My Baby in a Flying Saucer', 1989), none have discussed how the way it has been touted as a culmination of feminist theatre renders invisible and insignificant an entirely different, even opposing, movement in feminist theatre, a movement with its roots, ironically enough, in the consciousness-raising groups that Wasserstein ridicules.

The New Feminist Theater, based in New York City and founded in 1969 – the same year as the Los Angeles Feminist Theater, whose aims and approach belonged to an altogether different trend – was the first spark of an explosion of feminist theatre collectives that would erupt throughout the country over the next several years. The group's statement of purpose was echoed by many to come. The company, it declared, sought to:

> contribute to the liberation of women from centuries of political, social, economic, and, above all, cultural oppression. By this we mean to just "to give women a chance" in the arts, though necessarily, feminist theater will be composed mostly of women, but primarily to give dramatic voice to the new feminist movement.
>
> (dell'Olio, 1970, p. 101)

This radical imperative fueled countless groups that spontaneously burst forth – and then sometimes vanished just as quickly – in a remarkable proliferation of grassroots activity. This was a theatre of proclamations and manifestos. Few came to life without announcing their noble aims in brochures, flyers or pronouncements from the stage. And though many were convened by women with experience in the theatre – usually the experimental theatre – their ranks were often filled by women without theatrical training. Their works often served a cathartic function – for audiences and performers alike.

By Linda Walsh Jenkins's count (Chinoy and Jenkins, 1987, p. 276), there have been more than 150 feminist groups in the US since the late 1960s, more than 30 of them still active in the 1980s – and that's not counting such already established radical theatre groups as the San Francisco Mime Troupe (1959 to the present), the Caravan Theater (1965–78) and the Omaha Magic Theater (1968 to the present) which were presenting a feminist point of view in plays on a variety of topics. Feminist collectives, though, were usually made up of women only, and many performed for all-women audiences. When Dinah Leavitt writes, in *Feminist Theater Groups*, one of the first works to document such theatres, that though these groups 'are rarely affiliated with any official movement organization, they have absorbed the consciousness of the movement and applied it to their theaters' (1980, p. 93), she misses much of the point: these theatres *were* movement organisations.

Like activists in any political movement who realise that merely handing out flyers doesn't much move people, women have long seized on theatrical techniques to gain attention for their causes, whether in the form of staged dramas – such as the 'bloomers' plays of the suffragettes – or in the form of protest spectacle – as in 1886, during the unveiling of the Statue of Liberty. When women were barred from the festivities celebrating the largest female image in the world, the New York Women's Suffrage Association rented a boat, decorated it with banners, and circled the statue chanting protests. In the 1960s, picketing the Miss America contest and throwing high heels into a garbage can or burning bras, served as histrionic emblems of women's refusal to limit themselves to roles dictated by men.

All such uses of theatrical devices in the service of feminist protest – and there have been too many to count – can be seen as a kind of feminist theatre – and such activity continues today. (In April 1989, a group called No More Nice Girls demonstrated in Washington, DC for abortion rights – along with half a million other protesters – by dressing in pillow-created pregnant bellies, black frocks and chains.) But these guerrilla theatre actions do not add up to a feminist theatre *movement* that develops new organisational and aesthetic forms, forges links among similar groups, and rides the crest of a political wave, as did the feminist theatres that began to emerge in the early 1970s. Such groups exploded onto the scene in response to the gathering momentum of the women's movement – and, just as important, of the burgeoning experimental theatre – and then dwindled as that movement lost ground to the rightward shift of the Reagan era.

In the first, heady days of the women's liberation movement, as it was then known, consciousness-raising groups emerged both as a means of analysis and as a method of organising, spurred, largely, by such groups as New York Radical Women, one of the first in the country. That group, Kathie Sarachild recounts in her 1973 essay 'Consciousness Raising: A Radical Weapon',

> decided to raise its consciousness by studying women's lives by topics like childhood, jobs, motherhood, etc. We'd do any outside reading we wanted to and thought was important. But our starting point for discussion, as well as our test of the accuracy of what any of the books said, would be the actual experience we had in those areas.
>
> (1973, p. 132)

They assumed, she continues,

> that most women were like ourselves – not different – so that our self-interest in discussing the problems facing women which most concerned us would also interest other women. Daring to speak about our own feelings and experiences would be very powerful.
>
> (p. 134)

Indeed, daring to speak was so powerful – not the silliness that Wasserstein portrays – that this format organically engendered a radical feminist theatre that essentially took the process and results of the C-R experience and made it public. Plays were based on women's actual experiences of 'childhood, jobs, motherhood', and so on, and were developed through a C-R procedure of discussion.

As C-R groups gave women a chance to speak about their oppression, discover that they were not alone, and become angry, theatre based on this revelatory procedure sought the same effects on a larger scale. Founded in New York in 1970, the It's All Right to Be A Woman Theater used this technique most sharply, trying, as their leaflets put it, 'to make women feel that the condition of being woman (not individual women, but collective woman) is *all right*' (Rea, 1972, p. 82).

The group's performances were based on the actual experiences of the group's members, experiences that had been revealed through the company's own C-R process. Naturally, then, their plays dealt with subjects that came up in C-R groups all over the country: abortion, women's dependency, motherhood, sex role stereotypes, rape, lesbianism – and these themes were taken up in much of the work being created in the early 1970s.

Not surprisingly, some of the earliest plays produced by feminists were agitprop pieces arguing for legalized abortions, a central battle in the women's movement. (That fight proved victorious with the 1973 Supreme Court decision on *Roe* v.*Wade*, but the decision was partially reversed in July 1989 when the Supreme Court gave individual states certain rights to limit access to abortion; feminist theatres will no doubt be taking on the issue again.) In 1969, one of the plays that would serve as a model of much of the work in the feminist theatre movement was presented by the New Feminist Theater as a benefit for the abortion rights activities of the feminist group, Red Stockings: Myrna Lamb's *But What Have You Done for me Lately?*, using the tried-and-true comic device of reversal as its starting point, followed the trials and tribulations of a man who becomes pregnant and searches desperately for a safe abortion.

As the women's movement revealed and reacted to the astounding frequency of rape in American, theatre groups responded with such plays as the 1971 *Rape-In*, a series of four one-acts by Gwen Gunn, Sally Ordway and Dolores Walker produced by the Westbeth Playwrights' Feminist Collective, a writers' workshop created in 1970 by women living in the same Manhatten apartment complex. Such plays focused on the experience of rape from the survivor's point of view, shocking audiences – and validating the feelings of women spectators – with the sheer commonality of the experience of rape, more than they analysed the social forces that give rise to such common violence.

A year later, the Minneapolis company, Alive and Trucking, presented *Pig in a Blanket*, a collectively created play that combined mime, dance, drama, audience participation and improvisation in what the group wryly subtitled 'A tender, poignant drama about young love'. Most of its disjunctive eighteen scenes about male and female roles were comic: in one, three men and three women careened around like Ken and Barbie dolls, sputtering nonsensical 'masculine' and 'feminine' patter about cars and fashion, respectively. In the middle of the first act, however, the mood changed when one actress, in a highly stylised scene, was gang raped. From there, the play returned to its ironic depictions of schoolgirls, sexuality and Superman.

Perhaps the most sophisticated work to deal with the subject was *Raped: A Woman's Look at Bertholt Brecht's The Exception and the Rule*, the premiere production of Minneapolis's At the Foot of the Mountain theater in 1976. ATFM used actual testimony of women who had been raped as interventions in and ironic comments on the Brecht play. Examining how economic forces permitted such violence against women, the play made room for public testimony by inviting women audience members to yell 'stop' at certain points during the action and tell their own rape stories.

The Circle of the Witch, also based in Minneapolis, took on the issue of rape along with sex-role stereotyping, mother–daughter relationships, and the narrow, male-defined standards of female beauty in their 1974 vaudeville revue, *Sexpot Follies*. Here, institutions such as the nuclear family, government and church were represented as rapists who exploited women.

This form – a series of scenes, monologues and comic romps – served many feminist groups well as satire proved a powerful weapon in battling sexism, misogyny, and in some cases, racism and homophobia, and as a non-linear structure, developed in the experimental theatre, provided room for drawing connections among related problems without having to spell them out in a contrived plot. The New Feminist Theater's *Cabaret of Sexual Politics* used improvisational material to build a collage of funny, critical scenes; Spiderwoman, a company of Native American women, used clown-like characters in wild costumes built of household appliances in their 1975 slapsick play, *Women in Violence*; The New York Feminist Theater Troupe, founded in 1973, relied on humour to engage a number of serious issues in, for example, *But Something Was Wrong with the Princess*, a rolicking composite of circus, slapstick and improvisation that featured such sideshows as Abortion Annie, Birth Control Bonnie, 'Lectric Lizzie (who had survived electric shock treatment) and Wonder Woman – the perfect housewife. Meanwhile, in Atlanta, the Red Dyke Theater, as their very name suggests, took a sharply satirical approach to lesbian invisibility and oppression.

While there were some instances of conventional, naturalistic dramas among these theatre troupes – Circle of the Witch's 1975 work, *Lady in the Corner*, for instance, was a realistic play about a mother and her two daughters – the majority of plays by feminist companies in the 1970s experimented in form as well as content. Like polemical theatre of any period, they used broad, presentational techniques to make their points clearly, but they were also very much influenced, in style and procedure, by the experimental theatre of the 1960s – and many women who worked in feminist theatres cut their dramatic teeth in experimental theatres. These artists formed what could be called a second wave of radical feminist theatres in the mid-1970s, consciously combining a feminist perspective with a radical aesthetic.

Roberta Sklar, co-founder with Sondra Segal and Clare Coss of New York's Women's Experimental Theater in 1976, was an original member of Joseph Chaikin's Open Theater which broke new ground in exploring the relationship of an actor to his/her role and to the audience. Along with its charter of fostering women's culture, WET also sought to develop a feminist actor, one not hemmed in by the stereotypes perpetrated on traditional stages. Drawing from workshops and interviews with hundreds of women, WET's earliest plays looked at the *Oresteia* and asked, 'What happened to the women?' The result was *The Daughters' Cycle Trilogy* (1976–80), a series of three plays about motherhood, relationships between sisters, and domestic violence. A later cycle, *Women's Body and Other Natural Resources* (1980–85), looked at women's relationship to food and their bodies. Again, the group developed the plays through workshops and interviews, using humour, as Sklar has said 'to ameliorate the pain of seeing the experience of women in patriarchy. Our intention was to disturb, to challenge ourselves and other women, and to create good times' (Chinoy and Jenkins, p. 306).

Martha Boesing had already been working with the radical company Firehouse Theater for several years and had already published some dozen plays when she helped form At the Foot of the Mountain in 1974 with three men and two other women. That group folded and the company re-emerged as an all-female troupe in 1976 with the mission, as their brochure put it, of trying to:

> relinquish traditions such as linear plays, proscenium theater, non-participatory ritual, and seek to reveal theater that is circular, intuitive, personal, involving. We are a theater of protest, witnesses to the destructiveness of a society which is alienated from itself, and a theater of celebration, participants in the prophesy of a new world which is emerging through the rebirth of women's consciousness.

Such theatres did not function as a women's auxilliary of the experimental theatre movement; instead, they borrowed and elaborated on techniques of the experimental groups, shaping them to specifically feminist means and ends.

Many feminist theatres, for instance, created plays collectively, using improvisation, Grotowski-inspired physical exercises, theatre games and group discussion, but extended such methods to reflect a feminist interpretation of anti-hierarchical principles. The It's All Right to Be a Woman theater sought 'a theater without separation of roles . . . a theater without a stage to separate audience and players' (Gillespie, in Chinoy and Jenkins, p. 284). Womansong Theatre, in Atlanta, went so far as to omit the names of individual performers from its programmes. Indeed, for a number of such groups, the process of developing a work was deemed far more important than the product. Like many other feminist groups, At the Foot of the Mountain called its work 'process-oriented'.

This position called into question traditional standards by which theatre was commonly judged. Early on, feminist theatre troupes for the most part didn't much care that the mainstream press ignored them. After all, the sanctioning conferred by almost entirely male reviewers in what was considered the 'patriarchal' press was irrelevant to a theatre attacking the very foundations of that patriarchy. According to Patti P Gillespie, between 1969 and 1977, Women's Interart was the only one, of fifteen active feminist theatres in New York, to be reviewed by *The New York Times* or *The Village Voice* (Chinoy and Jenkins, p. 278). Of course the feminist press – women's newspapers sprouted like mushrooms during the early 1970s – covered local theatres, but rarely reviewed them in standard form, preferring, instead, nonjudgemental, descriptive articles that were sometimes based on interviews with performers, sometimes on the reviewer's identification with the play's subject matter.

During this same period, parallel developments in feminist theatre were taking place, rarely converging with the work of these radical collectives. In the experimental theatre, which had opened up old organisational structures, women were seizing artistic opportunities unavailable before. The *auteur*-director who was born in this theatre, not only wrote performance pieces, but often directed, designed and acted in them as well. Along with such artists as Richard Foreman, Lee Breuer and Robert Wilson, this method produced important women as well, among JoAnne Akalaitis of Mabou Mines, Liz LeCompte of the Wooster Group and Meredith Monk of the House.

Women playwrights, meanwhile, were creating organisations to help get their work produced in an environment that rarely noticed them. (Only 7 per cent of the plays produced in New York between 1969 and 1975 were by women, according to a survey by the Action for Women in Theater – see Patti Gillespie's 'Feminist Theater: A Rhetorical Phenomenon' in Chinoy and Jenkins, pp. 278–86.) The Women's Theater Council was formed in 1972, for instance, as a support group for such avant-garde women playwrights as Maria Irene Fornes, Julie Bovasso, Megan Terry, Rochelle Owens and Adrienne Kennedy. Though not all these artists would define themselves as feminist playwrights (Fornes once wrote in *Performing Arts Journal* that she looks forward to a time when 'the gender of the playwright will be the last thing we think of' [Fornes, 1983, p. 90]), the experimental nature of their work distinguished them from another aspect of activity of the time – organisations devoted to redressing the imbalance between men and women in the commercial theatre, to creating affirmative action programmes for women in theatre.

Groups like the Los Angeles Feminist Theater, the Washington (DC) Area Feminist Theater, and New York's Women's Interart and Women's Project were all producing plays by women in an effort to promote their writing, create more roles for actresses, employ women in other fields such as design, stage management and directing, and to encourage economic and social reforms that would put women on equal footing with men in the traditional theatre. As networking organisations that didn't produce plays, the Women in Theater Network and the League of Professional Women in Theater have served similar causes. In some ways, these groups, many of which still exist, have sought their own obsolescence, looking toward a time when their efforts would no longer be necessary. Their stance is moderate, their methods accepting of the organisational and aesthetic structures of the male-dominated traditional theatre. Julia Miles, founder of the Women's Project, has said that her organisation was not based 'on feminist notions' (Dolan, 1986, p. 11).

That these organisations still operate while most of the theatre collectives have vanished reflects the absorption of the women's movement itself into a kind of bourgeois feminism that seeks equality in the boardroom,and rejects the more radical question of why the boardroom should be so valued in the first place. In many respects, the feminist movement in the US remained white and middle class – which is not to discount the efforts and contributions of working-class women, women of colour, and lesbians, many of which still continue in community centres for health, self-defence, shelter from battering, or rape crisis intervention. But as a sweeping movement, feminism in this country failed to align itself with an agenda wider than equal rights, and, in an effort to appeal to mainstream women and to make headway *within* male bastions of power, did not take up the connections between women's oppression and racism, classism, and homophobia.

This is easy to understand given the shape of the left in general in America – unorganised, powerless, divided into a number of fringe factions, widely derided on principle. (Just look, for instance, at how damning it was during the Presidential campaign of 1988 for George Bush to label Democratic candidate Michael Dukakis as a liberal.) There's not been much for the feminist movement to connect with in organisational terms, and this lack, necessarily, is reflected in what has happened to the radical impulses of the feminist theatre movement. Without an active tradition of democratic socialism in the US, for example, its theatre has not produced a tradition of political play-writing like that of Britain. And just as America has had no David Hares, John Ardens or David Edgars, it has not had the structures in place to produce any Caryl Churchills either. Michelene Wandor can draw her theoretical conclusions about British feminist theatre inductively in *Understudies*, referring to feminist groups 'working in a growing socialist theater movement' (Wandor, 1981, p. 29). There's been no such thing in the US.

Indeed, despite the presence of an experimental theatre movement, the feminist collective theatres developed in an atmosphere at best indifferent, but more often hostile, to the very idea of political theatre. (The black theatre movement of roughly the same period – which also aimed at redressing stereotypes and exposing and expressing outrage at pervasive bigotry – suffered a similar fate. The Living Theater, perhaps America's most influential political company, spent most of the last thirty years outside the US.) From the very beginning, political theatre in the US has been stunted by redbaiting. The Federal Theater, for instance, initiated in 1935 with a $6 million grant from the government as part of the post-Depression New Deal, was killed off four years later by a Congress that objected to its radicalism. Within a decade or so, McCarthyism hammered the final nails into the coffin, going after playwrights, actors and directors most ferociously in its attempts to root out 'communism' from America. The country – and its theatre – has never recovered; the wedge between art and politics was driven in too deeply.

One result has been a general suspicion toward and devaluing of any theatre that is rhetorical, didactic or agitprop. Indeed, in American dramatic criticism, 'agitprop' is more often used as a pejorative than as a genre classification. That radical feminist theatre flourished at all in such a climate is remarkable, and it was able to do so only because it had a vibrant political women's movement as a context. As that movement petered out, so, naturally, did its theatres, tainted by anti-political biases even among its greatest allies. In *Feminist Theater Groups*, for instance, Dinah Leavitt only encourages an *a priori* distaste for political theatre when she suggests that the earliest feminist groups 'failed to produce collectively any significant drama, perhaps because of their overtly didactic content and their reliance on the skits of the political theatres' (Leavitt, 1980, p. 21).

As the agitated 1970s gave way to the corporate 1980s, feminist institutions, such as alternative healthcare and daycare centres – and theatres – folded. Before the 1970s were over, such important groups as the Washington Area Feminist Theater, Minneapolis's Lavender Cellar Theater, New York Feminist Theater Troupe, Westbeth Playwrights' Feminist Collective, Circle of the Witch, It's All Right to Be a Woman Theater, New Feminist Theater – and countless others – had all disbanded.

But if the golden age of feminist theatre collectives came and went in a fleeting decade, new feminist groups, writers and performers emerged in response to new cultural forces, and those companies that did remain in place, such as the exemplary At the Foot of the Mountain Theater, expanded beyond the white, middle-class limits of the movement's earlier years. Holding onto its first principle that the personal is political, and maintaining its dedication to craft, ATFM consciously sought to change shape in the early 1980s to become a more multigenerational, multicultural and multiracial theatre.

Around the same time, festivals of feminist theatre brought together work from all over the country, and in some instances from around the world, in a celebration of the previous decade's developments and in preparation for the work to come. From 1981 to 1985, the National Festival of Women in Theater took place annually in Santa Cruz, California. On the east coast, the Feminist Amerikan Theater co-produced the Boston Womyn's Theater Festival in 1980 and 1981. Since 1985, the festival has continued annually, under the rubric the Boston Women in Theater Festival – the change in title reflecting changes in the political climate. The Women's One World Festival in New York in 1980 and 1981 placed performers from Europe on the same stages as women from the emerging East Village performance scene in downtown Manhattan. When the festival ended, local women established the WOW Cafe to keep the energy generated by the festival going. Now a vibrant, largely lesbian, women's community theatre, WOW produces as many as thirty new works a year, many exploring sexual politics with a raucous, gender-bending style that to a large degree rejects what this new generation of artists considers the sanctimonious 'political correctness' of their forebears.

Meanwhile, the feminist movement in the visual arts (which, perhaps because it is a less social discipline, started out earlier than the feminist theatre movement and still remains strong) fed the theatre as painters and sculptors began turning the galleries that displayed their work into performance spaces. Theodora Skipitares, for instance, turned from sculpture to large murals and body coverings, and then to life-sized puppet spectacles to present alternative views of history that include women's contributions. Rachel Rosenthal, who danced, painted and acted in the experimental movements of the 1960s has emerged as one of the most important political performance artists of the 1980s, presenting her vision of eco-feminism in such compelling pieces as *L.O.W. in Gaia* (1986) and *Rachel's Brain* (1987). Jerri Allyn, a generation younger, has moved from painting to the creation of performance installations, such as *American Dining: Labor in the '80s* (1987), in which stories she has recorded about waitresses were installed in the little jukeboxes in booths at diners around the country.

Some performances by women trained in the visual arts have intersected with one tendency in the feminist theatre movement toward ritual performance. In the absence of a strong materialist feminist movement in the US, much of the theatre work that continued beyond the flush of the first five years, posited an essential female experience that derived from a pre-patriarchal world of goddess worship and female power. Such cultural feminism has been celebrated in theatrical rituals by groups like Karen Malpede's New Cycle Theater of Brooklyn, which, founded in 1977, named itself after the cycles of the female body and of the earth, with which it associates the female body. Though they might make fewer claims for the capacity of female biology to resolve political problems, performance artists like Linda Montano, Carolee Schneemann, Pat Olezsko and Karen Finley have used their own bodies as a medium for addressing the issue of objectification.

Oddly enough, as feminist performance artists have created one-woman pieces based on their own lives, their work has paralleled a development in the far more mainstream women's theatre – the one-woman historical play. Organisations such as the Women's Project, with, for instance, its 1986 series, 'Women Heroes: In Praise of Exceptional Women', has encouraged a spate of one-acts in which a woman impersonates a historical figure who has not been given her due. Though such works tend to stick to the conventions of naturalistic drama, like their cousins, autobiographical performance art, they address the problem of the lack of significant roles for women to play in the traditional theatre. In addition, they cope with the increasing unavailability of funds for theatre: one-woman shows tend to be cheap.

But at the same time, some artists, such as Suzanne Lacy and Leslie Lebowitz, have collaborated with literally hundreds of women to create huge public spectacles that have carried the notion of feminist theatre into new territory. Starting in the late 1970s, Lacy and Lebowitz worked with other women as 'Aridane: A Social Art Network', creating such works as *Three Weeks in May*

(1977), a piece about rape, and *In Mourning and Rage* (1977), a massive street performance protesting the murder of women by the 'Hillside Strangler' in Los Angeles. Lacy's San Francisco piece, *Freeze Frame: Room for Living Room*, brought together a hundred women from widely divergent backgrounds, and divided them into small groups in the wall-less 'rooms' of a furniture showroom. There, women discussed survival, their actual conversation mixing with choreographed sequences. More recently, Lacy collaborated with At the Foot of the Mountain in the creation of a huge Mother's Day pageant.

Whether in such public spectacles, in the burgeoning of a community-based lesbian theatre, through developments in performance art, or through women directors who have emerged as important leaders of experimental theatres, feminist theatre continues despite an increasingly inhospitable climate and an ever-decreasing availability of funds. As this work has grown and developed, the feminist academic community has begun to take note. Building on a decade's work in literary and cinematic feminist criticism, feminist theatre theorists have begun to write about contemporary feminist theatre. In 1983 *Women & Performance – A Journal of Feminist Theory* started publication, focusing on women in the performing arts. (It continues to be published semi-annually by the Department of Performance Studies at the Tisch School of the Arts, New York University.) Since then, such writers as Sue-Ellen Case and Jill Dolan have published books that blaze new trails in theatrical theory, and Lynda Hart has edited an anthology of essays that carry this project further.

Though cynics might say that such a proliferation of theory is a sure sign that activity in the area being theorised is dead, it's clear that is some respects, feminist theatre is facing new beginnings. Wendy Wasserstein and other conventional women playwrights may be able to win Pulitzers, but women still plugging away in collectives, small performance clubs, downtown lofts and in the streets, demonstrate that feminist theatre is still an alternative theatre, and will remain so at least as long as we live in a patriarchal culture.

As long as At the Foot of the Mountain continues its multicultural collective explorations in Minneapolis, and the New York-based lesbian company Split Britches continues to deconstruct gender in its distorted narrative style; as long as California performance artist Rachel Rosenthal keeps reclaiming the image of the crone

242   *Contemporary American Theatre*

with her intense stage persona, and New York actor and writer
Robbie McCauley keeps building her vision of African-American
history on a feminist foundation in her compelling autobiographical
performances; as long as feminist theatre makers continue to
examine the boundaries of gender, race and class as they are
constructed in American culture, Wendy Wasserstein's Heidi
can beam all she wants at her new baby as if to say, 'now
women really do have everything', and many in the audience
will know better.

BIBLIOGRAPHY

Case, S-E. (1988) *Feminism and Theatre* (New York: Methuen).
Chinoy, H. K., and Jenkins, L. W. (1987) *Women in American Theatre*
    (New York: TCG). A section on feminist theatre includes articles
    on the Caravan Theater, Omaha Magic, Washington Area Femin-
    ist Theater, Women's Interart, New York Feminist Theater Troupe,
    Lavendar Cellar, At the Foot of the Mountain, Spiderwoman, Women's
    Experimental Theater, and Split britches, on which this study relies
    heavily.
dell'Olio, A. (1970) 'The Founding of the New Feminist Theatre', in
    Shulamith Firestone (ed.), *Notes from the Second Year: Major Writers
    of the Radical Feminists* (New York: New York Radical Feminists),
    pp. 101–2.
Dolan, J. (1986) 'The Politics of Feminist Performance', in *Theater Times*,
    July/Aug.
———. (1989) *The Feminist Spectator as Critic* (Ann Arbor: UMI Research
    Press).
Fornes, M. I. (1983), statement on the 'Woman Playwright Issue', *Per-
    forming Arts Journal 21*, vol. VII, no. 3, pp. 90–91.
Leavitt, D. L. (1980) *Feminist Theatre Groups* (Jefferson, N.C.: McFarland).
Rea, C. (1972) 'Women's Theater Groups', *Drama Review 16*, pp. 79–89.
Sarachild, K. (1975) 'Consciousness Raising: A Radical Weapon', *Feminist
    Revolution* (New York: Redstockings) pp. 131–7.
Stone, L. (1989) 'The Women's Movement Carried Off My Baby in a
    Flying Saucer', *The Village Voice*, 13 June.
Wandor, M. (1981) *Understudies* (London: Methuen).

PART IV

Further New Directions

13

Poets of Bohemia and Suburbia: The Post-Literary Dramaturgies of Farabough, Harrington and Shank

JIM CARMODY

Laura Farabough, Laura Harrington and Adele Edling Shank are representatives of what can be called a post-literary movement in contemporary dramatic writing. Influenced by the non-textual theatrical creations of the last twenty-five years, their work displays an aversion to traditional dramatic form, particularly as it has congealed into the predominantly literary modes of American realism. Post-literary writing for the theatre employs a hybrid dramaturgy influenced by visual art, media and music that is rich in recognisable detail as well as surreal transformations of what the traditional theatre represents as 'real'.

The theatre of Farabough, Harrington and Shank is fundamentally a poetic theatre, a theatre of images rather than of plots, a theatre of unresolved ambiguities – a theatre, finally, that demands a certain kind of active collaboration on the part of the spectator in the creation of meaning. This chapter does not attempt to discuss all of the plays, screenplays, translation and librettos written by these artists during the 1980s. Instead, it examines a representative sampling of their work in an effort to describe their themes and isolate some characteristic features of their individual poetics.

LAURA FARABOUGH: ADVENTURES IN DREAM-TIME

In each of her plays, Laura Farabough blends a complex visual and verbal score to investigate human behaviour at the level of idea and fantasy, collapsing the habitual distinction between these twin poles of mental activity. Her spectators are invited to speculate on the relationships between word and gesture, video image and the physical presences of the stage. In their often ambiguous juxtapositions, text and image seem to play off each other, avoiding either explanation or illustration. The soft, bemused voice Farabough so often adopts in performance is, in fact, representative of her art as a whole. That she herself sounds puzzled or intrigued only intensifies the allure of the puzzles she creates.

Farabough's dramaturgy revolves around a 'principle of multiplicity'. Typically, her pieces combine an interest in multimedia techniques with the complex presentation of character. In Farabough's work, character is composed of a number of voices or image sequences. She presents her characters through an external, social voice as well as through the internalised voice of consciousness. Both voices are frequently further fragmented. Similarly, she stages characters in their physical and social environments as well as in their fantasy environments. Often these environments blend into each other. She shows her characters as they appear to strangers, to each other and to themselves.

Technically, these multiple manifestations are accomplished through a combination of live and recorded voice and live and recorded action. The live and recorded images rarely double each other, which introduces yet another level of multiplicity into Farabough's pieces: she asks her audience to pay attention to several stories or several points of view simultaneously. Yet another level of complexity is added by superimposing live action and live video (the technicians and their equipment usually remain in full view of the audience). Events and characters are thus presented through at least two different mediations at the same time. In this way she creates both an aesthetic and intellectual puzzle for her spectators.

Femme Fatale: The Intervention of Personality (1980) already reveals an interest in the multifaceted nature of the self that comes to dominate her work during the 1980s. The play tells the stories of two celebrated *femmes fatale*, Mata Hari and Greta Garbo, tracing their passage from obscurity through fame and notoriety to death and silence. The two stories intersect historically in 1926 when Garbo plays the title role in *Mata Hari*.

The two stories are framed by a structural device that has become one of the most versatile and interesting elements of Farabough's poetics – her use of a 'documentary voice'. In *Femme Fatale*, this voice belongs to a character called The Narrator (played by Farrabough) who imparts 'information' about the development of ladies' fashions during the two World Wars. It is difficult to tell if Farabough is using excerpts from periodicals of the period or creating her own pastiche of that kind of writing. The documentary voice in this and other plays is characterised by a dispassionate, measured manner.

After the house lights dim, two television monitors show the concluding dates for the stories about to be enacted. Stage right, Mata Hari's side, the monitor shows 1917, the year of her death. Stage left, the date is 1941, the year of Garbo's retirement. The dates fade to be replaced by still photographs of women wearing undergarments from the two periods. Two maids, one in each half of the divided scenic space, go through a series of identical actions in rearranging their clothing. In unison, their taped voices say: 'The quality of my uniform details the condition of my role'. Farabough thus invites the spectator to pay attention to the semiotics of clothing as one of the key subjects of *Femme Fatale*. In this play, clothing is either uniform or costume, consciously designed to signify in specific ways. Some moments later, the Narrator offers this commentary:

> Today, it is quite the style among a certain set of Parisian women to look disreputable. . . . The purpose of such fashions is to endow the garments themselves with the sex appeal which nature perhaps omitted to give the wearer. The advantage is that any woman can purchase as much sex appeal as her purse can afford.

The impartial and impersonal tone of the speaker ironically makes the ideological nature of the content unmistakable. The 'narrative' continues to punctuate the development of the two parallel stories, framing Garbo's and Hari's individual experiences with the history of sexuality from the period of the two World Wars as reflected in the clothing of the times. Farabough shows us how the identities of Garbo and Hari were constructed as *femmes fatale* at the same time as she exposes the prevailing ideologies that generated those constructions.

Hari creates her own sexualised identity as a fiction that initially enables her to survive in difficult times but which finally leads to her execution. Garbo, on the other hand, has her identity molded by a film director to satisfy his personal search for a sexual ideal. Her career succeeds as long as the sexual ideal she represents retains popularity. With the advent of the Second World War, her popularity begins to wane and she chooses to remove herself from public life. Farabough's plotting reveals the extent to which the *femme fatale* is an identity that results from an historically determined process.

In *Obedience School* (1983), Farabough approaches the nature of the self from a different perspective by exploring the relationship between control and fear, a theme that she returns to in subsequent plays. *Obedience School* recounts the events of a weekend at the home of The Model and her husband, The Pilot. The events of this 'weekend' include a barbecue sequence in which The Model cooks a hamburger with a blowtorch, a fantasy sequence in which she imagines herself being assaulted by a man wearing a dog mask (or perhaps it's a game they play together), and an argument about getting a guard dog. As the play progresses, it becomes increasingly difficult to distinguish between what belongs to The Model's dream world and what is 'merely' dream-like. In the end, the distinction becomes immaterial. Fear and apprehension pervade this dream-like world. Her husband tells her to 'get it under control', but moments later we learn that this admonition springs from his own fear: 'Her fear is like a magnet, it pulls me down'. In The Pilot's system of values 'The worst thing that can happen is to lose control'.

Like her other work, *Obedience School* is written for multimedia presentation. In this play, Farabough uses video to create a second level of narrative that at times doubles the live on-stage action. Early in the play, for example, the live actor (The Pilot) enacts a flying sequence using a working model of an F-15 fighter while the video screen shows film of 'real' fighters taking off and performing other manoeuvres. In such sequences, the stage world seems to offer a more artificial representation of reality. Later in the play, however, dream images appear equally artificial on both stage and screen. Indeed, fragments of dreams seem to cross back and forth between the two media unimpeded. The boundaries between fantasy and reality that seemed to have been established early in the play now appear illusory. Reality takes on some of the characteristics of dream and vice versa. In this fluid image world, the characters do not differentiate between what they see with their mind's eye and what they see with their physical eyes: for them, the conceptual *is* the real, the imagined *is* the experienced.

With each succeeding play through the 1980s, the video component becomes increasingly important, culminating with 1987's *Bodily Concessions*, a 'solo work for a woman performer and video'. *Bodily Concessions* may be Farabough's most complex investigation into the self to date. It begins by recounting the steps taken to verify that she is, in fact, a sleep-walker. From there, the play goes on to recount a number of apparently autobiographical experiences, both conscious and subconscious. These experiences include a story about growing up in a Freudian household (accompanied by an amusing disquisition on Freud's theory of the nose as a sexual organ), a sexual fantasy about being raped by soldiers in a church (the Religious Mysteries of Latrinism), and a story about attending a party (while sleep-walking).

Bodily Concessions combines live performance with recorded video. Video images appear on a television monitor and are also projected on a screen that forms the backdrop for the acting area. Farabough performs solo on stage and in each of the videos. The identity she enacts as performer is thus mediated in three different ways, each of which represents a different facet of the character that Farabough herself performs. Throughout the play, Farabough (the performer) speaks about herself (the subject of the narrative) in both the first and third person. Here, she applies her 'documentary voice' to the description of her own experience.

In a coda to the performance, Farabough removes the bandages that obscure her face for much of the latter part of the play and improvises a monologue that addresses the issues of the play from yet another perspective. The monologue begins by returning to the idea of control, which was the subject of the live performer's final line:

This is an exercise in control.
I believe I am in control. . . .

It pleases me to think that my body can respond with exquisite precision
to my mental commands: I think my life depends on it.
Perception.
Interpretation.
Reaction. . . .
My understanding that my ability to perceive the world around me,
to interpret this information, and then to react to that translation
is the basic activity and process of my life . . .
is new to me.
And I am fascinated, obsessed with this structure.

The 'I' of this final monologue may be closer to the 'I' of Farabough the playwright than the character embodied by the live performer during the play. When the play comes to an end, the live performer seems to have subsumed the other two characters, suggesting a provisional reintegration of the self. This newly reintegrated self appears, for instance, much less disturbed by her sleep-walking than the character on the monitor. She also sees the question of control in a different way – the monologue ends with a joke about control in which Farabough exercised 'control' by calling for her final light cue.

The woman who speaks the final monologue of the play does not, however, suggest that 'integration' has been achieved once and for all. If anything, she seems to suggest that her sense of herself moves back and forth among a number of different perspectives, some of which are intuitive and some rational. Indeed, *Bodily Concessions* itself is a synthetic work created by nesting two earlier works within a subsequent analytical framing narrative. Farabough added this analytical narrative (largely the story of the monitor lady) and the live performer to two earlier video pieces, an installation entitled *Twelve Stations of the Latrine* and a piece she created in Japan called *Investigation Through a Window*. *Bodily Concessions*, then, represents an investigation of Farabough's own imaginative production, an investigation whose own results are then subject to a further imaginative reconstruction. Here, the three core activities and processes of Farabough's life – perception, interpretation and reaction – oscillate continuously as both subject and poetic technique.

ADELE EDLING SHANK:
COMFORTING RITUALS, VISIONS OF DISTRESS

Armed with the cool, dispassionate vision of a cultural anthro-
pologist, Adele Edling Shank wrote a six-play cycle during the
first half of the 1980s that explores contemporary California life.
The series includes *Sunset/Sunrise* (1979), *Winterplay* (1980), *Stuck*
(1981), *Sand Castles* (1982), *The Grass House* (1983) and *Tumbleweed*
(1986). The locations of these plays range from a suburban home
and a freeway in the San Francisco Bay area to an ocean beach, a
cabin in a northern California forest and a house in the southern
California desert.

The subtitle for the first two plays in the California series,
Sunset/Sunrise and *Winterplay*, is 'A Hyperreal Comedy'. 'Theatrical
hyperrealism' (the term is Shank's) grew out of her interest in
the work of a group of American painters (Bechtle, Mendenhall,
Eddy, Goings, Estes and others) whose work has been variously
called hyperrealist, photo-realist or super-realist. Their painting
is characterised by its unemotional depiction of elements from
the everyday urban and suburban world with an unprecedented,
'photographic' attention to detail. In dramatic terms, hyperrealism
'creates a distance which tends to keep the focus on behavior, on
appearance, rather than on psychology, social analysis, or emotion. . . . Spectating becomes more an act of perception than emotional involvement' (Theodore Shank, 'Director's Note', *Stuck*).

The individual plays cohere around contemporary rituals such as
a Christmas dinner (*Winterplay*), a backyard cookout (*Sunset/Sun-
rise*), a vacation at the beach (*Sand Castles*) or a wedding (*The
Grass House*). These rituals gather together individuals who do
not normally share everyday life with each other (although some
of them may belong to the same family). These gatherings allow
individuals to interact in a number of permutations according to
the 'rules of association' that govern such groups of people. Shank
is particularly interested in exploring how 'rules of association' condition and are conditioned by social roles. Her characters manifest
a variety of ritualised behaviours as they try to cope with what
happens on a moment-to-moment basis.

Sunset/Sunrise is set in the same 'Suburban California' as *Winterplay*, in the home of James, a tax attorney, and his wife, Louise.
Family, friends and neighbours gather on a hot afternoon for a
barbecue in the backyard. In the course of the afternoon and even-

ing, couples drift apart, a husband and wife decide to try living together again, families try to reconcile, and James and Louise's daughter, Anne, decides to leave her self-imposed quarantine. While every element of the play is grounded in a rigorous fidelity to observed suburban reality, with all the diversity of heterogeneous detail that such fidelity implies, the overall impression is one of a surprisingly homogeneous culture that succeeds in forging significant links that connect and reconnect these individuals to each other despite the transitory emotional peaks and troughs, problems real and imagined that form the texture of their lives.

This overall impression of connectedness springs from Shank's skill at moving groups of characters in and out of focus. She is adept at creating dramatic effects with great economy, and many of the conversations in *Sunset/Sunrise*, for example, are made up of no more than five or six exchanges. Because there is a good deal of activity on stage, the viewer is usually obliged to watch more than one thing at a time. From the very beginning, Shank hints that the spectator needs to watch as well as listen (her visual images are as meticulously crafted as her dialogue) because the physical actions will not necessarily be explained by the dialogue. Shank's writing facilitates this expanded range of attention by using storylines that are, like the subjects of the hyperrealist painters, familiar, even banal.

But hyperrealism, especially in Shank's work, frequently transcends the banal. Like the hyperrealist painters, she transforms the reality she observes and, in the process, produces effects that are both distancing and disquieting. Many hyperrealist painters prefer the gleaming, translucent surfaces of new objects to the tarnished surfaces of those damaged by use and time. The use the airbrush to recreate this shine of the new, giving their images an unreal, dreamlike aspect. Shank, too, frequently polishes her fragments of observed reality to create strange, implausible, sometimes nightmarish images.

At times, she creates mildly surreal effects by strategically undermining the audiences expectations. A good example of this is her treatment of Iris in *Sand Castles*. During the first act, Iris, an unusually beautiful young woman, sits in her beach chair enjoying the sunshine and flirting with Stephen. Stephen is shocked when her servant Fritz (dressed in leather and wearing a studded collar and wristbands) arrives to serve her champagne. He is even more astonished at the end of the act when Fritz picks Iris up and sets her down in her wheelchair. Traditionally conceived realism insists on exposition to justify such behaviour.

At the endings of her plays, Shank often creates even more nightmarish images by carefully nurturing the anticipation of a traditional comic ending only to shatter the resolution with an unexpected entrance. At the end of *Sand Castles*, for example, the Aussie enters 'bloody and limping. . . . He stops, looks at the ocean, then comes down the steps. He howls in anguish as he disappears toward the water' (p. 324). The Aussie appears just as Paul and Anemone have kissed for the first time (they also appear in *The Grass House*, where they get married, and in *Tumbleweed*, where they finally separate). The traditional romantic resolution of the Paul/Anemone story is juxtaposed with the unexpected entrance of this violent character. The almost surreal apparition of the Aussie frames the ending of the play in a disquieting way: Shank pairs a kiss with a howl of anguish.

Tumbleweed, the sixth play, ends with a picnic on the exposed concrete slab of a burned-down house in the California desert. A card table is set up on the slab and covered with a lace tablecloth and silver place settings. As they sit down to eat their turkey, Alice, a spry, old neighbour says grace: 'Dear Lord, we thank you for this food which you have provided. May it nourish our bodies that we may work to purify out souls' (p. 95). This ritual celebration dinner gathers together a strangely disparate group of people whose paths have crossed at what they all recognise is a turning point in their lives. This final dinner, with its ironic evocation of the first Pilgrim Thanksgiving, recalls the many meals and other shared consumptions of food and alcohol that mark the passage of time through the six plays.

But it would be a mistake to read this ending as a reaffirmation of the pilgrim work ethic or a turn toward the consolations of religion. Like any other character in these six plays, Alice does not speak for Shank. Her prayer does not imply that the members of the group have developed a new belief in the Christian God. What it does imply, however, is a shared need for a specific gesture that marks the ceremonial, ritual aspects of this picnic. Like the other characters in the California plays, these people eat and drink together (often to excess) because there appears to be no other civilised alternative. Indeed, such eating and drinking is the very mark of their civilisation, the only significant social interaction possible for a heterogeneous group of individuals in this late twentieth-century culture.

In *Rocks In Her Pocket* (1988), Shank turns her attention to the subculture of academia. *Rocks* presents the farcical events of a single afternoon and evening at the Winterbourne Hotel on the Isle of Wight. For a brief time the home of Charles Dickens, the hotel now hosts an international conference on the subject of artists' suicides. Although the location is borrowed from the real world, Shank treats this room with its pair of doors, fireplace and French doors leading to the balcony as if it were one of Feydeau's *boudoirs*.

Like the setting, the characters are 'borrowed' from real life, even if three of them are returning from the grave. Shank's premise is that Virginia Woolf, Sylvia Plath and Diane Arbus are compelled by the laws of the afterlife to attend conferences at which their work is being discussed. This obliges Woolf, for instance, to listen to a paper on *To The Lighthouse* entitled 'Semen in the Flotsam: Preventing Premature Conceptual Closure' by Jacques Foucault from the Institute of Advanced Philosophical Analysis in New England. This is, at first sight, a transparent references to Jacques Derrida, who has taught occasionally at Yale University in New Haven. Also conflated into the character's name is a reference to Michel Foucault. But Shank's Foucault is clearly the playwright's creation. None of his pronouncements resemble any of Derrida's or Foucault's. Nevertheless, Shank's characterisation of this arrogant academic rings true, as does her treatment of the others: Trish Cowley, the sociologist who organised this conference; O G Washington, a black feminist who teaches in the Women's Studies Department of a California university; Max Gill, a middle-aged New York art critic; and Sheila Higgs, the young maid at the hotel.

Like her earlier plays, *Rocks* is far from being a vehicle for easy laughter, even though it contains many of the playwright's wittiest lines (the caustic humour in this play is on a par with Noel Coward's). While the topic of suicide provides grist for the comic mill, it is also the source of profound pain (there is less her than in Shank's earlier plays). O G claims to have discovered Sylvia Plath's suicide journal 'The Bell Jar, Volume Two: A Diary of Despair'. She has, in fact, written this journal herself – it is a diary of her own despair. During the thunder and rain that accompanies much of the second act, O G is prevented from drowning herself by the three ghosts who send Sheila off to the rescue. Sheila returns with O G, soaked to the skin. In the final moments of the play, as the chaos of the day's events resolve into calm, Plath encourages O G to forget about suicide, change the ending to her book, and publish it under her own name instead of Plath's. At the same time, Arbus burns the negatives of her own suicide, happy that she has 'cheated the tabloids'.

In the farcical context of a play like *Rocks*, it is easy to miss the accuracy with which Shank has recreated the subculture of academia (here, she concentrates on the 'back-stage' aspects of the academic conference ritual). She uses physical comedy and savage wit (particularly the three ghosts') to force a confrontation between the formalities of academic behaviour, especially its specialist vocabularies and fascination with the arcane, and the more prosaic desires and problems of the individual characters. Images such as Trish behaving as if her dead dog, Paulina, were still walking at her heel may appear outrageously unrealistic and implausible, although this character is certainly no more implausible than Anemone, who pimps for her mother in *Sand Castles*. Unlike conventional realists, Shank is quite unconcerned with a superficial plausibility – a lack of concern that is, perhaps, one of the principal reasons why her work remains so fresh.

LAURA HARRINGTON: FIGURES OF LYRICAL DESIRE

As opposed to the relatively cool, 'objective' dramaturgies of Laura Farabough and Adele Shank, Laura Harrington's poetics provoke her audience's emotional involvement. She wants her spectators to empathise (particularly with her female characters), to be caught up in the vortex of desire and emotion that are her characters' existential situation. What makes Harrington's work compelling is her ability to combine familiar music and plots into complex, lyrical dramas of passion and transcendence.

The Wrong Man (1985) provides a useful entry into her work as it concentrates in its three and a half pages a number of characteristic features of her writing:

1 self-consciously poetic treatment of language with special emphasis on condensation of expression, musicality and rhythmic patterning of speech;

2   ambiguous or enigmatic presentation of character, event and context;
3   thematic preoccupation with desire and the problem of knowledge;
4   fluid, non-realistic treatment of time and space.

A woman is dancing alone on a balcony. A man enters and begins to dance with her. Moments later, he attempts to introduce himself but she stops him: 'Tonight we're going to do something new. . . . Instead of the usual banalities we're going to lie to each other' (p. 25). Nadia suggests that they tell each other what their first meeting was like. Each in turn articulates a fantasy of an idealised erotic or romantic encounter, interrupting when the other person's images are not to their taste. In the end, their stories have diverged to the point that John retreats, insisting that she is thinking of 'Another man, another time' (p. 27).

The audience never learns who these people are (their names are never spoken), where they are, or even whether they know each other or not. Although the opening moments suggest that the two are strangers, the intricately patterned dialogue is suggestive of a kind of dance between two people who know each other's favourite moves very well indeed. Whether this dance is interpreted as an encounter between two strangers attracted to each other or as a game played by two lovers, the final outcome remains the same. These people desire different things. Whatever the status of their relationship, they remain unalterbly separate. She has not been 'pulled out of [her] skin' and he has 'not talked until [he has] no breath left' (p. 27). The presence of the other, the mere existence of the other, makes it impossible to pursue a fantasy to its pleasurable end. On the plane of desire, Harrington rearticulates Sartre's perception that 'hell is other people'.

Although *The Wrong Man* suggests no larger world to which these characters might belong, the action is not without context. One might, at first, mistake the offstage music for an indication that there is a party going on. But music is never merely atmospheric or decorative in Harrington's dramatic world. Indeed, it is often difficult to tell which comes first, the music or the characters. (Since 1986, she has been commissioned to write three opera librettos.)

Jazz provides both a cultural frame of reference and a medium of communication for the two characters of *'Round Midnight* (1984). Seven well-known jazz songs are sung during the play and

Harrington suggests that additional incidental music be taken from Billie Holiday, Ellis Larkins, Thelonius Monk or John Coltrane.

Two sections of Harrington's opening stage directions are worth quoting. The first describes the space, the second how the actor should treat the language:

> Both spaces [a bar and Sal's room] are stark and unornamented, with only the most essential objects in evidence. It is a space you could dream in. . . .

> SAL and LEO often riff off each other with slang. They use language as they would use music.

Scenic spaces 'you could dream in' and using language like music are features common to all of Harrington's writing for the theatre. Her stage is often a void out of which images emerge and to which they return.

'*Round Midnight* begins with Sal performing the Thelonius Monk song 'Round About Midnight'. After the song, Sal refuses to recognise Leo and suggests that if he wants to talk to her, he should 'try the present'. Later, when she tires of playing the 'strangers meeting in a bar' game, she relents and agrees to discuss their past. We learn that years ago, Leo (a jazz musician) left her with a permanent emotional scar when he returned to his wife.

Music pervades their public and private lives; it is a part of their shared language. Scene Three (Sal's apartment, 4am) begins with a long musical sequence in which Leo and Sal express their feelings to each other through song. Leo initiates the conversation with 'Come Rain Or Come Shine', accompanying himself on the piano. Sal breaks in with 'Downhearted Blues'. Leo cuts in with 'You've Changed' and Sal in turn interrupts with 'I Gotta Right To Sing The Blues'. At this point Leo begins to accompany her, 'riffing off her singing until she stops him'. He then breaks into an 'upbeat version' of 'Love Me Or Leave Me'. Sal continues with 'Fine and Mellow' and sings the song through to the end. 'This time', Harrington comments, 'she is singing for real'. This lengthy sequence of songs divides the play into two almost equal parts and plays a pivotal role in the play's structure. Here we see Sal and Leo communicating to each other through their common language of music. The spectator cannot know, except in very general terms, what the substance of their conversation might be. Dramatically, what seems to be going on is a seduction, and Sal does finally begin to give her emotions free rein. In terms of the overall movement of the play, however, the musical sequence marks a shift away from Leo being the more aggressive of the two. In the second part, Sal's passion seeks its own expression. The musical sequence also works to increase the emotional temperature of the scene, moving the action onto a heightened emotional plane where Sal's desires can finally emerge.

The second part of *'Round Midnight* moves into the darker realms of human desire as Sal searches for a way to create an unbreakable bond between herself and Leo. She asks him to cut her, to give her a scar on her face that will mark her as belonging to him. Sal's desire to have Leo mark her by scarring her with a razor blade is quite upsetting. Equally disquieting is her willingness to cut him if he refuses. In the end, she makes him hold the blade while she marks her own face. *'Round Midnight* us a typical Harrington piece: erotic, musical, lyrical, dealing with the very limits of feeling, knowledge and self-knowledge.

Like *'Round Midnight*, *Angel Face* (1986) is set in a contemporary bohemia. Its characters live in the low-rent districts of metropolitan America. They are pimps, hustlers, whores and would-be artists. Harrington's bohemia, however, has no counterpart in any actual city; this milieu is a district of the mind, an imaginative transformation of sordid reality into a glittering *demi-monde*. Uninterested in sociological issues, her themes are the nature and limits of human passion and the exploration of the limits of the self in situations of extreme stress.

Gabriel, a man with a scar on his face, and Lil narrate rather than enact their story. They take turns telling their story through a series of poetic monologues that eventually resolve into alternating short speeches. In its essentials, the plot is centuries old; only the setting and some of the incidental detail is contemporary. The power of the play resides almost exclusively in its poetry and in the lyrical flights of passion that poetry conjures up. These two character are caught in a web of images that represent the extent to which they have merged their identities. They are both angels, both fascinated with flight, both aching to melt into each other. At the heart of this fantasy of transcending the limits of the self is the recurring image of the knife slicing through skin, an image that appears in other plays: 'We slice skin. / Our blood mingles. / Our heart beats become one. / She enters me. / Her wings enter me'. This is a love that is sado-masochistic, lyrical and mythic all at once. The poetry blends the biblical with the modernist, the sacred with the profane, in a disturbing oratorio to human desire.

Night Luster (1986) also features a man with a scarred face, Sharkey, who gets injured trying to save his lover, Mink, from a life of prostitution. Although this is a play about dreams of escaping, escape itself is a complex idea and means different things to different characters. For the three principal characters, Mink, Sharkey, and Mink's best friend, Roma, escape means getting away from their current unsatisfactory day-to-day routine. Mink and Sharkey dream of amassing enough money to escape a life of prostitution and gambling. Roma dreams of finding a man in the music industry who will give her singing/songwriting career the start it needs.

As the play begins, Mink is dancing alone in her lingerie in a spotlight, singing 'Touch Me'. Her first words are 'I want you to touch me'. We have no idea who this woman is or who she wants to touch her. We learn that Mink is herself seeking answers to the same questions. For much of the play, it seems that Sharkey's touch is not enough for her. At the end of the play, however, as he lies bleeding on the stage, she realises that Sharkey was the right man for her all along, that he has 'touched' best of all.

Harrington has structured the play around a paradox: Mink wants to be touched; men want to touch Mink; Mink doesn't want the men to touch her. Mink allows men to touch her in the course of her work, even though she is afraid of potentially dangerous clients. She likes to feel 'safe' yet she refuses to stay home. She doesn't want to miss 'the shine of the evening', even though Sharkey tells her that he now has enough money for them both to quit their street lives and move on to something 'better'. She hangs onto the streets because they are 'slick with possibilities', because they promise that elusive 'dark', 'deep' happiness that Harrington's women seek.

Mink's quest parallels that of Sam, the principal female character of *Freefall* (1985). The title refers to the moment at the beginning when Sam, a stunt pilot trying to land in the fog at a remote airport on the coast of Maine, cuts the engine and waits for the plane to touch down. During those brief seconds of silence and waiting, the plane is in freefall. Although the plane crashes this time, such moments provide the kind of excitement that Sam is addicted to. For Sam, 'freefall' is a state of mind, a space beyond the normal limits of her experience, a way of transcending her own identity. Much of the plot is concerned with Sam's husband, Lou, trying to persuade her to retire from this life in which being in freefall is an all too frequent danger. The title also describes what is happening to Lou throughout the play. No longer able to fly (he is afraid of taking control of the plane), he gradually slides into depression. A third possibility, the title describes the slow dissolution of the marriage between Sam and Lou. Perhaps, paradoxically, freefall describes both extraordinary, transcendent experience and the everyday, mundane effects of gravity, physical and metaphorical.

Harrington sets *Freefall* in a dreamscape airfield on the very edge of the continent. The characters step out of their apartment, 'a cross between a quonset hut and a trailer', directly onto the boardwalk. The audience views the action from 'offshore'. This is a liminal space, at the border between sea and land, land and air. It is also a mythic space – the country airfield, unchanged since the barnstorming days of the early aviators. This airfield has a kind of iconic presence, conjuring up the early days of flying, reminding us that the air was once a romantic space. Equally iconic and mythic, perhaps, is the boardwalk as a space of social interaction. Sam, Lou, and the other characters inhabit a space of familiar elements of Americana. These elements combine to evoke two different sets of fantasies. One is the fetishistic idiom of leather jackets, high-heeled shoes, and other alluring clothing (Sam and Lou disguise themselves as the more rapaciously sexual Rita and Nick). The other is the cultural fantasy of 1950s Americana, now greatly dilapidated. Unlike her other work, the marginal world portrayed in *Freefall* is utterly lacking in 'shine'.

CONCLUSION

In different ways, Laura Farabough, Laura Harrington and Adele Edling Shank break free from the prevailing realisms of American dramatic writing by refusing to see the playwright solely as a purveyor of dialogue that can be evaluated according to the traditional criteria of dramatic literature. In this, their writings reflect a commitment to the practices of both dramatic writing and scenic writing – their scripts contain notations for a variety of scenic events, musical and visual as well as verbal. Fundamentally, however, their work moves away from traditional dramatic representations because the have rejected the aesthetics on which those representations are based. And, like playwrights of previous generations, they have gone to other art forms for aesthetic ideas that help them rethink their approaches to their own art of playmaking.

BIBLIOGRAPHY

Farabough, L. (1981) *Femme Fatale: The Invention of Personality.*
———. (1982a) *Locker Room.*
———. (1982b) *Surface Tension, West Coast Plays,* vols 11/12.
———. (1982–3) *Obedience School.*
———. (1983) *Sea of Heartbreak.*
———. (1983–4) *Beauty Science.*
———. (1984) *A Liquid Distance/Timed Approach.*
———. (1984–5) *Under Construction.*
———. (1985) *Baseball Zombie.*
———. (1987) *Bodily Concessions.*
Harrington, L. (1983) *The Listener.*
———. (1984a) *Cheat.*
———. (1984b) *'Round Midnight.*
———. (1985a) *Freefall.*
———. (1985b) *The Wrong Man,* in Stan Chervin (ed.) *Short Pieces From The New Dramatist,* (New York: Broadway Play Publishing).
———. (1986a) *Angel Face.*
———. (1986b) *Night Luster.*
———. (1986c) *Secrets,* screenplay (WCVB-TV, Boston).
———. (1987) *Ah!,* screenplay.
———. (1988) *The Original Colored House of David,* screenplay.
———. (1989a) *Lucy's Lapses,* opera libretto.
———. (1989b) *Martin Guerre,* opera libretto.
Harrington, L. and Baillargeon, P. (1985) *Sonia: A Film About Alzheimer's Disease* (National Film Board of Canada).
Shank, A. E. (1979) *Sunset/Sunrise: A Hyperreal Comedy, West Coast Plays,* vol. 4.
———. (1982a) *Winterplay: A Hyperreal Comedy, New Plays USA 1* (New York: TCG).
———. (1982b) *Stuck: A Freeway Comedy,* Plays-in-Process Series (New York: TCG).
———. (1983) *Sand Castles, West Coast Plays,* vols 15/16.
———. (1984) *The Grass House,* Plays-in-Process Series (New York: TCG).
———. (1985) *War Horses.*
———. (1986) *Tumbleweed.*
———. (1988) *Rocks In Her Pocket.*
Shank, T. 'Director's Note' to *Stuck* by Adele Edling Shank.

14

Not Either/Or But And: Fragmentation and Consolidation in the Post-modern Theatre of Peter Sellars

DON SHEWEY

Peter Sellars is a pivotal figure in contemporary theatre. His work is both a product of twentieth-century avant-garde theatre and a departure from it, overleaping the high-tech obsessions of his immediate predecessors for a more classical vision of theatre.

Born in 1957, Sellars began his stage career at the age of ten by apprenticing with a marionette theatre in Pittsburgh, where he learned as much about French surrealism and Oriental theatre as about *Jack and the Beanstalk* and *Rumplestiltskin*. After high school, he spent a year in Paris, where he encountered the work of Giorgio Strehler, the Bread and Puppet Theater, and Andrei Serban's *Fragments of a Greek Trilogy*, all of which had a powerful, formative effect on him. He launched his professional career while still an undergraduate at Harvard, and within a decade he had created a remarkable and influential body of work without ever having a major production in Manhattan. An assiduous student of theatre history as well as of such admired peers as the Wooster Group's Elizabeth LeCompte and Robert Wilson, Sellars has applied his extraordinary energy and erudition to mounting radical productions of Shakespearean tragedies and Mozart operas as well as lucid productions of lesser texts by Brecht and Sophocles, not to mention outright obscurities such as Velimir Khlebnikov's *Zangezi*.

By the time he began his career as a mature artist in the early 1980s, the innovations and the groundbreaking of the older generation of avant-garde artists were a *fait accompli*. For him tradition was not Tennessee Williams, Neil Simon, and Broadway musicals but the Wooster Group, Robert Wilson, and the Bread and Puppet Theater. His aesthetic is based less on innovation than on applying innovations from the recent past to the canon of theatrical literature. In that respect, what *New Yorker* dance critic Arlene Croce wrote of his erstwhile collaborator, choreographer Mark Morris, could as easily apply to Sellars: 'He's the clearest illustration we have, at the moment, of the principle of succession and how it works . . . each new master assimilates the past in all its variety and becomes our guide to the future.'[1]

In the evolution of art, every period of intense innovation is a response to – a revolt against – established tradition. And this response is always followed by a period of consolidation, in which a sort of cultural triage takes place: classical culture is re-evaluated in the light of recent developments, and the value of recent experiments are weighed against the truth and usefulness of art that has remained vital across centuries and continents. The collage that results is the basis of a new tradition, against which future innovators will inevitably rebel. The cycle is as simple (and violent) as nature itself.

For instance, after the Second World War there occurred a levelling of the cultural landscape – a Hiroshima of the arts. Reinterpreting Marcel Duchamp's Dadaist dictum 'Anything can be art' for post-war America, John Cage declared that the purpose of art was 'not to bring order out of chaos nor to suggest improvements in creation, but simply to wake [us] up to the very life we're living'.[2] Cage's influence inspired countless experiments which effectively reduced art to the tiniest increments of human activity, glorifying everyday behaviour. This was the logical and perhaps inevitable extension of modernism's quest to locate the essence of each art and to express only that essence. But minimalism transformed the notion of purification into a reductive impulse, and that impulse could go too far, and often did.

Oppressive as a tradition, minimalism did leave a clean slate for artists. Just as computerisation found a way to convert all forms of information into bits of electronic 'memories' that can be stored in and quickly retrieved from a machine, modernism broke down the individual art forms into a pool of elements available to all artists. It was originally performance artists who took up the challenge of recombining speech, song, images, movement and modern technology in new ways. It could be said that the real tool of performance art is 'the media', more powerful in today's society than any one art form, but that would be underestimating the importance of the human presence activating the performance. On a microcosmic level, performance art acts out the twentieth-century struggle between man and machine. This metaphysical struggle takes place, however, not on Beckett's barren landscape – the stark, post-apocalyptic terrain inhabited by minimalist composers and choreographers in the 1960s and 1970s – but on a rich, dense, lively technoscape capable of yielding entertainment and information as well as destruction.

More and more, the use of media technology (film, video, sophisticated sound equipment) has become a hallmark of experimental theatre, which has merged the visual discipline of performance art with the verbal discipline of drama into something that might be called media-theatre. The works of media-theatre artists such as the Wooster Group, Mabou Mines, Laurie Anderson, Robert Wilson, Richard Foreman, Meredith Monk, and Ping Chong exemplify a new art form (with antecedents in twentieth-century avant-garde art) that demands from its audience a peculiarly modern mode of perception – an ability to synthesise visual, verbal and aural material in new ways. All contemporary media-theatre has been influenced to some extent by the theories of post-modern criticism and the practice of performance art, as well as movies, television and rock music.

Performance art and other reflections of the post-modern impulse toward cultural collage could be said to mark the beginning of an era of consolidation – a period of assimilating the lessons of modernism's minimalist last gasp. And its completion can be seen in the work, for instance, of Mark Morris (in dance), the Kronos Quartet (in music), and Peter Sellars (in theatre), who apply their creativity to consolidation rather than innovation – not to suggest that there's nothing new under the sun, but to establish that there's value in drawing attention to old things.

In contemporary American theatre, Peter Sellars represents the demise of the 'either–or' proposition. The previous generation of great theatre-makers – the Michael Bennetts and the Tommy Tunes, the JoAnne Akilaitises and Elizabeth LeComptes, all in roughly the same age and talent bracket – had to make vast choices early on that defined and in some way limited them: working 'on Broadway' versus 'off the beaten path', being 'popular' versus 'avant-garde', art versus entertainment, and all that implies. Sellars recognises no such constraints. Given a choice, he is most likely to embrace both options, and of all the work he has done in the professional theatre, there is no better example than *Hang On To Me*, which was produced at the Guthrie Theater in Minneapolis in 1984. A literal translation of Maxim Gorky's 1904 play *Summerfolk*, into the text of which Sellars introduced sixteen songs by George and Ira Gershwin (mostly from *Lady Be Good* and *Treasure Girl*), *Hang On To Me* was both a play and a musical. It took place simultaneously in the past and the present, in Russia and in America, and it was entertaining as well as highly experimental, not least because the cast of twenty-six ranged from avant-garde stalwarts David Warrilow (a founding member of Mabou Mines) and Priscilla Smith (the leading actress of Andrei Serban's Great Jones Repertory Company) to Broadway veterans like Susan Browning and Marianne Tatum.

The connection between Gorky and Gershwin can only be called a poetic one. That mating had its origin in the year Sellars spent preparing the Broadway musical *My One and Only*, an adaptation of the Gershwins' *Funny Face*, before he was dismissed as director. The Russian connection came partly from Sellars' delight at the similarities in playfulness and sentimentality between Mayakovsky's populist poetry and such Ira Gershwin lyrics as 'You've got/A lot /Of personali-TNT' or 'I'm feeling/No fooling/I'm falling, dear/I fell at the moment I found you'. Unable to put the Gershwin material to rest and obsessively agitated that the Gershwin theatre songs 'have always been seen in a dramatic context that barely comes up to their ankles', Sellars cast about for a Russian play to couple it with and found not only Gorky but a chance to make a more urgent political connection between Russia and America.

Summerfolk, a 1904 work by the father of Soviet realism (best-known for *The Lower Depths*), is an almost slavishly Chekhovian portrait of middle-class professionals on vacation, who spend four virtually aimless acts drinking, arguing, having love affairs, mounting amateur theatricals and discussing life. Written the year before the first Russian revolution, the long-winded and unnaturally eloquent speeches by one character after another nonetheless sounded in 1984 astonishingly contemporary in their concern for the responsibility toward children in a society whose future is uncertain, the polarisation of the classes, the widening gap between elitist and popular art, and the failure of political activism.

Just as he wouldn't think of doing Gershwin without giving it a social context, Sellars made Gorky fun with the Gershwin music; the songs corrected the play's cerebral talkiness by letting the characters voice the romantic sentiments that spur the real moon-June-spoon action going on amid the philosophising. But Sellars didn't indulge the entertainment value of the production at the expense of the very real, immediate concerns at the heart of his adaptation of *Summerfolk*. Upstage, where one would usually find birch trees in a Russian pastorale stood a line of huge cut-outs of peasants whose looming presence made the lounging summerfolk seem like complaining children. And around the back of the theatre on the audience's side were huge election-year posters of various presidential candidates (as well as Mao and Nixon). No verbal reference was made to these two rows of figures, but they sent a sort of electrical energy through the theatre, giving the play a heightened physical–political context. And there was just as much political content in Sellars' insistence on staging scenes in the aisles or leaving teh house lights on: he wanted the audience to feel alive in the theatre, good practice for being awake in the world.

The jumble of pop, classical and avant-garde references in *Hang On To Me* epitomises Sellars' theatrical palette. Both before *Hang On To Me* and after, he has never gone very far in one direction without making a gesture in the opposite direction. His career is littered with mixed signals and multiple ambitions, a sense of two roads travelled at the same time, a dilettante's restless imagination and curiosity as well as a burning intellect's desire to know the world. At Harvard's American Repertory Theatre, he made his professional directing debut with an extravagantly visual production of Gogol's well-known comedy *The Inspector General* and followed it the next year with a rarely performed uncut version of Handel's opera *Orlando*. In the wake of his disappointing experience with *My One and Only* (he was fired before previews of the Broadway tryout began in Boston), Sellars returned to the theatre by inaugurating the newly opened La Jolla Playhouse in San Diego with a production of Brecht's *The Visions of Simone Machard*, but not before staging Gilbert and Sullivan's

The Mikado at the Lyric Opera in Chicago. His first experience of running an institution involved an archtypically provicial theatre, the Boston Shakespeare Company, where his own productions included both *Pericles* and Peter Maxwell Davies' chamber opera *The Lighthouse* and those by guest artists ranged from Tim Mayer's adaptation of *Mother Courage* starring Academy Award-winning actress Linda Hunt to the Wooster Group's *L.S.D. (. . . Just the High Points . . .)*.

After one year at the Boston Shakespeare Company, Sellars accepted the directorship of one of the most august artistic institutions in the country, the Kennedy Center in Washington, DC. Exercising his trademark eclectic taste, he mounted productions of two familiar classical works – an adaptation of Alexandre Dumas' hoary melodrama *The Count of Monte Cristo* and a new translation of Chekhov's *The Seagull* (which Sellars and his translator, Maria M Markof-Belaeff, in a somewhat pugnacious but linguistically justified gesture, renamed *A Seagull*) – and two surprise choices not from the standard theatrical canon, Robert Sherwood's *Idiot's Delight* and Sophocles's *Ajax*. During the same period, contractually barred from producing opera at the Kennedy Center, Sellars embarked on a major cycle of operas – Handel's *Julius Caesar* and three by Mozard, *Cosi Fan Tutte*, *Don Giovanni* and *The Marriage of Figaro* – which he directed at the Pepsico SummerFare in Purchase, NY. At the same time that he was immersed in staging these opera house staples, Sellars was engaged as a crucial collaborator on *Nixon in China*, an opera composed by John Adams with libretto by Alice Goodman and commissioned by the Houston Grand Opera, that was received by critics and audiences with the kind of immediate enthusiasm rarely accorded contemporary operas. Shortly after the world premiere of *Nixon in China* in Houston, Sellars' production appeared as part of the Brooklyn Academy of Music's Next Wave Festival. Not content with mere popularity, Sellars was also represented in the same festival by his staging of Velimir Khlebnikov's Russian futurist poem-play *Zangesi*, which he originally created for the opening of the new Museum of Contemporary Art in Los Angeles. Never the familiar without the obscure; never the avant-garde without the mainstream. Not either/or but both/and.

Certain crucial influences provide important keys to Peter Sellars' work. He has always cited his exposure to puppetry as a major influence, both his own involvement in the Lovelace Marionette Theatre as a child in Pittsburgh and his observation of the Bread and Puppet Theater, whose four-hour performances in Paris he saw six times. These imprinted on him the value of visual design and music to the theatre experience. It was while working with the Lovelace Marionette Theatre that Sellars encountered the scenography of Joseph Svoboda: 'Suddenly, I was doing all these wild, abstract things, these sets that were all white when I was 13 or 14, *Rumpelstiltskin* with a very modern unit set based on Svoboda's *Romeo and Juliet*'.[3] In an interview with Ron Jenkins published in *Theater*, Sellars described the experience of staging *Jack and the Beanstalk* in department store windows:

> That's when I first learned that music is one of the main keys in figuring out the level of which drama is lyrical and has musicality as its center. When it comes to the chase down the beanstalk, [you learn that] "Night on Bald Mountain" will help. You learn that words only connect in a certain way, and that beyond the words there has to be this musicality, or you have something that is exactly what it says it is, which isn't much.[4]

Music plays a role, often a central role, in nearly every Peter Sellars production. His Kennedy Center productions of *The Count of Monte Cristo*, *A Seagull* and *Idiot's Delight* all prominently featured live musicians onstage, as did *Hang On To Me*, *Pericles* and *Ping*. (It's worth noting that Sellars' use of Alfred Schnittke's String Quartet No. 2 for dramatic underscoring in *The Count of Monte Cristo* predated by nearly two years any major American recognition of the contemporary Soviet composer.)

Throughout his work, Sellars has pursued a policy of casting black, Asian, Latino and other actors in non-traditional ways. He's certainly not the first to do so; he had seen and admired works by Peter Brook and Andrei Serban that employed multiracial, cross-cultural casts. But he once cited a specific turning point in his thinking about actors: the opening scene of Meredith Monk's *Specimen Days* (performed at the Public Theater in New York during the 1981–2 season), in which each actor was given a costume that signified gender and an armband that signified race. 'The way the white person with the black armband enacted the suffering of a black person represented how we're all alike

at heart.'[5] Sellars assembles racially mixed casts for nearly everything he directs; he has, for example, employed the classically
trained black actor Ben Halley, Jr, in such disparate roles as a
French poodle in V R Lang's *I Too Have Lived in Arcadia*, the
title character in *Pericles*, and the title character's teenage brother
in *The Visions of Simone Machard*. But Sellars' multiracial casting
cannot be said to be 'colour-blind'. He frequently casts non-white
performers specifically for the cultural references they invoke, be
they theatrical, musical and political. That is to say, it was no
accident that Carmen De Lavallade, who played *Hang On To Me*'s
militant doctor and moral spokeswoman, bore some resemblance
to Coretta Scott King; Sellars surely intended for the audience to
make the connection between Gorky's character and a contemporary figure representing social responsibility to all races and
classes. Similarly, the casting of Zakes Mokae, an actor closely
associated with the plays of Athol Fugard, brought to *The Count
of Monte Cristo* a sense that the drama might reflect the present
situation in South Africa. Sellars has also made it a point to
hire actors of professional backgrounds: avant-garde actor David
Warrilow and Richard Thomas, best-known as John-Boy from the
TV series *The Waltons*, both appeared in *The Count of Monte Cristo*
and *Two Figures in Dense Violet Light* at the Kennedy Center.

Non-traditional casting was crucial to one of Sellars' most important productions, the staging of Sophocles' *Ajax*, which ended
his tenure at the Kennedy Center and later toured to the La
Jolla Playhouse and several festivals in Europe. Sophocles' play
portrays the decline and suicide of the Greek hero of the Trojan
War who, feeling insufficiently rewarded for his efforts, goes
crazy and attacks a bunch of livestock, having been deceived by
Athena into thinking they are his fellow generals. Robert Auletta's
adaptation, commissioned by Sellars for the American National
Theater production, set the action in the very near future, after
an American military victory in Latin America.

The setting was explicitly the Pentagon, a military hearing
presided over by Athena, who appeared in a slinky blue gown
and whispered into her hand-held microphone like a disco deity.
Tecmessa, Ajax's foreign 'spear-won bride', was Vietnamese. The
chorus consisted of five actors – three black, one Asian, one
white – in camouflage fatigues who also double as Odysseus,
Agamemnon, Menelaus, Teucer and the Messenger. Most startling, Ajax was played by Howie Seago, a leading actor with the

National Theater for the Deaf, whose signing was translated by various members of the cast. (This bit of casting clearly recalled *The Gospel at Colonus*, Lee Breuer and Bob Telson's mating of Sophocles with black church music, which featured blind gospel star Clarence Fountain as Oedipus.) Sellars' copious programme notes illuminated the connection between a deaf actor's signing and Greek choral dancing and explicated his allegiance to the Greek ideal of theatre as public discourse. *Ajax* premiered at the Kennedy Center just two months after Robert Wilson's staging of Euripides' *Alcestis* had its debut at Harvard's American Repertory Theater, and the contrast between these two productions further defined the degrees to which Sellars followed and departed from avant-garde theatre traditions. Both productions were formally stunning and visually splendid. Yet in Wilson's aestheticised distillation of the Greek myth the contemporary references were exclusively private – even cryptic – rather than public, while Sellars insisted that every interpretive choice have political resonance.

Translation, both as a literary form and as a method of critical interpretation, is one issue of concern to post-modern critical thinking that has influenced Sellars significantly. Perhaps the strongest influence has been the work of the Wooster Group under Elizabeth LeCompte's direction, with its stripped-down, highly interpretive deconstructions of such classic American texts as *The Cocktail Party, Long Day's Journey Into Night, Our Town* and *The Crucible*. Director Elizabeth LeCompte's ability both to boil these works down to their essence and to recast or reinvigorate their meaning through radical and often deeply personal theatrical juxtapositions has clearly emboldened Sellars in his staging of classic plays and operas. The mixture of classical music (Debussy and Beethoven) with pop music (five blues songs by Elmore James) in his staging of *Pericles* seems directly influenced by the Wooster Group's *Route 1 & 9*, in which a piece by Charles Ives ('The Housatonic at Stockbridge', from *Three Places in New England*) carries as much weight as Thurston Harris' gritty rhythm-and-blues dance tune 'Little Bitty Pretty One'. In the 'Fascinatin' Rhythm' number from *Hang On To Me*, Sellars had a band of amateur theatricals, played by children, pantomime a thirty-second version of *The Three Sisters* – a witty tip of the hat to the Wooster Group's *Nayatt School*, which featured an excerpt from T S Eliot's *The Cocktail Party* enacted by children. And George Trow's *The Bob Hope War Zone Special*, the mad satire play that Sellars attached to *Ajax* (and pulled after opening night in Washington), openly emulated *LSD (. . . Just the High Points . . .)* in its irreverent satire and its frenzied performance style.

Though much if often made of the bizarre anachronistic scenery in Sellars' work – the *King Lear* staged around a Lincoln Continental, Handel's *Orlando* set in Cape Canaveral and on the moon, *Julius Caesar* ostensibly set in contemporary Beirut – there is a distinction to be made between this work and the kind of conceptual theatre production that 'updates' a classic play to the present or moves it from one historical period to another. Sellars is careful to avoid making glib associations or one-on-one correspondences when making anachronistic references; he's prepared to utilise whatever scenic devices are necessary to set up the spiritual or philosophical or intellectual journey the work offers, but finally his productions don't take place in any specific time or place beyond the given moment. Most important, perhaps, he doesn't replace one set of references with another but usually finds a way to let the original stand alongside the updated version – supplying to the audience for his *Julius Caesar*, for instance, both his own detailed production notes and a facsimile of the bilingual (English and Italian) libretto given out at the first performances of Handel's opera in London in 1724.

Sellars' production of Wagner's *Tannhauser* at the Lyric Opera in Chicago in 1988 received much media attention on the basis of its concept. Wagner's hero, the knight and minstrel who must seek redemption from the Pope for the sin of sensual passion, was played as a contemporary televangelist involved in a sex scandal, as Jimmy Swaggart had recently been. But as the production played itself out, it went beyond the jokey concept to reveal the underlying drive of Sellars' scenographic method of translation. He set the final act of *Tannhauser* in a deserted American Airlines terminal, where Elizabeth – Wagner's representative of pure human love – waits for the return of Tannhauser, and the mating of the banal setting familiar to every sophisticated opera-goer with Wagner's psycho-spiritual anguish elevated the former to Wagner's plane of inquiry and gave the latter the poignancy and urgency of real life.

Liviu Ciulei once described Peter Sellars as 'a director who writes poems with stage elements'.[6] His search for objective correlatives and his critical approach to a text manifest themselves in clear, even corny gestures that are like puns taken to their most theatrical extremes. He uses bold lighting effects (almost always designed by key collaborator James Ingalls) to transform conversation-stopping monologues into soliliquies by isolating the speaker in a pinspot, and he makes pictures that dredge up the psychological subtext of a scene. The multiracial casting of *Ajax* led to a striking image of Ajax's death attended by a black goddess, a black angel and an Asian musician – a tableau which, intentionally or not, suggested the symbolic death of the white man, the end of white hegemony in world power, the recognition that coloured people make up most of the earth's population.

Possibly the most important influence on Sellars' work was his visit to the Taganka Theatre in Moscow in early 1984, shortly after the dismissal of Yuri Lyubimov as the theatre's director. Sellars, who witnessed some of the last performances of Lyubimov's productions before they were removed from the Taganka repertory forever, has said, 'This was the most important theater I have ever seen in my life'.[7] In an interview with Mark Bly, published in *Theater* (Spring 1985), Sellars minutely described Lyubimov's productions of *The Master and Margarita*, *Crime and Punishment* and *The Three Sisters*, among others, noting at least three elements that have since turned up frequently in this own work:

a   Expressionistic lighting. "At various points in the evening when Lyubimov thought it was appropriate, special banks of lights permanently trained on the audience would be brought up just to let us know that we were in this too and to acknowledge that there was one room, and we were all alive at one moment in what was reality." Sellars uses this particular effect in many productions – *Hang On To Me*, *Ajax*, *Don Giovanni* and *Cosi Fan Tutte*, to name a few.

b   Referential density. "One of the examples of Lyubimov's stagecraft that I like to cite is the moment when there is a pounding in Raskolnikov's skull. It starts as a knocking on the door and becomes a pounding in his skull. He is terrified and doesn't want to answer the door, but the pounding becomes ovewhelming. Meanwhile, Lyubimov has the landlady making soup downstairs (borscht) and two or three people passing on the street. Suddenly, Raskolnikov works up the courage to open the door, and with a supreme moment of intensity, hurls himself at it. At the same moment, something terrifies the people in the street and the landlady. The soup flies out of the woman's hand, and as Raskolnikov flings open the door, there is borscht dripping down the front of the door, looking just like blood. Then he slams the door shut. Typical of Lyubimov, it all happens in seconds. That is the way in which Lyubimov layers images and adds a kinesic immediacy to the novel. I think it is rather interesting that, as a rule, he doesn't direct plays; he directs prose pieces. His sense of time and space operates on many levels simultaneously and most playwrights can't accommodate that vision. Those levels of diachronism are typical of the novel."

Sellars' production of *The Count of Monte Cristo* can be seen almost as a direct response to Lyubimov's *Crime and Punishment*. The text that Sellars staged was James O'Neill's adaptation of an English translation of Dumas' play, into which Sellars interpolated not only excerpts from the King James Bible and writings of Lord Byron but string quartets by Beethoven and Alfred Schnittke. In addition, almost every aspect of the scenically extravagant, multiracial production conjured references that had associations to some, if not all members of the audience. Some references were political (Steve Biko, Nelson Mandela, Jacobo Timerman), some were literary (*Othello*, *Endgame*, *Threepenny Opera*). Others were entirely theatrical: the make-up recalled Kabuki, the choreography *Einstein on the Beach*, the lighting Lee Breuer's staging of *Lulu*, the set Hal Prince's productions of *Sweeney Todd* and *Pacific Overtures*. Whether self-conscious quotations (in the manner of contemporary appropriation art) or homage to Lyubimov, these references gave the piece the dramatic sweep and density of an epic novel. Although Sellars' technique in making these references in *Monte Cristo* resembled pastiche, they had a cumulative effect through the evening so the successive images began to overlay one another, achieving the simultaneity of Lyubimov's work:

c   Religiosity. Probably the most important influence on Sellars was Lyubimov's open presentation of religion, not nearly as acceptable on the Soviet stage as social or political commentary. "In *Crime and Punishment*, Lyubimov had Dostoyevsky onstage the whole evening, setting scenes up for the characters, trying to help them along, and most movingly praying for them. To watch the author praying for his characters' futures and his nation's destiny was one of the most immensely generous and heartbreaking images. Somewhere one hoped that maybe our Author was praying for us."

American theatre is equally squeamish about the sincere treatment of religious drama. Sellars himself, a practicing Christian Scientist, is one of the few major theatre artists whose work betrays explicitly Christian imagery again and again. His staging of *Das Kleine Mahagonny* linked Brecht and Weill's song cycle to a series of Bach church cantatas; he seems fond of works which deal with resurrection (Mayakovsky's *The Bedburg*, *Pericles*, *Zangesi*, *The Count of Monte Cristo*). And just as his production of *Idiot's Delight* ended with a group of mortally fearful luxury hotel guests singing 'Onward Christian Soldiers', his staging of Mozart and da Ponte's *Don Giovanni* for Pepsico SummerFare zeroed in on the opera's morality-play essence. The scenic design placed the characters on a street corner in Harlem: Donna Elvira appeared in leopard-skin tights and a punky hairdo, Don Giovanni put on a ski mask to pass for Leporello (played by a black actor) in the dark, Donna Anna shot up with a syringe during her aria, and Don Giovanni feasted on a last supper from McDonald's. But the most pertinent images that occurred periodically, insistently throughout the production, were a white neon cross over the neighbourhood church and a spotlit red door, representing the struggle in Don Giovanni's soul between Heaven and Hell. At the stunning finale, the street opened up to reveal an open grave, a little girl appeared in the door of the church and walked across the grave, and pushed Don Giovanni, stripped to his underpants, down a manhole to Hell. From the open grave, a chorus of naked souls drenched in red light rose up from purgatory to sing the final verses of the opera as the house lights came up, implicating the audience in the soul-wrenching drama.

However recognisable his influences may be, Sellars has digested them and recycled them in a highly idiosyncratic manner that has had a profound effect on his peers and his students. A chief characteristic of any Sellars production is its insistence that everyone – including the director, the performers, the designers, and especially the audience – rise to the challenge a work of art poses. Conventional wisdom says that it you're going to throw something difficult of scary at an audience, you have to give people something safe or familiar to cling to throughout the trip: a story, a star, recognisable furniture. Sellars tends to dispense with such niceties. His productions are sometimes like graduate seminars where the prerequisites might include a working knowledge of Russian culture of the revolutionary era, Shakespeare, Beckett, the Bible, Tantric imagery, and the landscape of downtown Los Angeles. The class may grumble at the workload and suspect that the teacher is only one step ahead on the reading list. But at a time when almost every kind of culture comes predigested for a demographically targeted audience, when the level of writing for the theatre is so degraded the Neil Simon's tiniest departure from mechanical one-liners is hailed as a breakthrough in American drama, Sellars' theatre demands and rewards an active intelligence.

Of course, there is a thin line between advocating awareness of history and other cultures for the purposes of combating ethnocentricism and merely shopping at what critic Elinor Fuchs calls 'a Bloomingdale's of empty signs from ever more exotic sources recombined to create an artificial and dehumanized culture'.[8]

Sellars' career in the theatre is instructive because it embodies several impulses that relate to other contemporary theatre artists whose work similarly points toward the future. These include aesthetic concerns (a renewed interest in staging classics, the influence of electronic media on theatrical narrative) as well as practical considerations that have impact on aesthetics (the ease of air travel, the resurgence of interest in theatre ensembles).

Renewed interest in staging classics

Because of the omnipresence of the media, any new development in contemporary theatre gets pounced upon and dissected; there are no secrets; any promising artist's further development takes place under a blinding spotlight. So what's new swiftly gets old. It's one of the reasons that it seems that many of the most original, creative artists working in the late 1980s embraced the classics, exploring a desire to connect with the history of the world through the history of literature. The work of directors such as Anne Bogart, Des McAnuff, Robert Woodruff and Garland Wright represent a reaction to innovation and a movement toward consolidation. The previous generation of theatre-makers, those were seen to be moving the theatre forward, had put a premium on creating their own work, taking at best a critical attitude toward classical texts. But the way Richard Schechner adapted, say, *The Bacchae* in *Dionysus in '69* or the way Elizabeth LeCompte interpolated *The Cocktail Party* in *Nayatt School* was very different from Peter Sellars' staging of *Pericles* or *A Seagull*. In contrast to theatre's avant-gardists of the 1960s and 1970s, Sellars and others of his generation gravitated toward classics because they were starved for verbal eloquence and dramatic content.

'Our generation doesn't have anything to say because we've lost the ability to talk about things', says Anne Bogart.

I think I know why, too. It's specifically political – it goes back to the McCarthy era, when artists were destroyed for being politically involved. We've been brought up thinking art and politics don't mix, so what do we have to talk about? Ourselves. I have this theory about plays, that they're little pockets of memory. Like a Greek play about hubris – if you do it now, it's a chance to bring that question into the world and see how it looks at the time you're doing it. We've lost the sense that theater has this function of bringing these universal questions through time . . . Now we think it's all about inventing, making something new. But how can you create something if you don't have anything to talk about but yourself?[9]

Similarly disturbed by theatre's contribution to 'the murder of language and the destruction of text', director Des McAnuff has analysed this tendency in the context of American education:

Look at any paper's ads for private schools – they don't talk about the arts, won't talk about the humanities, they'll talk strictly about computers. Increasingly, we're getting generations of young people who have not been given the vocabulary to appreciate art, music. Therefore, they've lost interest. In a sense, we've perpetuated that by discouraging ideas onstage and replacing questions either with simplistic ideological statements or simply images, pictures, laughs. We need to turn it around. We need to be discussing issues onstage, asking questions, encouraging people to think, to accept the fact that they don't have to sit there and like it necessarily, they can make up their own minds. There needs to be content in what we do. The times in which we live demand it.[10]

The pull toward classics links young American directors like Sellars, Bogart and McAnuff both to European masters such as Giorgio Strehler, Lucian Pintilie and Liviu Ciulei and to new vaudevilleans such the Flying Karamazovs, Bill Irwin and Fred Curshack, all of whom are attracted to images but need them to speak. Their need/desire for Shakespeare is the search for a new voice/eloquence/articulation in response to the anti-narrative, non-linear work of the great avant-gardists of the 1970s (Foreman, Wilson, Mabou Mines, Wooster Group).

Interdisciplinary collaboration

Sellars frequently hires artists to design sets, draws inspiration from Giotto frescoes and Bruce Naumann sculptures, uses Handel in one piece and Elmore James in another, and borrows ideas about lighting from Hitchcock movies. In doing so, he hews to the tradition of directors such as Wilson, Foreman, Lee Breuer, Elizabeth LeCompte and JoAnne Akalaitis, all of whom embrace a vision of theatre that depends upon cross-disciplinary exchange to battle the insidious effect that photography, film and television have had. Television in particular encourages viewers to judge the value of art by its achievement of a literal representation of reality rather than some artistic expression of the human spirit. And the more theatre focuses on the literal representation of reality, the less room it has for collaboration with other art forms; American drama in particular has become very attached to living room sets. Thus it is that the best-known American theatre of this century is the O'Neill–Miller–Williams–Albee strain of naturalistic drama, which relies in no crucial way on exchange with visual artists, composers, *et cetera*. Yet the most fertile periods of culture in the twentieth century have involved artists communicating across disciplines: Russian futurist performance, French surrealist performance, and in America the Black Mountain College collaborations. In the 1970s, media-theatre artists resurrected the Wagnerian ideal of *gesamtkunstwerk*. The influence of visual art on contemporary theatre cannot be underestimated; is has emboldened directors of classical texts to tell more with compressed images and distilled poetry, a corrective in many ways to the logorrhea of television.

The effect of electronic media on contemporary notions of narrative

The continuous bombardment of scattered, splintered images and fragmented narratives have affected not only contemporary playwriting but also the audience's capacity for concentration. It's fascinating to see playwrights who in another era, even ten years earlier, would have been writing exremely conventionally crafted dramas exhibiting the influence of avant-garde theatrical and literary techniques. The plays of A R Gurney, Jr, practically epitomise bourgeois dramaturgy, with their unit sets and familial concerns; yet the sly self-referentialism of plays such as *The Dining Room*, *The Perfect Party* and *The Cocktail Hour* lodge them firmly in the post-modern period, when no picture accurately reflects contemporary reality without somehow pointing to its own frame. Likewise, Craig Lucas' work – *Blue Window, Reckless, Three Postcards, Prelude to a Kiss* – cross-breed superficially cheerful TV-style conversational dialogue with challenging theatrical techniques clearly inspired by experimental theatre; in *Blue Window*, the set simultaneously represents six locations, and in *Three Postcards* a trio of women lunching in a trendy restaurant play themselves at every stage of life, from infancy to senescence, without changing clothes or make-up.

The influence of structuralist narrative can be seen in musical theatre as well – for instance, *Sunday in the Park with George*, Stephen Sondheim and James Lapine's portrait of pointillist Georges Seurat. Seurat's vision, of course, had exactly to do with creating a whole picture from dots of colour and light, counting on human perception (eye and brain) to make the whole out of parts. The first act shows Seurat creating his masterpiece *A Sunday Afternoon on the Island of la Grande Jatte*, ruminating in the show's finest song, 'Finishing the Hat', on the irony of secluding oneself from the world to reproduce it in art, abstracting reality to see it more clearly. The second act presents a contemporary artist, the putative great-grandson of Seurat, who spends more time making deals than art; the irony is that while Seurat encountered resistance because his artistic vision was new, the present-day artist battles the craving for novelty and has to separate himself from the cries of 'Do something new!' in order to rediscover the classical virtues of order–design–tension–balance–composition–light–harmony.

The resurgence of interest around the country in forming ongoing theatre ensembles

In response to the decline of commercial theatre production and diminished opportunities for well-paying work, theatre artists have been banding together to produce their own work – a practice popular in the countercultural 1960s which didn't have much currency in the 1970s. This movement has natural leaders such as Robert Brustein of the American Repertory Theater (formerly Yale Rep) and Adrian Hall, founder of the Trinity Square Repertory Company, now director of the Dallas Theater Center, who have devoted their lives to the resident theatre companies they founded twenty years ago. But it also includes less formal examples, such as the unusual gang of actors who've worked with playwright-director John Jesurun, the NYU students who flocked around Anne Bogart (before she entered the institutional theatre as artistic director of Trinity Square), and the multidisciplinary performers associated with the works of Ping Chong. The word 'ensemble' means something different to these groups, though, than it did to the previous great wave of ensembles. In the Living Theater–Open Theater-Performance Group heyday, 'ensemble' went hand in hand with 'avant-garde'. Ensembles rarely did conventional plays – the work was collectively created, often based on group improvisations. Sometimes there was a verbal text sometimes not. There was also an implied political engagement with the movement and the assumption of shared views on the Vietnam War, sex, drugs and abortion. Above all, the avant-garde ensembles of the 1960s were an alternative movement, rejecting the standards of mainstream society in general and mainstream theatre in particular – whether that meant Broadway musicals or traditional regional theatre productions of classics.

The 1980s ensembles are all over the map, both artistically and geographically. In lieu of a common theatrical vocabulary or political solidarity, ensembles formed in the 1980s share a healthy pluralism, a willingness to leave the options open, and an ability to synthesise techniques and aspirations that formerly were ascribed exclusively to Broadway, the avant-garde or regional theatre. 'Professionalism', a dirty word to 1960s ensembles, now describes a seriousness of commitment rather than a mercenary slickness. And 'the mainstream' is no longer considered some bourgeois fraternity that one can only get into by compromising one's individuality – it is the platform from which the leading artists in our culture can address the widest possible public, a situation to which most visionary artists aspire. To work only in mainstream theatre, of course, might breed a tendency to embrace yuppie complacency; to stick to avant-garde theatre would be to accept left-wing marginalism. Most theatre ensembles seek a healthy balance, rejecting an either–or situation.

It's always interesting to note the differences between Peter Sellars' theatre productions and his opera work. Many of his opera productions – including all those presented at the Pepsico SummerFare – the employed musical director Craig Smith and several of the singers such as Susan Larson, Sanford Sylvan and James Maddelena who make up the Opera Company of Somerville, an informal repertory company that has worked together for years. (The name is an in-joke, Somerville being a working-class suburb of Boston.) Whether performing Handel or Maxwell-Davies, Mozart or John Adams, the singers achieve an autonomy within the performance – based on their formidable knowledge of the music and the trust developed among longtime colleagues – where even the most talented actors new to Sellars' work would be struggling simply to keep up with the director's ideas. Clearly, even a brilliant director like Sellars can get a certain kind of performance only in an ensemble situation.

The energetic eclecticism coming from a generation of young directors who refuse to accept conventional distinctions between avant-garde and mainstream theatre, high art and pop culture. Companies run by directors in their twenties and thirties bring a vital eclecticism to the theatre because it's in their blood. They represent a generation that grew up on rock, music, TV and movies, as well as theatre, and they don't recognise distinctions between high art and low art used to separate the cultured classes from hoi polloi. They trust what stimulates them, whether it's Springsteen or Shakespeare, Prince or Prokofiev, the Greeks or the blues. When this collapsing of barriers occurs, audiences – especially young audiences – begin to realise that theatre isn't a secluded art form shrouded in mystery and accessible only to the elite, the educated, the initiated, but something that can speak to them.

NOTES

1. A. Croce, 'Championship Form' (review of Mark Morris at the Brooklyn Academy of Music), *The New Yorker*, 17 December 1984, p. 138.
2. John Cage, 'Experimental Music' in *Silence* (Middletown, Conn.: Wesleyan University Press, 1973) p. 12.
3. P. Sellars, quoted in Don Shewey, 'Alive in the Theatre, Awake in the World' (review of *Hang On To Me*), *The Village Voice*, 12 June 1984, p. 87.
4. P. Sellars, quoted in an interview with Ron Jenkins, *Theater*, vol. 15, no. 2, Spring 1984, p. 47.
5. P. Sellars, in conversation with the author, September 1983.
6. L. Ciulei, in conversation with Shewey.
7. P. Sellars, quoted in Mark Bly, 'Lyubimov and the End of an Era: An Interview with Peter Sellars', *Theater*, vol. 16, no. 2, Spring 1985, p. 10. The subsequent Lyubimov quotes are from this interview.
8. E. Fuchs, 'The Death of Character', *Theater Communications*. vol. 5, no. 3, March 1983, pp. 5–6.
9. A. Bogart, quoted in Don Shewey, 'Bogart in Space', *The Village Voice*, 18 December 1984, p. 126.
10. D. McAnuff, quoted in Don Shewey, 'In Search of the New Mainstream', *American Theater*, January 1985, p. 7.

Index

283